Encountering Education through Existential Challenges and Community

Directly inspired by Indian British activist Satish Kumar's 2013 seminal work 'Soil, Soul and Society', this book rethinks education in line with thoughts around the current climate crisis, the purpose of education in a post-pandemic world and the mental health of children, teachers and youth across societies.

Acknowledging the realities of a world battling with the after effects of COVID-19, the author envisions a future for education that realises real-world solutions to contemporary existential, ecological and societal challenges that might otherwise be limited to an imaginary or idealist space. Offering a novel approach through a combination of narrative-based enquiry and auto-ethnographic study, the book provides a synthesis of ideas from both Kumar and political philosopher Hannah Arendt not usually linked to debates in sustainability education.

Ultimately providing a critique of a predominantly Western-orientated, global education movement, this interdisciplinary book will appeal to scholars, researchers and post-graduate students involved in education theory and the philosophy of education, as well as indigenous and sustainability education more broadly.

Giles Barrow is a self-employed teacher, trainer, consultant and ecologist.

Theorizing Education

Theorizing Education brings together innovative work from a wide range of contexts and traditions which explicitly focuses on the roles of theory in educational research and educational practice. The series includes contextual and socio-historical analyses of existing traditions of theory and theorizing, exemplary use of theory, and empirical work where theory has been used in innovative ways. The distinctive focus for the series is the engagement with educational questions, articulating what explicitly educational function the work of particular forms of theorizing supports.

Series Editors

A Pedagogy of Equality in a Time of Unrest
Strategies for an Ambiguous Future
Carl Anders Safstrom

Moral Emotions and Human Interdependence in Character Education
Beyond the One-Dimensional Self
Agnieszka Bates

Indirect Education
Exploring Indirectness in Teaching and Research
Herner Saeverot

Encountering Education through Existential Challenges and Community
Re-connection and Renewal for an Ecologically based Future
Giles Barrow

For more information about this series, please visit: www.routledge.com/Theorizing-Education/book-series/THEOED

Encountering Education through Existential Challenges and Community

Re-connection and Renewal for an Ecologically based Future

Giles Barrow

Routledge
Taylor & Francis Group

LONDON AND NEW YORK

First published 2024
by Routledge
4 Park Square, Milton Park, Abingdon, Oxon OX14 4RN

and by Routledge
605 Third Avenue, New York, NY 10158

Routledge is an imprint of the Taylor & Francis Group, an informa business

British Library Cataloguing-in-Publication Data
A catalogue record for this book is available from the British Library

Library of Congress Cataloging-in-Publication Data
Names: Barrow, Giles, author.
Title: Encountering education through existential challenges and community : re-connection and renewal for an ecologically based future / Giles Barrow.
Description: Abingdon, Oxon ; New York, NY : Routledge, 2024. | Series: Theorizing education | Includes bibliographical references and index.
Identifiers: LCCN 2023010807 (print) | LCCN 2023010808 (ebook) | ISBN 9781032517315 (hardback) | ISBN 9781032526638 (paperback) | ISBN 9781003407751 (ebook)
Subjects: LCSH: Environmental education. | Sustainability. | Environmental responsibility.
Classification: LCC GE70 .E534 2024 (print) | LCC GE70 (ebook) | DDC 333.7071--dc23/eng20230715
LC record available at https://lccn.loc.gov/2023010807
LC ebook record available at https://lccn.loc.gov/2023010808

ISBN: 978-1-032-51731-5 (hbk)
ISBN: 978-1-032-52663-8 (pbk)
ISBN: 978-1-003-40775-1 (ebk)

DOI: 10.4324/9781003407751

Typeset in Sabon
by KnowledgeWorks Global Ltd.

To David Farrow

(1934–2009)

Contents

Preface

I think it is often assumed that arrival is welcomed. It somehow anticipates the completion of a journey with a corresponding sense of relief, as if only after arriving we have the possibility of comfort, ease and fulfilment. Furthermore, that the assumption is that the journeying might have been discombobulating, unsettling, full of uncertainty, and that glimpsing first sight of arrival promises an end to the ache for stability. The root of the word itself – arrivaille – refers to a French term meaning 'disembarkation from a sea-bound journey'; stepping onto dry land. I can imagine that sense of sure-footedness following swaying with the swell, and where arrival would indeed be welcome.

For the purposes of this writing, I am more interested in a less than welcome sense of arrival and want to look at the combination of 'arrival' with the concept of interruption. I will explore these ideas in the context of my own informal educational experience, undertaken several years ago when I moved from south London to rural Suffolk. At the heart of this narrative, which extends throughout the following pages, is an encounter between myself and an elderly neighbour, David, who had spent his life in farming. This section you are reading is the first in a series of five that interleaves between the substantive chapters and which explores ideas that are central to my perspective on education. The relationship between myself and David will feature throughout these episodes and the purpose of the telling is to illuminate specific educational ideas, not necessarily the unfolding of our respective biographies (although at times this interweaves powerfully with a theme, as will be revealed later). In the following vignette, arrival is considered important to the opening of the educational encounter. I refer at times to a journal I kept at the time, and I will begin here with its first entry.

26th September, 2006

In most respects the lawn has been the biggest challenge. It had been used as an exercise ring for training horses, comprised of sawdust, consequently it had no body or nutrition. First it was broken up and turned, then seeded but didn't take. For our first summer, brief, sparse blades wilted and the bald dusty bowl remained. Since August we have seeded three times, fed it and added topsoil. Slowly we have seen the grass appear in solid spreads. Now we can see that we are there at last. A kind of arrival, and reclamation.

David and I made the agreement last Sunday. He and I were admiring the newly seeded lawn. Fresh, bright green shoots darted out of the ground creating a bristle of grass. Again he was urging patience, explaining that regardless of its chaotic, vigorous growth, the lawn should be left until next spring before first cutting. 'I would like most of all, if I might, cut it then', David said, adding, 'If I am still here, and well enough.'

As I copy this out, I am mindful of three things; the coincidence of the reference to 'arrival', second, the significance of what becomes a substantial 'reclamation', that of the dilapidated farm, and third, in David's closing words, the premonition of how this story will end. For now, it's the importance of arrival that draws me in. By this point, I had known David a year or so and we were clearly on good speaking terms, but there had been a stage, when I had first moved to the area, when this was not the case and this earlier, difficult time warrants closer scrutiny.

I had not truly wanted to move to the country. My reluctance proved such that I remained in London with my daughter, whilst the rest of the family moved into the farmhouse with its derelict yard. Even the property was not properly chosen; it just happened to be one of the few left at the time that was available for rent. This transition was neither fully planned nor welcome. After eventually deciding to join the family and to settle in the new home, I did so with no intention of being a student, let alone to be 'taught by'. For my part, the move was an unwelcome disruption in what, for me, was a familiar lifestyle the function of which was to confirm the world as I had grown to know it. Not only an external sense of the world, but also an internal sense of how I existed within it, and in which I had no notion that there was some other way in which I might exist. No notion of another view of myself, or an expanded version of 'me'. David's intervention as a teacher took the form of an educational interruption and from its first moment beckoned me into discomfort – but I am getting ahead of myself – let me go back a little.

Prior to our arrival, David had experienced the bereavement of his wife. They had been moved out of his family home a year before in order that the landlord could refurbish the property in readiness for the rental market. He and his wife were resettled in a small tied cottage across a quiet lane, just opposite their old home. Both were ill with cancer and two weeks before we moved in his wife died. It was from this experience that David had to bear seeing us, city newcomers, take over his old home, situated in the dereliction of a farm he had managed for 40 years. Bitterness and anger, sadness and loss, a toxic combination, that kept him from saying as much as a 'good morning' when we passed each other. (I hasten to add that I knew nothing, at this early point, of his recent hardship.) Suffice it to say, mine was a most unwelcome arrival for him of a different kind.

The land drew me in quickly. A three-acre meadow, growing itself out, seedy and weedy, lay just beyond the backdoor. Grass up to my chest, nettles higher. After a few months, it was ignorance that led me to putting sheep out to graze it. I started with two fattening lambs and expanded to six more when I dimly wondered how many it would take to gnaw down the woody forage (they never did, nor could ever have done so). With my city eyes I saw nothing, understood even less and threw myself at tasks as they arose. A polytunnel seemed a good idea and I set about digging the trenches which would be backfilled to tension the polythene sheeting. It took an entire weekend working the heavy clay and perhaps had I known better I would not have started the task, but significantly, I was unconsciously incompetent, blissfully ignorant. This term – ignorant, ignorance – is associated with the term 'to be unacquainted', and this captures precisely my experience, in relation to the soil; if I were to be acquainted, I needed a teacher.

What I had not noticed during these initial months was that David had been watching me or, to be more exact, had decided to watch me. Furthermore, he had begun to move around me, checking my readiness, perhaps, or aptitude. Later, I often saw David take stock of individual animals on the farm. Once when we bought our first cow he spent an hour or so in its barn, slowly stepping around it, pausing for several minutes, murmuring reassurance, occasionally growling if it looked restless. He was weighing up the will of the beast, prepared to meet it with a regard for its own power, intention and volition; literally 'taking stock'. It was after the weekend hauling clay that he approached me, and that he chose me. 'I'll teach you all what I know', he declared. It was not so much a question, or invitation; it was an interruption, 'a breaking in of some action', a 'break in the continuity' of my life as I understood it. Later, David would tell me of how he had waited to see if there was a resilience in me, not only an enthusiasm. He had no idea if I could be 'taught by' him, or indeed, if I were 'teachable', but by the end of that weekend of digging, he decided to choose me as a student. A choice was now mine, and this is such a profound educational point and I feel it keenly as I write now. The option to walk away, remain on the edge of my familiar world, resists the call of the teacher. Nothing external was pushing me to become the student in this relationship and yet I felt so compelled, it was irresistible; how so? How had this desire to reach towards newness formed?

I recognise now that to be chosen by the teacher is a most potent transaction, perhaps we might call it the primal educational transaction. For me it carried both a parental and paternal psychological promise of support, containment and the power that arises from knowing where you come from. But a psychological incentive is insufficient to fully describe this experience. There was a sense of another world coming to me through this exchange, through this person as teacher, and that this could matter to me. It was not so much him – David – that would matter, but the promise he carried on behalf of the world; he was an ambassador for the world. I do not mean by this any kind of literal world, but a symbolic one that refers to more than the other person, but the universe which lies outside of myself. He was representative of what lay beyond the continuity of my experience of the world and held a key to my further belonging within it.

I am aware, as I write these lines, of the potential idealisation of the teacher and the grandiosity that comes with the role as I am describing both my experience and reflect on David's as teacher. If I stay at the symbolic, rather than psychological, level and I begin to recognise the significance of what the teacher might claim. That there are times, albeit brief and passing, when no-one else but I as a teacher will do. This is exactly what David enacted when he spoke of teaching me; at that point, he was irreplaceable as he interrupted my world, and he demonstrated how he as the teacher takes his place; not just any teacher but this one.

There is a sideline to this tale. It may be apparent here that the onus is on my tutelage, my apprentice to his role as teacher. It may appear as a one-way transaction, a purely altruistic act on David's behalf but it becomes clear that this is not the case. Our relationship is symbiotic and the educational gift reciprocal, a topic I will return to when considering the final chapter, 'Implications for an education orientated towards connection with the existential, social and ecological domains' For now, my submission into studentship transforms David's life, and he lives longer than he ought.

To think of arrival as educational raises a question for me as to with what authority does the teacher choose to arrive? There is also a close focus on the connection between the arrival itself and the event of subjectification of the student, but what my experience with David highlights is the significance of his own experience of subjectification, as teacher. David was utterly confident in himself as he stood with me that day, certain of what he knew, owning his competence; more importantly, he was sure of who he could be for me as his student. Crucially, he was aware of the risk he took in neither obliging me into servitude to his 'sovereignty', nor fearing his will would be diminished if I were to step back.

What I also discover in writing this piece is that arrival, as with natality, is fuelled by a wilfulness. Whilst life may appear of itself, its capacity to endure more than a moment requires engagement, relationship and expenditure of energy, even at least at a biological level. This can be understood as a type of agency, physis, a sense of individual volition in relationship with the other, held in the context of place. Embedded in that sentence I recognise the threefold educational vision presented in what follows, an education that is orientated towards soil, soul and society.

Acknowledgements

This book emerged out of a research study forged through a series of educational encounters. Such experiences were rooted in powerful locations, including the fields of east Suffolk, the rich, animated landscape of Schumacher College and the more distant and potent land of Bhutan. I am grateful to each of these and all the other places encountered in between. My experience with David has been a gift that has continued to yield a harvest and though he has long since passed, I acknowledge his presence both then as an astonishing teacher and now as an ancestor to all that has followed since.

More central to the writing itself, I am indebted to my supervisor and mentor, Gert Biesta. I cannot properly acknowledge the full extent of what it has been to be supported by Gert, but I will try nevertheless. Through Gert's subtle, and at times, imperceptible guidance, I discovered what it means to live subjectification from the 'inside out'. Rarely the subject of his direction, but as a result of Gert's presence, I have spent several years being encouraged to make my own decisions about how my ideas and experience might exist in my writing, something for which I am extremely grateful. At several moments in the educational journey, there were key inflection points, each of which was fundamental to shaping the content and format of the final study. Gert's teacherly gesture, his capacity to witness and sense of 'grown-up-ness' have impacted me both during the mentorship process and since then too. Thank you.

I have been fortunate to have been supported by others along the way, beginning with fellow travellers on the Schumacher College Right Livelihood programme in 2016, students from numerous groups, including at the Berne Institute, Kegworth, UK, here at the farm in Suffolk and various schools across the country. I appreciate the early supervisory support from Anne Chapell at Brunel University, and many colleagues in the transactional analysis community.

Finally, it is customary for authors to thank their partners and wider family for their support and this is certainly heartfelt on my behalf. However, this has not been so much a writing project but more an experiment in how to live life. I am grateful to all my family for having faith – Food of the Earth.

Arrival

A critique of product-orientated education and a rationale for an alternative vision incorporating sufficiency, homonomy and emancipation

Walking the Land

As I sat down this morning to begin to write, the phrase 'walking the land' comes to mind. This is what I do each day, often as the sun is rising, or at least, whilst it is still fresh in the sky. There's a purpose to it and especially for those of us who keep livestock. This is the time to discover what the night left behind and what the morning brings, new births perhaps, or an escapee. There is a practicality to walking the land which has necessity to it and, to an extent, is literally about taking stock. There's something else though – walking the land has a ritual quality to it. There is a familiarity that comes from coursing around the field boundaries, and the feeding of stock, and it takes on what some might call an act of worship, and what others might find an experience in mindfulness. There's honouring to be had in walking the land, a recognition of what has come before and will endure. A wondering in how, through the elegant simplicity of soil, water and sunlight, such abundance is possible, despite the entropy of autumn and the challenges of winter. Perhaps, psychologically, walking the land also provides a reassurance about belonging, not so much to people – kin – but about belonging to place – kith. That 'walking the land' resolves what it means to belong, and that here, on this planet, we can find our place. Taking account, and witnessing the gift of the morning, walking the land has potential for 'reckoning up' and deepens the connection with the soil, out of which lives are fashioned. How might an education look if born out of such a place?

Introduction

In this opening chapter, I set out the parameters of the book, a 'walking of its land' so to speak, and identify the core questions, and problems addressed in the work, followed by a rationale for resolving a series of issues associated with creating a vision of education fit for contemporary challenges at the personal, social and ecological level. The book takes the form of a philosophical consideration of a particular existential aspect of educational discourse, central to which is the work of Biesta (2014, 2017). The guiding

DOI: 10.4324/9781003407751-2

thread throughout is an exploration of the kind of education that supports a triad of connection which I suggest are currently critically endangered and relate to soil, soul and society. I will present what I regard as a fundamental problem with education, as it is generally understood and practiced, which, to put simply, is a tendency for education to be orientated towards production, a term that I treat specifically, and which has, what I suggest, are anti-educational implications. My concern is that an education orientated towards production impinges on themes which have a particular resonance in education, namely autonomy, freedom and the notion of growth. In this opening chapter, I will set out the basis of a critique of these three concepts and indicate how there are significant consequences when these are assimilated into an education that emphasises production. I will lead out from such a critique to a second dimension, which focuses on the question of what is at stake when education is understood primarily as a means of production. This is where the attention shifts from the abstract and towards a reckoning up of why such an enquiry matters and considers the consequences of discounting ecological and existential aspects, and the limitations that come with regarding education as a purely sociological activity. It is at this point that I draw attention to the wider context of planetary climate crisis, inequality and hyper-normalisation (Yurchak, 2006) and emphasise that educational effort has become embedded in the problem it might otherwise resolve, which might be framed as enabling individuals 'to be at home in the world' (Arendt, 1994). This chapter offers an initial consideration of why this concern of product-orientation is so important and in doing so highlights three disconnecting consequences which lead to my interest in soil, soul and society in the educational encounter. Finally, this opening chapter concludes by outlining the central objectives of this book, highlighting the key questions associated with addressing the theme of (dis)connection and education.

The argument of this work has arisen out of what I regard as a common preoccupation in which education has been understood as orientated towards production. What I mean by this is that what is referred to as 'education' is an activity which is understood as having a singular purpose, namely to generate some 'thing'. I set out shortly what kind of education I am referring to when I talk of it being product-orientated and explain how this understanding becomes important in the wider context of the book. This chapter is divided into three sections, the first of which outlines the concern, or problem that I will be seeking to address and resolve. The second section, 'What's at Stake?', sets out the kind of education I will suggest as a resolution, or response, to the problem of education presented in the first section. Finally, the third section begins to indicate why an alternative view of education is needed, in effect introducing the intention of my work. These sections set out both the parameters of the book – its landscape – and indicate the ideas, thinkers, writings and themes which are at play in its subsequent chapters.

Soil, Soul and Society

I want to offer a brief explanation as to my references to 'soil, soul and society' as it will become increasingly familiar motif to the reader as the book unfolds. This alliterative phrase originates in the work of Satish Kumar (2013), the full title of which is Soil, Soul, Society: A New Trinity for Our Time. Kumar sets out a view that encourages connection, or re-connection, as a basis for life that is distinct from other 'trinities' that have been historically influential, for example the Christian triune of Father, Son and Holy Spirit or the French Revolution's Liberty, Equality and Fraternity. Citing other ancient and contemporary examples, Kumar comments that 'none of them represents a holistic and ecological world view in an explicit manner. They are either spiritual or social but they are mostly anthropocentric and fail to highlight our relationship with nature or the connection between the social and spiritual' (Kumar, 2013, p. 16). Kumar cultivates his vision out of his personal experience as a Hindu monk and pilgrim, drawing on the tenets of the epic text, Bhagavad Gita. Whilst 'soil, soul, society' is associated with Kumar, the concept of a tripartite frame of connection is also apparent in the writing of Alistair McIntosh, a community activist, Quaker and ecologist from the Scottish Isles. He writes of the triune basis of community which comprises three dimensions:

Community with nature,
Community with the divine and
Community with another

(McIntosh, 2008, p. 49)

McIntosh recognises that in conversation with Kumar the alliteration of soil, soul and society 'wonderfully sums it up' and goes on to remark that 'This triune basis of human ecology or human community can be glimpsed in teaching and stories from all over the world' (McIntosh, 2008, p. 49). For my own interests, 'soil, soul and society' has been a guiding motif, an anchoring point so to speak, for my thinking and development of ideas. I have held the phrase lightly in developing the writing in the sense that it intimates the broad range of domains with which the following vision of education is concerned. (It is perhaps worth noting that I first came across the term when testing out the possibility for my research when I attended a programme of study at the Schumacher College in Devon, which was established by Kumar for the development of holistic disciplines.)

I encourage the reader to also hold the themes of soil, soul and society lightly when navigating the book. When I refer to society, I am doing so in a general philosophical sense, with societas in mind, in other words, a reference to a fellowship or gathering of persons. I am not intending to refer to a specific sociological conceptualisation. Similarly, when using the term 'soul' this is not within a theological or metaphysical frame of mind, but one which has a more existential quality. Finally, I am using 'soil' to denote what might be best understood as an earth-based position and not a literal, naturalistic ontological perspective. My hope is that by prefacing the work in this way, the reader might enjoy the sufficiency that comes with Kumar's delightfully ingenious phrase.

The Problem of 'Education'

There are arguably many problems that might be cited of education so my purpose in this discussion is to be more explicit about precisely how education is problematic in the context of what follows. I talk of the problem of education, not the problem with education in order to emphasise that the concern of my enquiry has been about how education exists, as opposed to the more technical questions of theory, method and practice. The problem of education draws attention towards defining education conceptually. This is the first way-marker as we 'walk the land' of the book and in some respects the task of defining education is held in abeyance throughout. For now, I want to offer a view of education that commonly persists and shapes how it is discussed, developed and practised and what I will refer to as product-oriented education. This term requires a degree of explanation in order to better frame my motivation for the wider argument and its alternative vision for an education orientated towards soil, soul and society.

Product-Orientated Education

Throughout this work, I have found it necessary to adopt a term by which I can refer to a type of educational task that crystallises much of what is problematic in building a rationale for my work. Options have included 'process-orientated', 'technical education', 'managerial' or 'technocratic', and whilst each of these carries an element of what I have been looking for they have caveats and limitations that curtail the scale of the concern in what follows. Product-oriented education may be ungainly but it is more precise in capturing the essential problem. The two components – 'product' and 'orientated' – are well suited to defining the reason for why my argument is necessary. For a 'product' to exist it requires manufacture, a process from which something is created. To be 'orientated' refers to 'tailor' or adapt to specific circumstances or direction. To put this idea in a broader philosophical context, the concern in this work is that education is a reductive form of poiesis, the 'production of things'. Originating in Aristotle, this refers to a specific understanding of the nature of things, or rather more precisely, how the nature of things might be manufactured, or not. In referring to the practical business of living, there is an obvious value in creating products to navigate the various everyday tasks. However, this has implications when applied to the educational task, because how something comes into being is originated in the intention of the manufacturer and not in the 'product' itself. I argue that the basis of contemporary Western education is understood as a process of manufacture, governed by particular circumstances and which is dependent on adaptation. I am intentionally generic in this opening definition; I have resisted dropping into references to students or teachers, or 'teaching' and 'learning'. My point in doing so is to keep the idea of product-orientated education sufficiently 'open' in that both educator and 'educand' might be regarded as objects in the educational task. In other words, that the product being manufactured might refer to the objective for either and both partners in the educational relationship.

The use of the term 'product' in relation to education is potentially ambiguous, because of its generality and the potential for misunderstanding, so again, for the purposes of clarity, I want to set out the parameters of how the term is being used here. Anticipation is key to conceptualising the idea of 'product'. However, the product is defined, it implies prior expectation of its existence, before the process of manufacture begins. Such pre-determination is one of the components in thinking about product and production. In the context of the educational task, the product is most explicitly expressed, for example, in terms of 'learning' objectives. This in turn often originates, or is frequently associated, with the teacher, although as I indicated earlier, the teacher's performance may also be the object of what is anticipated within particular circumstances, an aspect dealt with later in relation to alienation and objectification. The central point at this stage is that production is 'realised step by step' (Arendt, 1958) and is distinct from the capacity of nature to appear of itself, a phenomenon that becomes significant in the later discussion of physis (Berne, 1957; Arendt, 1958; Jantzen, 1998). For now, 'to anticipate' is a pre-requisite of production, necessary to the tasks of design, implementation and assessment which are integral to the process of manufacture. Orientation, which refers to the capacity to tailor or direct the production process, similarly implies a navigational intention, which renders education as a 'strong' concept, with the consequence 'that education become strong, secure, predictable, and risk-free, and to see any deviation from this path as a problem that needs to be "solved", therefore misses the educational point in a number of ways' (Biesta, 2014, p. 2). In the context of education, the implications of an orientation towards product are paradoxically both far reaching and restrictive, and in the following section of this chapter, I will set out the possibility of an alternative 'education point'.

In using the term product-orientated as I have described, it will become increasingly apparent that this perspective permeates a diverse range of educational philosophies, theory and practice. The tendency to limit the application of a product-orientated education to the model most commonly found in post-industrial societies is understandable where mass schooling and tertiary education are generally focused on meeting standardised learning objectives, for example, and I discuss this in more detail shortly. However, it is important to emphasise that when I am referring to product-orientated education, this applies to more than the familiar, contemporary approach.

In many respects, the current preoccupation with standardising and regulating education accentuates the features of product-orientation. In developing my rationale, I am not limiting my focus to this dominant educational frame of reference, doing so would restrict the scope of my critique as well as the significance of what I am suggesting is at stake when education is regarded solely as a process of manufacture and production.

To broaden the range of argument, I am suggesting that even where approaches to education incorporate objectives which are more broadly defined, or open to negotiation, there is, nevertheless an underlying assumption of product-orientation. Examples of this include transformational learning (Mezirow, 2000), which offers a radical educational model aimed at increasing social activism, and anticipate an end 'product' in the form of a shift in power differential, and a commitment to social justice. Meanwhile, those promoting humanistic education (Rogers, 1968; Noddings, 1984) set out an intention to increase personal growth and development. Closely aligned to humanistic approaches, the holistic education movement (Miller et al, 2019) maintains a more elaborate, but nonetheless pre-determined goal governing the educational task.

To manufacture a product is founded on something other than a random act or in the absence of anticipation. An intention is formed out of circumstances from which the product is designed to have some purpose. Take, for example, a product such as a garden shed, which arises from a need to store tools or cultivate plants. Furthermore, there is also an understanding about the particular context. It is an unlikely product intended for someone living in a high rise apartment, for instance. The intention and subsequent design of the product and manufacturing process reveals the significance of the context of the 'manufacturer'. In turning back to the specifics of education, this raises interesting questions about the conditions which give rise to particular variants of product-orientated education. The contextualising of the current direction in educational policy foregrounds what I suggest is a contamination of education and heightens an understanding of the need for the type of alternative vision of education which lies at the heart of my work.

The conceptualising of education as product-orientated is not inherently a problem, but in the current context it is, I argue, a central concern, and I will set out how I see it as prone to becoming problematic. Clearly, having an objective for the educational process can be highly beneficial, for example, in terms of attaining a certificate to practise dentistry, or to drive a car. To be assured that the person installing the heating system, or in preparing financial accounts, has achieved the requisite training is important to our daily lives. In this respect, the concrete benefits of a product-orientated education process are not in dispute. Even where outcomes are expressed in less technical terms, product-orientated education has some justification, as in the case of humanistic pedagogy. Outcome can be described in this approach, for example, through the process of cultivation. The process of the students' personal unfolding is more subtle, or open, and involves tolerating a degree of ambiguity as to the precise nature of the outcome, or 'product'. Nevertheless, there is an underlying trajectory that envisages the student being in a process of maturation, one in which the individual is 'learning to be human' (Macmurray, 2012), moving from point A to point B. Describing these two types of product-orientated education – concrete and discrete – highlights two valid dimensions of the educational task, which correspond with two of Biesta's educational domains of socialisation and qualification (2010). I am drawing attention here to the validity of accreditation and enculturation simply in order to emphasise that there is a legitimate place for product-orientated education. However, in relation to the central themes of connection to soil, soul and society, product-orientated education is highly problematic.

The Problem of Product-Orientated Education

To understand the premise of what I propose, product-orientated education is regarded as both pivotal and problematic, and in the following discussion, I will present what I see as some of the most significant issues. The context for this opening commentary on product-orientated education is that it can be characterised as globalised, post-industrial and neo-liberal. Furthermore that my argument is centred on the basis that education is subject to rapid and extensive commodification due to it being rooted in a capitalist context, and that the tendency to promote product-orientated education has compromised the capacity of education to effectively address ecological, individual and social challenges. Shortly I will introduce the work of several writers, each of which has addressed different limitations of this kind of education policy, including, amongst others, Biesta (2010), Pring (2013) and Sahlberg (2012). Each of these writers has been interested in pursuing a specific enquiry, whether it be the threat to democratic education, reductionist implications of standardisation, or the homogenisation and limitations of education research. What emerges as a common concern is the prevailing culture of a global education reform movement (GERM), a term originated by Sahlberg (2012) and which captures the essential character of a post-industrial educational model that dominates policy and practice across sectors of schooling and tertiary education.

Global Education Reform Movement (GERM) and Product Education

As will become clearer, I am taking a position opposed to the dominant view of education as it occurs as product-orientated. Understanding the characteristic features of its socio-political context will be important to bear in mind when I discuss why such a critique is important and propose an alternative perspective on education. Sahlberg's introduction of the GERM (2012) presents a treatment of contemporary education that identifies concerns with an educational perspective deeply embedded in global policy and practice. For my purpose, Salhberg's presentation is important because it describes a version of education that is firmly product orientated and, in fact, might be argued to be the quintessential form of this kind of educational approach, or perhaps, its ultimate end point as an educational idea. Sahlberg's argument is that for the past 30 years in many European and American systems, government decision-making has pursued policies that are increasingly similar, focused on effectiveness, efficiency and which bring about a homogenised global model of education. The GERM is founded on five principle features; the introduction of competition between schools and colleges in order to generate more choice for consumers; standardisation of education as manifested in a focus on outcomes-based education; a focus on core subjects, namely numeracy, literacy and natural sciences; test-based accountability, for both students and teachers; increasing school choice so as to create a diverse educational market-place (Sahlberg, 2015). The overarching impact of this global project is to ensure certainty in the educational task and, by implication, create a pervasive risk-averse educational culture. The significance of such a 'strong' concept of education (Biesta, 2014) is that it rules out what is 'in' the scope of education, and what is not, whether this refers, for example, to the exclusion of non-core subjects, non-typical students or 'errant' teachers.

Sahlberg's treatment of education provides a compelling indictment of how education has been rendered to a crude, simplified version of a product-orientated activity which continues to diminish how educational work might be understood. Despite its predominance, the durability of the GERM is not so straightforward. One of the challenges which the GERM has needed to respond to is how to maintain the objective of conformity, whilst simultaneously advocating that autonomy, growth and freedom are educationally plausible. As will be discussed shortly, these three concepts are core to the neo-liberal economic system that underpins and drives the GERM agenda. This tension – between establishing certainty of outcome, with encouraging individuals to exercise autonomy and freedom of choice as consumers – requires a complex negotiation of factors to avoid rupturing the implicit socio-political contract. One way in which this divergence can be accommodated is by increasing the language of choice in relation to selecting schools, courses, universities and other types of educational product and providers. By marketising the educational estate, introducing the economics of consumer choice, customer care and product delivery, the field of education is integrated into a broader context in which the civic sphere is privately owned and corporately managed. Managing the dissonance between the promotion of values – such as autonomy, growth and freedom – and the lived experience can be understood through the concept of hyper-normalisation. This term was originally used in reference to a delusional process described in relation to Soviet culture prior to the collapse of communism (see Yurchak, 2006). The phrase refers to how the general population were aware of the obvious disparity between political descriptions of reality and their lived experience. Whilst the failure was obvious, it was equally impossible to envisage an alternative. The consequence was a deepening engagement by all parties in maintaining the delusion which was a pretence of a functioning society. This 'fakeness' was understood as reality, and its effect was termed 'hyper-normalisation'. This idea is useful because it describes a disconnection which becomes increasingly central to my overall critique of contemporary education, and the impetus for seeking a more connective view of the educational task. The important disconnect at this point is that there is an increasing disparity between the dominant aspirational rhetoric about education and that of the lived reality for educators, students and other stakeholders, in addition to a limited capacity to articulate educational alternatives.

> What, in terms of political rhetoric, has been the message for selling 'education' to young people and their parents? For several decades, it has been that more education will maximise opportunity, ensure better jobs, create greater social mobility and raise living standards.
>
> What, then, if this is no longer the case – or even if it never was the case for many young people as they struggled to get qualifications which had no, or only marginal, financial returns? In the UK wages have not risen in real terms since 2005. Upward social mobility for some has meant downward social mobility for others. There can be no universal opportunity for betterment in such social and economic terms.
>
> (Pring, 2013, p. 29)

Pring's focus is on the future prospect for secondary education in the UK, hence the reference to vocational destination and the emphasis on education and its impact on earning potential. His argument continues with a more generally applicable critique of education, identifying four areas of doubt about the appropriateness of contemporary educational policy. These include the increasing number of students disengaging from formal education, the impact of a counter-culture of the social worlds that young people inhabit, the debilitating effects of social and economic disadvantage and the impoverishment of the culture in its accommodation to all (Pring, 2013, p. 71). My substantive point here is that aligning education within an economic frame of reference, and in particular with a model espousing the advantages of global capitalism, becomes highly problematic. Artificiality, either in terms of rhetoric or practice is part of the disconnective mechanisms which I will be identifying throughout this work. Maintaining a suspension of disbelief is required by many, including students, parents, teachers and school leaders in order to sustain the paradox which reduces the range of educational experience whilst promoting, for example, freedom (of choice), autonomy and growth.

I have already mentioned the importance of disconnection and there are two further general phenomena – objectification and alienation – which amplify the impact of the kind of disconnection created by product-based education in a market-driven environment (see Friere, 1970). Objectification refers to how an individual, or more precisely, aspects of an individual, serves the purpose or provides benefit to another more powerful individual or system. Whilst terminology might be used in relation to meeting the needs and ambitions of the individual student, for example, through 'personalised learning', or a 'bespoke curriculum', summative educational and regulatory priorities remain stubbornly fixated on the collation of data and an analysis focused on highly delineated and limited data sets in relation to precisely defined outcomes. Indicators of objectification include how students are referred to as 'clusters' of potential 'outcomes', and interventions are designed to 'progress' batched students from one grading level to another. Other groups of students might be either avoided, through selective admission arrangements, or abandoned via exclusion because of the threat to the overall success of the wider educational population. Alienation emerges as an impact of objectification on the individual. It refers to the absence of personal engagement in the educational task not only by students, but also teachers, in the face of systemic objectification. High levels of transition, both amongst students leaving school and college placements, and teachers seeking new careers, are further indicators of alienation which occurs in other sectors based on production and service supply in capitalist systems.

A further important difficulty with such a managerial and entrepreneurial product-orientated education is its limiting impact on educational research through its preoccupation with 'evidence-based' practice and the associated 'metrics' for gathering and analysing 'educational data'. It is beyond the scope of this book to explore in depth the ramifications of introducing causality into discussions about the educational task; however, much of the debate about such matters assume that teaching and learning are connected and that the teacher can assume to establish learning – or to be more precise, learner's – objectives, and that these are determined, or secured, through technical interventions by the teacher. In these conditions, educational work becomes frustrated as it is subjected to a causal frame of reference which has been appropriated from non-educational disciplines, for example, medical research. Biesta, in his critique of evidence-based research in education, continues to describe this false analogy.

> To begin with the role on causality: apart from the obvious fact that the condition of being a student is quite different from that of being a patient – being a student is not an illness just as teaching is not a cure – the most important argument against the idea that education is a causal process lies in the fact that education is not a process of physical interaction but a process of symbolic or symbolically mediated interaction .... While we may

want to refer to the activities of teachers as interventions ... we should not think of these interventions as causes, but as opportunities for students to respond and, through their response, to learn something from these opportunities.

(Biesta, 2010, pp. 34–35)

This resistance to causality and the limits of evidence-based approaches to educational research further highlight the problems for a product-focused education, which sets out to promote efficiency towards a pre-defined notion of effectiveness. Certainly in the English schooling system, the implications of this have generated a new kind of alchemy for which schools appoint 'data managers', often senior leadership positions, who undertake the specialist business of combining variables to predict outcomes, set programmes and instruct staff in manipulating technical interventions in order to improve educational 'productivity'. An extension of this practice is that individual teachers are reduced to technical operatives, a development explored by Ball (2003) writing in the early phase of GERM policy development. 'The novelty of this epidemic of reform is that it does not simply change what people, educators, scholars and researchers do, it changes who they are' (Ball, 2003, p. 215). With its emphasis on performativity, 'conflicting effects' emerge, on the one hand with an 'increasing individualisation, including the destruction of solidarities based on a common professional identity ... as against the construction of new forms of institutional affiliation and "community", based upon corporate culture' (ibid, p. 219).

My purpose in presenting these issues – alienation, objectification and hyper-normalisation, and the latter comment on research – is to fill out some detail of the limitations inherent in the educational landscape in which this work is situated and form something of the character of the landscape that is being explored. To summarise thus far, in scoping out the broad arc of this book, it is important to understand that product-orientated education, whilst ubiquitous in contemporary discourse, is problematic. Furthermore, that although it may be widely accepted as a way of framing the educational task, product-orientated education risks jeopardising the extent to which it – the educational task – can exist separately from the limitations of global economics. Given this context, I am interested as to whether education can be understood as useful in addressing the contemporary challenges of individual, social and ecological disconnection.

Growth, Autonomy and Freedom and Product-Orientated Education

I want to step back a little from the specific focus on the GERM and the capitalist culture that supports its dominant position and turn attention to three ideas historically associated with the aims of education and suggest further limitations of product-orientated education. For the purposes of my argument, growth, autonomy and freedom are multi-faceted ideas that provide opportunities to both critique product-orientated education and which might begin to inform an alternative vision of education. My aim here is to indicate how each of these ideas – growth, autonomy, freedom – can confuse the educational task when associated with product-orientation. The following critique is offered as a frame of reference, a view finder, to hold in regard to subsequent chapters.

The Problem with Growth and Education

Perhaps rather obviously, product-orientated education is based on the virtue of growth, with the development of the student being regarded in such a way that there is some kind of 'improvement' through the completion of the educational engagement. When this is related to the fact of physical maturation, any objection to growth, developmentally, would be regarded as unnatural or even an impossibility (although, in the context of this book, the process would not necessarily qualify as educational). However, when used more generally to justify what is happening in educational terms, the notion of growth is less straightforward. Initial questions I would raise would be about whose growth is being prioritised? what kind of growth? and to what end is it designed? Such questions begin to highlight how an educational process can be liable to misinterpretation or mis-direction. Furthermore, within a context rooted in capitalist objectives, an educational process promoting growth – however defined – will be prone to the assumption that all growth is 'good', an assumption that I will return to later in this section.

Before further investigating the problem with growth in education, I will clarify how I am using the term and in doing so draw on the work by Land, Grow or Die (1973), who distinguished three forms of growth. The first, described as accretive, refers to the simple act of adding to that which already exists, 'an accumulation of "sameness" simply extending boundaries and getting larger without changing the basic form' (Land, 1973, p. 11). Land's second form of growth – replicative – is more pertinent to my argument. This involves 'growth by influencing other things to take on the form of the initiator. Whereas accretive growth is sameness, replicative growth is "likeness"' (ibid, p. 11). In other words, there is an intention from the outset that the process of growth, its shape and designation is determined through the authority of the initiator, and here again there is the echo of the previous discussion of a product and design intention of the manufacturer. The intended trajectory, and particular character, of accomplishment is set in its 'authorship'. The relevance of this to education is important because it begins to indicate the limitations of growth as an ambition for the educational task. Re-creating the 'likeness' of the initiator, in this instance, that of the teacher as representative of what is possible educationally, delineates the boundaries of possible growth. Land, in a brief reference to discovery and creativity, claims that such ideas are 'wholly unlike our traditional concept of replicative education' (ibid, p. 57). In other words, set in the context of a dominant education policy framework characterised by the GERM, the student is capable of growth on condition that they conform to the standardisation embedded in the system. What this means practically is that students create – or 'grow' – individual responses for attaining what it will take to be successful in the economic market, engage as a consumer and, ideally, initiate further replication of a capitalist ideal.

Associated with this premise is an assumption that growth is also sustainable; that key indicators of successful growth such as accumulation (e.g. of knowledge), acquisition (e.g. of skills), with the capacity to increase consumption (e.g. through exercising 'free' choice), are all endlessly possible. The implications of these features of a growth-based, product-orientated educational philosophy are that such a model is vulnerable to the influence of marketisation, managerialism and commodification. Consequently, policy makers, education leaders and teachers embark on a campaigns to establish greater certainty, secure outcomes and minimise inefficiencies, for example by 'removing barriers to learning' and thereby 'raising achievement'. Such educational intentions are ostensibly benevolent – who would object to either obstructing development or reducing achievement? However, in the broader context of liberal capitalism, such language is educationally precarious; first, because it borrows too much from a free-market lexicon that leaves education vulnerable to a similar exploitation, whereby student agency is not free, but subject to direction and control by the teacher. Second, because the direction of what constitutes a valuable student 'product' is pre-determined by those who govern the means of this production – the teacher. In other words, the apparent benevolence of product terminology, incorporated in educational language, has subtle controlling implications for the teacher-student relationship and is covertly adverse to growth.

Typically, alongside the premise of 'growth is good', a product-orientated education also assumes that the student's starting point must necessarily be inferior to the intended destination. The pupil is envisaged as lacking in understanding, the adult learner is unpractised, the collective are regarded as oppressed, the community as impoverished. The need to instigate a hunger for a 'next best thing' is core to re-fuel the market-driven engine of a capitalist model, and education becomes a substantial provider. The notion of being incomplete prior to educational intervention reinforces the economic imperative that whatever one has is not enough. A further implication is that the prior experience of the student is somehow deficient and that it is growth, via education, that will satisfy the appetite (only to re-ignite the hunger post-attainment with a new, next 'must have' qualification).

Even where education is not driven by an economic imperative, the emphasis on growth remains troublesome. I suggest that humanistic and holistic educational perspectives also engage in a concept of growth that is problematic. Whilst there are interesting ideas to draw from in this educational lineage, and I will be doing so in later sections, the emphasis on personal growth in these approaches to education follow a similar trajectory to that of the more instrumental methods of product-orientated education. This is more subtle territory because whilst 'progressive' education objectives might have an appeal to teachers critical of their experience of technocratic education, the 'problem' of growth persists. The fundamental challenge regarding growth in education is that the definition of growth is pre-determined, or embedded, in educational 'code'. Furthermore, that by implication growth is set towards the end of the educational journey – it continues to take the form of a destination. The point is that many discourses on education imply a template for what is intended for the student, the authority for which lies with the educator.

A second feature of my critique of growth is that the pre-growth position is necessarily 'less than' what will be achieved as a result of an educational intervention. Whilst this is especially explicit in the marketised version of product-focused education, wherein attainment and qualification equip the student with increased currency, there is a similar tendency in how humanistic educators frame progress. The student is regarded as developmentally incomplete, or that their potential is 'unrealised', and therefore justifies the involvement of the teacher, or, more precisely what the teacher can do to, or for, the student.

The Problem with Autonomy and Education

Modern democratic and pluralist societies that rely on the market to play a significant part in economic and social life consider autonomy, or the ability of individuals to choose and follow their own conception of a life that they deem suitable for themselves, an indispensable condition of individual well-being .... It is hard to see how such societies could continue to exist in their present form were autonomy not to be available. Naturally then, one thinks that a society's education system is one of the key means through which individuals become autonomous.

(Winch, 2006, p. 1)

The argument for autonomy has had a longstanding claim as an educational aim, similar to growth and, as discussed previously, appears common-sense, and can be regarded as another kind of outcome associated with product-orientated education. I want to explore more closely the implications of autonomy as an educational objective and suggest that it becomes problematic in the context of product-orientated education especially when situated in a Western, Anglo-American tradition. For the most part educationalists (see, for example, Peters, 1965) have used autonomy in the classical sense of the term, defined generally as the capacity of the individual to be independent, living by one's own laws, specifically framed by Kant as the doctrine of the Will giving itself its own law based on conscience. I have found it useful in expanding my critique of autonomy to include reference to Berne (1964) and the link to individual agency. In doing so, I will argue that there is a close connection between the promotion of autonomy in education and its restrictive affect on the capacity of students and teachers to actually experience such a state of being autonomous in the world. Second, in referring to the important work of Angyal (1941), I want to suggest a fundamental flaw in choosing autonomy as a valid educational objective and argue that autonomy runs contrary to a possible educational alternative, which again I will discuss later.

Berne's definition of autonomy referred to the development of three human capacities, each of which echoes the classical Greek understanding that to be autonomous meant achieving an internal discipline by which to live one's life fully. Increased self-awareness, spontaneity in choice-making and greater availability for authentic, intimate relationship constitute the three features of Berne's idea of autonomy. He regarded this state of being in the world in contrast to living life according to external expectations, unquestioned norms and values, and beliefs and decisions determined by others. Berne's work on autonomy is typical of a wider cultural premise that development and accomplishment is framed in terms of the success of the individual; it is a job of work to be achieved alone and primarily for the benefit, or service, of the self. In cultures dominated by capitalist economic drivers, for example, those in the European and North American regions, the notion of autonomy is highly prized culturally. However, this is the very reason why autonomy becomes complicated with the acquisitive and individualistic qualities associated with consumerism. In addition there is a further problem, a deeper existential assumption at play, which is that the 'natural' and healthy human tendency is towards separation from the other. This assumption – pervasive in Western psychological and theological frames of reference – can be found in cultures that separate out the 'I' from the 'You'. This tendency can be identified with general concerns about the harm of symbiotic, co-dependent relationships and unresolved 'issues' regarding attachment patterns, both of which reflect a common-sense understanding that becoming separate and independent is a desired normative state. Such 'common-sense' aligns neatly with an economic model that encourages individuation, self-reliance and personal success formed on financial and material status. Promoting individual ambition via competition is intended to amplify the advantages of separateness and independence and attaining autonomy is a powerful mechanism for achieving this. Embedding autonomy as an objective of product-orientated education encourages, reflects and underpins a culture ironically 'dependent' on individuals striving for independence.

Andras Angyal's Foundations for a Science of Personality (1941) provides a different critical perspective on autonomy which exposes its problematic qualities. Born a Hungarian, studied in Vienna and practised as a psychiatrist in the US, Angyal refers to tendency, or trend 'toward' autonomous 'cravings',

> 'The goal of autonomous craving is always taking possession, domination, mastery of the object or, in general, the subordination of outside factors to the organism …. Autonomous behavior is characteristically restless and drives toward advancement ….
>
> (Angyal, 1941, p. 175)

In discussing the implications of autonomous cravings, Angyal offers a prescient comment given the link between capitalism and autonomy; 'The gratification of cravings is short-lived and is soon followed by renewed craving and one wishes it to be so. One does not merely wish to be satiated; one also wants to get hungry again' (ibid, p. 175). This never-ending appetite to consume, and the emphasis on separation, constitutes two significant reservations about autonomy as an educational objective. The Kantian notion that a law might be self-determined, internally ordained, reveals as much about how the individual is envisaged in isolation from others, as it does the advantage of autonomy as a desired objective. This brings into sharp relief the cultural specificity and limitation of autonomy and this is particularly problematic in the educational cause that I am interested in developing in the course of this book.

Whilst autonomy is regarded as a central educational objective in product-orientated education, it risks contamination by capitalist tendencies which mirror those described in the previous section on growth, namely, consumerism, commodification and accumulation, with those of the insatiable appetites of the individuated, atomised and idealised self. There is an echo here of Biesta's observations about desire in relation to the individual,

> The egological way of being is entirely generated by the desires of the ego, without asking – and this is the crucial distinction – whether, how, or to what extent such desires are desirable, both for the ego's existence in and with the world and for the world in and with which the ego seeks to exist.
>
> (Biesta, 2017, p. 16)

This matters in educational terms because, unchecked, the drive for autonomy promotes a disconnection of the individual from others; it jeopardises the possibility of envisaging different ways of being in relationship to self, others and the world. It turns the purpose of student agency inwards, towards satisfaction of the self and in doing so reduces the capacity for the student to discern how to 'be at home' in a pluralistic world (Arendt, 1994). As my argument unfolds, I will highlight the educational shortcomings of this in terms of a Western cultural bias and test out if autonomy may no longer fit as a legitimate educational purpose.

The Problem of Freedom and Education

My final critique is concerned with the concept of freedom in a product-orien-tated education. As with growth and autonomy, freedom might be regarded as a common-sense educational objective and certainly in product-orientated education the pursuit of freedom appears in a variety of forms. Whether it be freedom from ignorance through the acquisition of knowledge and under-standing, with the classic premise that education leads to a liberated citizen, or that students might be free from some kind of oppression as a consequence of an educational experience. The promise of becoming free from whatever existed before the educational process is integral to product-orientated edu-cation. Put bluntly, whatever you have now cannot be as good as what you will have at the end of this process called 'education'. At times, this promise might be utilitarian, along the lines of qualification (Biesta, 2014), resulting in a concrete outcome such as accreditation securing recognition in terms of competency. Whereas at other times, the outcome might be more 'open', framed as growing maturity, a successful process of socialisation (Biesta, 2014). My interest is that in these instances, freedom through education be-comes problematic when it has 'salvation' overtures. In a product-orientated frame of reference, the student is situated initially as incomplete and it is anticipated that this problem of incompleteness will be resolved through the educational intervention. Again, we can hear the pre-determined design of the manufacturer at work in this premise and that the educator is positioned as the rescuer of the student's incompleteness.

In addressing this issue, I will turn to Grace Jantzen – a feminist theo-logian – who offers a view on salvation in relation to human flourishing. Jantzen is at this point developing her ideas alongside those of Arendt's thoughts on action,

> 'Salvation', on the other hand, is a term which denotes rescue. One is saved from something: from drawing, from calamity, from loss .... To be saved means to be delivered from a situation which was problematic or even intolerable .... Salvation normally implies rescue by someone; there is a saviour.
>
> (Jantzen, 1998, p. 160)

Such terms might appear misplaced in relation to educational work; how-ever, I suggest that there is a great deal of figurative language in contempo-rary education discourse that resonates with salvation tendencies. One of the main justifications for additional schools' funding in impoverished areas, for example, is that education is regarded as the route out of poverty for students. A common refrain is that education provides an escape from the ghetto or the housing estate, and that that the student might enjoy a bet-ter life elsewhere. Be good, study hard and heaven awaits in another place.

Freedom, in this regard, is heavily conditional and deterministic. The educator is positioned as the gate-keeper, whether by supporting the pupil out of their down-trodden town, or facilitating adults overcome oppression.

In a product-orientated education, the teacher might be regarded as a Pied Piper figure, the folktale character who leads the children of Hamelin away from the ungrateful townspeople, never to return. In other words, 'freedom' disguises what is a pre-determined outcome and the student and teacher are caught in a trap of their own making, albeit one that is justified and enmeshed within a mechanistic, product-orientated education. Freedom, in this sense, becomes entrapment,

> One problem is that although emancipation is aimed at liberation of the one to be emancipated, it actually installs dependency at the very heart of the act of emancipation. After all, the one to be emancipated is dependent upon a 'powerful intervention' by the emancipator in order to gain his or her freedom.
>
> (Biesta, 2017, pp. 62–63)

There is a parallel between this account of educational entrapment in the guise of freedom, and the dependency behaviour associated with addictive consumerism, echoing my previous comments in relation to autonomy and growth. What is promoted as freedom, choice and an experience in (materialist) liberation eventually becomes a deepening exercise in reliance on a higher authority and what might be regarded as submissive or a surrendering of personal agency. In a similar way to growth and autonomy, the notion of freedom is compromised in the context of product-orientated education. This is particularly significant in reducing the student's connection with the core self, or subjectification (Biesta, 2014), and which will be a central theme in Chapter 3. The experience, ambition and trajectory of the student is defined by others who are positioned with the authority and power to do so.

In developing my critique of growth, autonomy and freedom, I have been indicating that each idea becomes problematic in the context of product-orientated education. The purpose of my commentary has been in part to highlight the different ways in which familiar, 'common sense' educational objectives can be contaminated and counter-productive when assimilated into an education where capitalism has been longstanding and which dominates the cultural and educational imaginary. There is, however, a second point to the critique that runs through my treatment of growth, autonomy and freedom, which is concerned with the theme of (dis)connection. This is arguably the more significant feature of my reservations about these three ideas; that there are implications for their use in product-orientated education which are instrumental in creating disconnections. Furthermore, that such disconnections damage the possibility for education to be relevant because it turns attention away from the crucial and difficult challenges of being in relationship to soil, soul and society.

What's at Stake: Why This Work Matters

I will turn now to introducing the rationale for why I believe the educational vision I am presenting matters and in doing so indicate the features and direction of an alternative which, I suggest, attempts to counter the problems and limitations of product-orientated education. Much of what I am setting out to do is to test the parameters and character of an education orientated towards connection, in ecological, spiritual and sociological terms. In addition, I am exploring a view of education that is centred on encounter (Bollnow, 1955), as opposed to the more familiar discourse of education as a longitudinal process. This, I suggest, brings my work into the existential territory of education and raises a question about how education exists, and what kind of education emerges when understood in this way, and why it is important to pay it attention (Biesta, 2014, 2017). In this section, I will highlight some of the conceptual ideas that might be important in establishing this educational alternative, most of which reflect what is so acutely lacking in the contemporary scheme of product-orientated education.

Before highlighting themes that relate to particular chapters, I want to focus on the two meta-concepts that run across the entire project, those of connection and encounter. Education understood as re-connecting the teacher and student with soil, soul and society is the heartbeat of the work presented here. The core problem with product-orientated education – epitomised for example by the GERM – is that it leads to an education that perpetuates disconnection of who we are, where we are and the basis of our relationship to one another. What is absent, or most at risk, in product-orientated education is for the teacher and student to experience themselves being rooted in place, founded in respect of each other's difference, and yet despite such difference, be in relationship nevertheless. There is more at play than this, but at this stage, I am wanting to introduce the complexity that comes when testing out a view of education that seeks to address this three-dimensional (dis)connection. The need to hold this complexity is necessary if education is to serve the contemporary circumstances where the finite nature of the planet is increasingly apparent and that the task of individuals to be at home in the world, with others, becomes similarly challenging. The disconnecting impact of product-orientated education works to accentuate and propagate the problems fuelling the crisis of climate collapse, and subsequently, the capacity of the human species to exist in the world, both literally and in existential terms. Consequently I am concerned with defining education as one which remedies this disconnection and promotes the advantage of an education vision that is a more direct response to the present challenges.

Connective education is predicated on the 'essence of community is the recognition, indeed the celebration, of interdependence between all parts' (Orr, 1991, p. 138). The premise of interconnectedness lies at the centre of all what follows and, I believe, will relate directly to a different view of the educational task. Unlike product-oriented education which is framed as an exclusively sociological, or anthrocentric activity (Buckles, 2018), I will be testing out an ecocentric perspective and, in doing so, argue that education becomes defined in relation to place. Put simply, all educational activity occurs somewhere, earth-bound, and I argue that this matters. Acknowledging interconnectedness as a key dynamic is important here in order to counter the disconnection inherent in product-orientated education. I intend to set out a rationale for why connectedness is a valid educational objective if teacher and student are to be a part of the world and not apart from it.

The second meta-concept I have in mind in establishing an alternative educational vision is the centrality of encounter which will be explored in more detail later, but for now I want to introduce how I am using the term. Historically, the word was used to describe an adversarial quality in the meeting of people, 'to counter' the other. It also includes the notion of being 'in front of' the individual, and this certainly captures an important aspect of the educational experience I will exploring. Education, from within the perspective of encounter, is where someone 'shows up' in the life of another, and that there is a moment, in which there is a possibility of the student being seen, called forth and where neither the teacher or student is replaceable. Such is the existential quality that comes out of conceptualising education as encounter, although as I have suggested this concerns more than a human-to-human engagement. The experience of showing up in the life of another is undertaken in the spatial environment. In pursuing this idea of encounter, I am bearing in mind Bollnow's development of the general use of encounter in educational experience;

> For Bollnow, encounter is a fundamental experience in which the subject meets something new, strange, uncontrollable, and (to the subject) incomprehensible. And encounter is a collision with everything outside one's understanding, not a meeting with the familiar. It is a meeting with something outside one's life-world. In other words, encountering a force outside subjective understanding results in a change to that subjective understanding; one recognises an entity that is not understood, and begins to learn.
>
> (Koskela and Siljander, 2014, p. 72)

This summoning up by the teacher of the student is quite different from the transactional exchange prevalent in product-orientated education. To 'summon up', etymologically, refers to the calling of another, and also to 'arouse, and excite to action', and which whilst might be in the 'gift' of the teacher, is not a promise that the student will 'appear', but that such a summons might be made. The nature of encounter as presented later on is, by implication, elusive, spontaneous and exists in the uncertain, liminal time and place of the education task. Conversely, in product-orientated education, the planning of each minute of a lesson and the concise structuring of activity and movement of students, the potential for encounter is limited. So, what is at stake in developing an alternative idea of education is one that incorporates emergence and possibility. The themes of connection and interconnectedness, combined with that of encounter, are central in my response to the concerns identified about product-orientated education.

Before moving further into my discussion, I am mindful that in addressing the importance of encounter in education I have not as yet referred to the significant early work of Martin Buber who also wrote specifically on the topic (1947). Referring to Begegnung as encounter, Buber's interest is in not solely the meeting, but in the relation, or Beziehung that occurs. I see a close connection between what I am interested in within my work and that of Buber's envisioning of the educational encounter. The recognition of the other as subject, rather than object in Buber's conceptualisation of I-Thou (1937), for example, is clearly aligned to my concern about objectification of student and teacher. However, for my purposes in developing a vision of education, and in my understanding of Buber's work, his intention appears to be focused on what is to be done out of such an encounter. That having engaged in relation via encounter, the point is then to forge community through, amongst other concepts, the centrality of dialogue. Genuine education, in my understanding of Buber's writing, is to set a course for building community, and that such an education is to develop the kind of character of the pupil by which this might be accomplished. I find this both compelling and highly important in a time of separatism and disconnection. However, my focus is on the encounter itself, and I am resisting a tendency to expand the remit into determining the end to which such a meeting is directed.

Beyond Growth, Autonomy and Freedom

I want now to return to the three ideas – growth, autonomy and freedom – which were critiqued earlier in this chapter. I had highlighted several ways in which these become problematic in the context of product-orientated education. I want to suggest now how growth, autonomy and freedom become re-framed and aligned with my exploration of education as a connected encounter.

To return to the concept of growth, I had argued that as an educational objective, it was problematic primarily on the basis that it can lead to an unsustainable appetite by which the world becomes the subject of acquisition and consumption, paralleling the features of capitalism. Instead, what I am interested in developing is a vision of education where sufficiency is a possibility. Whilst the notion of sufficiency might be generally understood, I want to explore more precisely its implications in educational terms. Its common definition refers to the condition of adequacy, or 'enoughness', and in its earlier usage referred to being adequate to an end purpose – a positive quality. In a contemporary context where 'good' is not enough, in terms of inspection judgement, for example, the notion of sufficiency can be construed as inadequate, a settling for 'second best'. Such a denigration of its original use exposes a tendency for striving that legitimises the pursuit of more 'growth', with a consequent emphasis on increased consumption on which capitalist economies are so dependent. Instead, I am interested in how sufficiency might be regarded as fundamental for establishing an ecological social imaginary (Buckles, 2018). This involves an understanding of sufficiency which recognises the importance of limits,

> Enoughness and too muchness become key limits, and this puts limits, ecological limits, on how much humans need to flourish. This then implies a refocusing of values not toward growth and progress, but toward quality of life and well-being, where more is not better. Implicit within this is a reworking of the ends of humankind, about purpose. A life of consumption and acquisition could destroy the very thing that gives life; a life of sufficiency may well enable the life systems to continue supporting life as it is currently constituted.
>
> (Buckles, 2018, p. 139)

'Enough', then, cannot be regarded as a neutral term and implies complex political consequences. When we start to think about the way it is deployed, in specific cultural situations and in particular historical moments, certain tendencies and contradictions within 'sufficiency' and 'enough' begin to emerge. To say that we have had enough of something might indicate a sense of being satiated, for example, with a good meal. However, it can also be used in a more declarative sense; 'Enough is enough!' in relation to the limits of tolerable behaviour, for example. By introducing sufficiency into my vision for education, I am interested in how it might encourage a discernment about desire, as mentioned in my earlier discussion. Not that the teacher's task is to define for the student how they might act differently, but that the educational encounter brings about an opportunity whereby the student is aware that such desire, and choices, in relation to it, exist,

> The educational principle here is that of suspension – a suspension in time and space, so we might say – that provides opportunities for establishing relationships with our desires, to make them visible, perceivable, so that we can work on them. This ... is not a process in which we overcome or destroy our desires ... but one in which we select and transform our desires so that we move from being subjected to ours desires to becoming a subject of our desires.
>
> (Biesta, 2017, p. 18)

Whilst Biesta does not refer specifically to how this 'suspension' and discernment might allow for sufficiency, or counter the unsustainability of growth in product-orientated education, the calibration of desire becomes increasingly useful when exploring the implications for establishing an education orientated towards soil, soul and society.

In turning to the topic of autonomy I suggest that what is most at stake, as it becomes problematic in product-orientated education with an emphasis on self-realisation and the promotion of autonomy, is that connectedness is diminished. In returning to the work of Angyal, a second tendency of living organisms, that of homonomy, is introduced, and this, I argue, is relevant in establishing an alternative vision of education. Homonomy, an unusual term and one that is quite absent in Western philosophical discourse, is explained as a trend away from the individual and towards the collective. Angyal suggests,

> The homonomous trend is toward the environment. Environment is the totality of those factors within the biosphere which do not follow the organism's determination, which are not centralised, do not depend upon the organism .... The environment from the point of view of the organism is largely a chaos and the autonomous tendency of the organism is to organise these factors and to coordinate them with the organism which acts as a governing center. The object of the homonomous trend is not the environment, not a collection of random and alien factors, but meaningful wholes of which he feels himself [sic] to be part or wishes to come part.
>
> (Angyal, 1941, p. 175)

Throughout this work, I will be advocating for a view of education that recognises interconnectedness as central and that homonomy, obscure a term though it might be, is one that will emerge in countering a general Western cultural bias. In practical terms, I will be interested in how homonomy is well established in non-Western ideas about education, most notably indigenous philosophies on education (Cajete, 1994; Petrovic and Mitchell, 2018).

Finally, in my critique on freedom, I emphasised how this can be corrupted in product-orientated education and creates an imbalance of power and authority in the teacher-student dynamic. I suggest that what is most at risk is an education where emancipation is possible. I am aware that in referring to emancipation there is a difficult balance to be struck. There is the possibility of emancipation being understood as another way in which the educator remains in charge of defining what is permissible or desirable for the student. I am mindful again, of Biesta's work (2014) in relation to emancipation and the link with action (Arendt, 1958) by which is meant the possibility for the individual to begin anew, or bring something new into the world. Freedom, in this sense, is understood differently from within a process of manufacture and product-orientation, and I will be associating it with natality, the matter of birth and becoming (Arendt, 1954; Jantzen, 1998). It is within this understanding of freedom that there is a possibility for the student to arrive, to choose whether, and how, to engage with the world, in relationship with others. It is out of this context of natality, that a further educational possibility emerges, dissensus (Biesta, 2017), which I will argue later in Chapter 5, can be associated with emancipation. So for the purposes of my argument, dissensus is predicated on an understanding of freedom which is in turn based on the premise of natality and that an educational encounter offers such an opportunity. This combination of ideas – natality, dissensus and emancipation – is to be tested later in my presentation when I focus on the issues of arrival and interruption in the education task.

To summarise at this point, what I am interested in exploring is a view of education that seeks connectedness, through encounter, and one which is orientated towards soil, soul and society. In doing so, alternative educational themes will be considered, including the importance of sufficiency, the necessity of homonomy and the possibility of emancipation. These then are the matters which are most at stake in establishing a vision of education and which are intended to counter both their absence in the dominant, product-orientated education and instead promote an education with which to live by in this current time.

What Is Needed: The Intention of an Alternative Vision of Education

Education as an interconnected encounter, orientated towards soil, soul and society, I suggest, remains beyond the familiar frame of reference that teachers hold about their work (even though it has powerful resonance when the concerns about product-orientated education are raised, and alternative possibilities shared). An implication is that teachers may feel a lack of control with regard to the design and delivery of their work, but also in their relational experience with students. The prevalence of product-orientated education renders the function of teacher to that of an operative engaged in ensuring that a mechanistic process is running efficiently. The professional preoccupation is on becoming increasingly competent (Biesta, 2014) to acquire the technical expertise required to increase effectiveness, within the parameters of an externally directed educational 'service'. However, with the notion of the educational encounter comes the possibility of an entirely different way of framing the role and impact of the teacher and this might be understood not as 'being in control' of what happens, but becoming irreplaceable – albeit briefly – in summoning the student, giving rise to the possibility of dissensus. My proposal is not to do away with the convention of product-orientated education, but to recognise that such encounters, even where the process is subject to powerful external control, an entirely different, and arguably where more significant, educational work takes place. It is one where the teacher might barely be able to claim to know what they teach, and even less so, what the student might learn. Herein lies a distinct sense of freedom for both student and teacher from within the confines of a product-orientated education.

To regard education as an encounter is intended in part, to re-energise and focus professional attention towards a reclaiming of vocational purpose and to encourage the cultivation of professional wisdom (Biesta, 2014). However, much more is at stake, in my view, and the aim of my work will not be solely to encourage teachers to think further about what they do and how they might be in relation to their students. It is through encounter that I hope to draw attention to the connections which this type of education can bring about. First, by providing an opportunity where the student can encounter themselves as a person. Second, that that the student is brought into contact with the wider world, via the teacher, and is challenged, or called to be part of it, yet not at the centre of it. In line with Arendt (1994), the intention is that such an education might raise an opportunity for the student to engage in a world in common, with all its plurality, and to find a home within it. Third, that the encounter occurs within a place, beyond the parameters of social relations. In others words, education has metaphysical and ecological components, in addition to being an anthropocentric activity. The Earth, so far, is the only place in which education can occur, and giving attention to the ecological context is increasingly important. The corrosive impact of product-orientated education is, in my view, becoming too significant, and to rely solely on such a model of education to address the contemporary issues of disconnection is evidently neither sustainable nor successful. Introducing the possibilities of encounter, combining the connections with soil, soul and society might provide alternative considerations for the thought-full practitioner.

Placing Myself

Before bringing this chapter to a close, I want to offer a few remarks on how I am placed in relation to the themes of the following education vision. I do so with a particular point in mind, which is that the idea of place is significant to the kind of education vision that I explore. The place where I began at the outskirts of this book are different to where I find myself towards the closing stages of this experience and I will return again to this in my closing chapter. I am keenly aware that there is a paradox in my creating an academic, philosophical educational journey, with its objective of completing the 'production' of a monograph. The irony of this is heightened when my interest is so explicitly focused on the limitations of product-orientated education. Even at this early point, there is the possibility that, as far as it exists as an object in the educational task, this work might be understood in addition to purely a 'product'. This is a matter I will explore in more detail in the later chapter on methodology.

I arrived to this journey several years ago as an experienced teacher, having worked initially in mainstream schools and a long period working in specialist education provision with students who had been excluded from school, many of which were regarded as having social, emotional and mental health needs. Eventually I became the head of services in a local authority in south London which provided individual and systemic support to children and families, teachers and school leaders. For the past 20 years, I have been working independently with teachers, school leaders and specialist educators on a range of themes including school culture, relational aspects of teaching and occasionally supervising complex educational casework. I mention this to highlight that for much of my career I have positioned myself in such a way that some might suggest I have been on the educational margins and looking into the mainstream world of education. However, for my part, I have often thought of the tendency to amalgamate 'education' with schooling and have felt that I have been more centrally located in education and looking, from a distance, at schooling. This book has been a way in which I have engaged in a personal exploration to understand what I mean when I refer to 'education', and myself as an educator.

In addition, over the past 15 years, I have been qualified in transactional analysis (TA) and I am a Teaching and Supervising Transactional Analyst (TSTA), which involves the education and development of professional qualification of others as transactional analysts. TA has its roots in the psychodynamic theory established by Eric Berne and which is practised predominantly in the clinical fields of psychotherapy and counselling. However, for several decades, non-clinical professionals have pursued training and qualification in the field of organisational development and, as in my case, the educational field of application. My commitment to this work has been significant and I have contributed widely to this approach and, in collaboration with other TA educators, have established a body of work and practice which nowadays is commonly referred to as educational TA (EdTA) within the TA professional community. Interestingly, during the five years of preparing this publication I had for the most part kept it separate my professional life as an educator in the TA community. It was only in the latter stages of bringing this work to a close that I recognised such a demarcation and considered the significance of such a peculiar oversight. I will return to this observation in my final chapter, For Whom is the Harvest? For now, I make mention of these personal observations because they relate to how and where I was placed and where I find myself at the outset and throughout as I have been writing. Location, as I explore in Chapter 5, is a thread followed in what unfolds.

Preparing the Ground

In this final section, I outline the sections of the book and explain the interleaving of different types of writing within its structure. Having established the context and rationale of the book in this opening chapter, I next discuss the how I have gone about creating a vision of education, in Chapter 2,

The importance of an ecological-phenomenological perspective in the educational encounter. This second chapter opens with a short passage which is the first example of anecdotal writing (van Manen, 2014). This type of writing appears at the opening of each chapter and is intricately linked to the design of the book. Chapter 2 provides an explanation of what I have done, how I have gone about it and, more importantly, why I have chosen this particular approach; it reveals something of the method in what may an appear unusual format. As I will make clear, I have found it necessary to create an approach that is congruent with the content of my argument. In this second chapter, I introduce a method that is aligned with the encountered educational experience which lies at the heart of the educational matter. One aspect of this is to share, in anecdotal form, episodes of encounter in an experience of my own education in relation to becoming a farmer, or aspects that have been significant in that experience.

Chapter 3, Natality, subjectification and the function of physis in education, explores the connections between a number of ideas, including subjectification (Biesta, 2014), natality (Arendt, 1958; Jantzen, 1998) and physis in the educational task. Again, the theoretical material is preceded by a second example of anecdotal writing that offers an experiential account of the themes explored in this third chapter. This chapter explains how arrival is an important starting point and is in itself 'arrivalistic', capturing the quality of the experience by which subjectification might occur and physis may find its expression through the education encounter.

Chapter 4, Liminality, place-based education and the role of myth and story, prefaced by a third example of anecdotal writing, looks to the themes of liminality (Turner, 1969; Conroy, 2004), and place-based education. I will be concentrating on the question; into 'where' does the student arrive? In some respects, this is the most 'liminalistic' section of the book in which I introduce material from the periphery of mainstream education discourse and includes insights from indigenous education (Cajete, 1994), eco-philosophy (Abram, 2017) and myth (Shaw, 2020).

Chapter 5, The act of teaching, 'grown-up-ness' and eldership in the educational encounter, turns to the role of the teacher and the art of teaching. My attention shifts from the student and importance of place and towards the experience of what it is to teach within an education that combines encounter with existential concerns. The ideas that inform this discussion include the concept of grown-up-ness (Biesta, 2017), eldership (Mindell, 2014), dissensus (2017) and the importance of gaze and gesture (van Manen, 2015).

A final example of anecdotal writing precedes Chapter 6, Implications for an education orientated toward connection with the existential, social and ecological domains. In some respects, this is the culmination of what has come before and I present more explicitly how I have been developing the educational vision through the preceding chapters. It might be regarded as the 'harvesting' of the work. However, I am also interested in re-framing what might be understood as an educational harvest and consider the ways in which this can have implications beyond the benefit to the student. Perhaps most importantly I raise questions about the underlying trajectory of educational thinking, suggesting that a move away from the commonly recognised linear view of product-orientated education, and towards an educational arc by which renewal becomes possible. In the closing sections of this chapter, I also consider tentative conclusions and possible limitations.

References

Abram, D. (2017) The Spell of the Sensuous: Perception and Language in the More-Than-Human World, New York: Vintage Books.

Angyal, A. (1941) Foundations for a Science of Personality, New York: Commonwealth Fund.

Arendt, H. (1954) Between Past and Future, London: Faber and Faber.

Arendt, H. (1958) The Human Condition, Chicago: Chicago Press.

Arendt, H. (1994) Understanding and Politics (the Difficulties of Understanding), in Kohn, J. ed., Essays in Understanding, 1930–1954, New York: Harcourt, Brace and Company, pp. 307–327.

Ball, S.J. (2003) The Teacher's Soul and the Terror of Performativity, Journal of Education Policy, Vol. 18, No. 2, pp. 215–228. DOI: 10.1080/0268093022000043065

Berne, E. (1957) A Layman's Guide to Psychiatry and Psychoanalysis, London: Penguin.

Berne, E. (1964) Games People Play: The Psychology of Human Relationships, London: Penguin.

Biesta, G.J.J. (2010) Good Education in an Age of Measurement; Ethics, Politics, Democracy, Boulder: Paradigm Publishers.

Biesta, G.J.J. (2014) The Beautiful Risk of Education, Boulder: Paradigm.

Biesta, G.J.J. (2017) The Rediscovery of Teaching, London: Routledge.

Bollnow, O.F. (1955) Begegnung und Bildung, Zeitschrift fur Pädagogik, Vol. 1, No. 1, pp. 10–32.

Buber, M. (1947) Between Man and Man, New York: Routledge & Kegan Paul.

Buckles, J. (2018) Education, Sustainability and the Ecological Social Imaginary: Connective Education and Global Change, Switzerland: Palgrave Macmillan.

Cajete, G. (1994) Look to the Mountain: An Ecology of Indigenous Education, Colorado: Kivaki Press.

Conroy, J.C. (2004) Betwixt & Between; The Liminal Imagination, Education and Democracy, New York: Peter Lang.

Friere, P. (1970) Pedagogy of the Oppressed, London: Penguin.

Jantzen, G. (1998) Becoming Divine: Towards a Feminist Philosophy of Religion, Manchester: Manchester University Press.

Koskela, J. and Siljander, P. (2014) What Is Existential Educational Encounter? Paideusis, Vol. 21, No. 2, pp. 71–80.

Kumar, S. (2013) Soil, Soul, Society: A New Trinity for Our Time, Lewes: Leaping Hare Press.

Land, G.T.L. (1973) Grow or Die: The Unifying Principle of Transformation, New York: Dell Publishing.

Macmurray, J. (2012) Learning to be Human, Oxford Review of Education, Vol. 38, No. 6, pp. 661–674.

McIntosh, A. (2008) Rekindling Community: Connecting People, Environment and Spirituality, Devon: Green Books.

Mezirow, J. (2000) Learning as Transformation: Critical Perspectives on a Theory in Progress, San Francisco: Jossey-Bass.

Mindell, A. (2014) Sitting in the Fire: Large Group Transformation Using Conflict and Diversity, Oregon: Deep Democracy Exchange.

Miller, J.P., Nigh, K., Binder, M.J., Novak, B. and Crowel, S., eds. (2019) International Handbook of Holistic Education, London: Routledge.

Noddings, N. (1984) Caring: A Feminine Approach to Ethics and Moral Education, London: University of California Press.

Orr, D. (1991) Ecological Literacy: Education and the Transition to a Postmodern World, New York: SUNY.

Peters, R.S. (1965) Ethics and Education, London: George Allen & Unwin Ltd.

Petrovic, J.E. and Mitchell, R.M. (2018) Indigenous Philosophies of Education Around the World, Oxford: Routledge.

Pring, R. (2013) The Life and Death of Secondary Education for All, London: Routledge.

Rogers, C. (1968) Freedom to Learn, Columbus: Charles Merrill Publishing Company.

Sahlberg, P. (2012) Finish Lessons: What Can the World Learn from Educational Change in Finland? London: Teachers College Press.

Sahlberg, P. (2015) Finish Lessons 2.0: What Can the World Learn from Educational Change in Finland? London: Teachers College Press.

Shaw, M. (2020) All Those Barbarians, Devon: Cista Mystica Press.

Turner, V.W. (1969) The Ritual Process, London: Penguin.

van Manen, M. (2014) Phenomenology of Practice: Meaning-Giving Methods in Phenomenological Research and Writing, London: Routledge.

van Manen, M. (2015) Pedagogical Tact: Knowing What to Do When You Don't Know What to Do, London: Routledge.

Winch, C. (2006) Education, Autonomy and Critical Thinking, London: Routledge.

Yurchak, A. (2006) Everything Was Forever, Until It Was No More; The Last Soviet Generation, Princeton, NJ: Princeton University Press.

Chapter 2

The importance of an ecological-phenomenological perspective in the educational encounter

From the Margins

From the Margins

Drive by rolling countryside and the gaze is often drawn to the bright yellow of pungent rapeseed, or the wave of barley in the wind, or the bright green that comes with rich grazing pasture. The patchwork extends for miles dominated by the swerve of greens and hues of yellow. It goes without saying that farmers spend hours maintaining these vast open tracts of land. Ploughing, spraying, seeding, rolling and harvesting all take copious amounts of energy and resource. Yet, whilst such effort is both obvious and productive, there's an entirely different range of tasks which the farmer attends to in order to ensure that the fields remain efficient; they have to maintain the margins. No field can exist without a margin, whether it be the stock fence, hedgerow or irrigation ditch, and the farmer knows that much depends on how well they manage the marginal terrain.

Left to its own, the land encroaches; it's in its nature to do so. Leave a field untouched for a year, let alone five, and you will see how what lies at the edge begins to reclaim what was once its own. If the arable field represents the mainstream domain then it needs to be noted that the corn never gains the hedgerow. Give it a couple of years and soon the blackthorn appear 5 feet from the fence line, the blackberry declares anarchy and throws a sucker root over to the other edge of the ditch. When we first set about re-fencing, one of the fields a 15 feet of pasture land was relinquished from the field boundary. Watch the landscape over a few years and eventually, after the tractors and combines have gone, there will come a time where the traffic waits (im)patiently whilst the hedge-cutting is carried out, leaving splinters on tarmac for days to come. Or the dredging bucket runs along the ditches, gorging on silted twigs and blackwater.

DOI: 10.4324/9781003407751-3

Whilst the passing passenger's gaze catches the crop, it's the margins which take my eye and there's good reason for it; wildness lives in those marginal spaces. Venture in to the heart of the hedge or ditch and let its world occupy you for a while. I did such a thing once, a couple of years ago on the hottest day of the year. It was at the height of summer and I had been walking across and along the edge of a meadow which was bursting with ungrazed grasses and flowers. I was taking my time, conserving my energy, yet in this early afternoon heat I was already sweating and looked about for shade. I found myself drawn to the wooded line of the meadow and having stooped into its shade saw the ground fall further into a ditch. It was damp, cool and dark and, despite the heat of the day, I could catch the scent of the rotting branches, wet wood and rich black earth underneath the low canopy of oak and hawthorn.

I cannot recall quite why I decided to hunker down in the ditch but I did so, uncomfortable at first whilst I adjusted my position so that I wasn't catching the wetness from the ground and yet might benefit from the cool breeze that ran along the culvert. At first, I found myself waiting, although soon recognised that there had been no sense that there was anything I needed to wait for. As my eyes got used to the dim light, I could see beyond the wooded edge and out into the sun on the grass beyond. Suddenly the meadow seemed irrelevant, or at least no longer as central as it had shortly before when I walked through it. What had appeared to be the world at large, now seem peripheral and I was utterly absorbed in this new world of the marginal. This place was not a single space but the meeting of places, not dissimilar from a crossroads, in the sense that whilst ahead of me there was the familiar meadow, behind me I knew that there was a second stretch of open land, and again, to my right, a third field. The place I had found did not belong to any of these three spaces alone, but to all three and to none of them.

I bent closer to the bottom of the ditch where the thinnest of trickling water could be seen, no more than an inch wide. Taking the excess water off the fields is one way in which the margins serve the main crop. Catching the debris that gets stirred and blown from the centre is another feature of the hedges and ditches; the margins swallow up what cannot easily be digested in the midst of the fields.

I find that I am no longer waiting but have begun to drift and my mind takes me to matters of the heart and the recollection of a woman I once loved, and then another whom I still do. I had lost any sense of purpose now, just a sense of dropping into the place itself. Maybe an hour had passed before what seemed most sensate was that I had become a part of this place. I have experienced this a few times now, a point where any notion of intention or objective melts away leaving me somehow absorbed into the place. I recall when I was fishing some years ago and after an hour had a similar experience. There was a brief moment when there appeared no separation between myself from the rod, line and float, or the bank opposite or the reeds or even the water itself. So again, I 'was the ditch' and I journaled, randomly, crouched on the stump of an old oak, merged into that place. Suddenly, I became aware of some kind of disturbance. It alerted me, energetically – I cannot say that I heard a noise or saw some movement. I just became acutely aware that something had changed in the place. I was now heightened and felt my hearing range expand and eyes strain. There was certainly a disturbance and now I could locate a sound, a breaking of twigs or scuffling of leaf mould. The noise increased and rudely broke the quite lazy hum of the deep summer mid-afternoon. There was a violence in the sound and a crashing too. I was startled, suddenly alarmed at whatever was coming, because it certainly was coming, and most definitely coming closer in my direction. I sat upright not knowing what to expect when the crashing of branches got close enough that I could now see them. Two young female deer, black deer, were racing through the wooded terrace straight towards me. As they broke through to the little clearing they immediately saw me and were startled. In a moment, no more than a second, we each took the other in – me in wonder and they in fright (or perhaps they too were in wonderment). They took flight to my left and within 2 seconds they had disappeared, a sound trail of leaves stirred in their wake. Such an encounter, I am sure, would not have occurred out in the field where it is too full of sun, too exposed. I discovered the wildness that runs in this marginal place and found myself mesmerised by its possibilities, held in both its fertile movement and mystery.

I travel home, pull myself out of the wooded boundary, clear of the ditch and back into the familiar territory of the open field, homeward bound. My work comes out of the marginal space, I realise. In so many ways, the symbolism of the threshold between the wild edge and the cultivated land suddenly speaks to me of the work that lies ahead. Perhaps this is an exercise in 're-wilding' of education, a process whereby the centre is provoked and altered by what wildness might still be found at its outer edge. I have been here before several times, when I think on this some more. The decision to move from the mainstream schooling system into alternative provision coincided with a shift in national policy towards social inclusion. For several years, those of us who had cut our professional teeth in the overlooked corners of educational work suddenly found ourselves called upon to innovate and develop inclusive practice. More recently, another wave of utilitarian policy, ransacking the dignity of the common classroom, eliminating the person in favour of the systematic, has run its course through many English schools. Now the ache for the human touch, talk of soul and role and – heavens! – even 'love' in education, draws me back towards the centre again.

How is it that it what lies at the edge is often what is called for to change the centre? Perhaps this book is part of my own effort to avoid making a marginal life out of a marginal experience. The work arises from the meeting place that crosses the ecological and the sociological realms with the existential territory, and it can be neither one, nor the other. It is in itself a kind of ecosystem, carefully balanced and integrating of these three inter-locking components, creating an alchemy that I hesitate to dissect with too sharp a scalpel. There are implications for grubbing up hedgerows and back-filling ditches; there's trouble ahead, and perhaps not the right kind of trouble, when the marginal is diminished or erased. So, I will let this marginality find its voice through my writing and stay curious and hopeful as to how it might re-wild a particular experience of education.

Introduction

In this chapter, I will set out the methodological basis of my perspective on education. In doing so, I will explain both the method itself and, as importantly, the key features of my approach which include the importance of congruity and parallel process. Before I launch into the detail of this, however, I want to open with some remarks about where this work is situated, following on from the prefacing text featuring marginality.

Having embarked on researching a possible vision of education, with several components, I have become aware that at times it could be challenging to understand quite where the work 'stands' in relation to the academic 'landscape'. At times it may find itself of 'no fixed abode' and adrift from a recognisable anchoring point. There are five significant concepts orbiting around this book; education, soil, soul, society and encounter. Such a combination has the potential to move in several directions including amongst others, the pedagogic, sociological, existential and ecological. Developing each of these domains has informed the book's shape and substance, and there are particular areas which have emerged as most significant during the development of the work. I would best describe the three spheres of educational discourse as existential education, indigenous educational philosophy and holistic education. In naming these three spheres, I want to acknowledge that others might prefer a different emphasis or include different discourses. As I hope to demonstrate, these spheres remain most pertinent to the view of education that I have chosen to explore. In recognising the three regions of indigenous, holistic and existential education, I see these forming a place of intersection. In other words, the work sits in the metaphorical hedgerows that meet at the edges of each of these three 'fields' of theory and practice but does not exist wholly in any one of them. This, I find, has been a useful way for finding the book's 'place' in the world. It has been founded in the marginal tract of ground that traces the outlines of indigenous, holistic and existential material, and my hope has been to discover what wildness might run through it.

Meeting at the Margins of Indigenous, Holistic and Existential Education

I will introduce briefly here each of the three spheres of educational discourse with a view to them becoming more apparent and embedded in subsequent chapters. As is usual when broadly categorising themes it is rare that there is not an overlapping of ideas and this is certainly true of how I discuss the three spheres of indigenous, holistic and existential education. Arguably it is helpful to begin with the existential theme, given that this is how my vision is most distinct from the product-orientated education that I have critiqued in the opening chapter. I don't intend to give an overview of existentialism in education as it is too broad a topic, although I think it might be useful to highlight what I regard as its salient features and how they relate to the direction of my work. So, for instance, the principle that human beings can exercise freedom in choosing how to live – as opposed to being subject to a higher force, or pre-ordained meaning by which to live one's life – is an important thread in the work. That this is an educational matter is even more so, and I have been aware of several writers who might justifiably align with this concern, including Saeverot (2012), Gordon (2016) and Todd (2012), in addition to the work of Biesta (2014) which is considered more directly and in detail in subsequent chapters.

There is a particular focus on the existential concept of freedom, which acknowledges the responsibility and possibility of the individual in determining purpose, and that this task precedes the notion of identity, or personhood. In other words, a first 'given' is in choosing how I might exist? and comes prior to the question of who I am? This latter question is more concerned with a person's 'essence' and to related discussions, for example, about a sense of true self. The existential challenge is to make meaning out of a world that offers no pre-set game-plan for living. The exercising of free-will, or agency, is an integral part of how I envisage the challenge for the student in education, recognising that this is no straightforward matter. First, the student must choose to exist with intention, and in the context of the world as it is, and not the one that they might prefer. In this respect, I have been influenced indirectly by Levinas through my reading of others, including, again, Biesta and Todd in addition to Jantzen (1998). What I have found most important in these accounts is the suggestion of irreplaceability for both the student and the teacher when the choice of whether to exist, and the responsibility to do so is heightened in the educational task. This encounter in which the student, put simply, is called forth to exist brings them into connection with the infinite possibilities that arise in a world of plurality. To be in the world, as a dynamic part of it, is central to this vision of education where (re)connection is such an important underlying theme.

As I have mentioned earlier, the sphere of existential education is significant because it offers a contrasting perspective on how education might be understood from that of a product-orientated view, and especially in regard to the limitations of concretising outcomes. To 'free' educational experience from the confines of realising particular teaching and learning objectives and instead to consider how else education might exist is, perhaps, an existential exercise in itself. The existential sphere is representative of what might be whimsically referred to as the 'home field' of this book, which is the land that lies closest to the farmhouse. It is the field that gets most attention and is the first point of contact for the farmer as they set out to work each day. Likewise, as the book unfolds the questions about how might education exist, what conditions give rise to the student choosing how to live in the world and, what role the teacher can play in this dynamic, will become familiar and common ground to the reader. However, whilst this might be the home field, it is not the only, nor most extensive field along which this book explores.

I have become increasingly aware of how much of my work has centred around and is informed by the broad and varied discourses concerning holistic education. Now, this is an unwieldy term to use and one that I hold lightly as I approach this topic. I have wondered if the phrase 'ecological pedagogy' might be more appropriate because of its implied reference to the natural world but have settled on 'holistic' as the generic description of which the ecological is a part. Certainly, in turning now to a commentary on holistic education, I am wanting to separate out two strands, or schools of thought, that are important in my visioning of education.

Holistic education is a phrase that is arguably the most efficient way of describing the kind of education associated with an emphasis on personal growth in its widest sense. Often in the literature, holistic education is sharply contrasted with liberal, or classical education, models typically found in most mass schooling systems. In these contexts, education might be caricatured as being concerned with the student from the 'neck-up', with an emphasis on building cognitive capacity, increasing knowledge and understanding and academic performance. Holistic education, with the implicit commitment to holism, broadens its concern with the emotional, social and spiritual aspects of the individual, in addition to the cognitive and intellectual.

In some respects, the origins of holistic education share similar influences of classical education. The objective of bringing about eduamonia – individual flourishing – was a consideration of Aristotle and one which is reflected in early religious communities that established some of the earliest models of education and, latterly schooling. The splitting off of the purely cognitive, or academic, tendencies is a relatively recent shift in educational philosophy and practice, brought about for the most part by the advent of scientific rationalism in the seventeenth and eighteenth centuries. In Eastern regions, a similar holistic perspective had also been understood in the dominant Hindu and Buddhist religious traditions.

For my purposes, here it might be useful to distinguish it within the wider domain of humanistic education. Teachers might be acquainted with the experience of humanistic education even if the term itself is unfamiliar. Rooted in the notion that education is about human growth and flourishing, humanistic education practice often has an emphasis on nurturing emotional literacy, deepening self-reflection, experimentation through group relationship and exploring new ways of exercising one's selfhood in the world. These interventions comprise the central components of a humanistic educational perspective that is essentially sociological. In other words, that education is primarily an activity that takes place between persons and is socially concerned, by which is meant improvement in the quality of social relations and betterment of society at large. Herein lie the limits, in my view, of a general humanistic approach in comparison to holistic education.

Miller et al (2019) present arguably the most recent and comprehensive account of holistic education available. The compilation of contributions covers the history and practice of holistic education since its early formation in the eighteenth century in Europe and even earlier in terms of indigenous practices. It's the work of John Miller particularly that tracks various themes in holistic education, principally the metaphysical, for example his work on spirituality (Miller et al, 2005) and soul (Miller, 2000), whilst David Orr has published a similar range of work that tends towards the environmental dimension of holistic education (Orr, 2004). In addition to these more explicit reference points, much of the humanistic education literature supports the holistic focus, and the works of Rogers (1968) and Noddings (1984) are examples of work sympathetic to holistic educational aims.

For advocates of holistic education, there are two features that distinguish it from a broader, humanistic approach. First, the inclusion of a spiritual sensibility, and second, the extension of the social into the ecological domain. To ignore – or discount – the spiritual experience, in the framework of holistic education, is to fail to understand the disconnection brought about in the individual by the academic emphasis in conventional schooling. A starting premise is that human beings have capacity for spiritual experience and that this might be nurtured and understood more fully as part of the educative process. Holistic education literature frequently refers to the 'soul' of the educator, the student and indeed of education itself. The spiritual self is a focus in educational practice alongside, or integrated with social, emotional, physical and intellectual development. For those educators embedded in contemporary schooling, this explicit reference to the spiritual domain might have a jarring affect or appear as inappropriate, perhaps belonging outside the familiar boundary of what education should be concerned with. However, in terms of holistic education, attending to the spiritual experience is crucial and interventions are designed to encourage, reconnect or awaken an associated sense of awe and wonder in the student.

A second principle of holistic education is that it assumes that people are part of an interconnected web of relationship which extends beyond the only-human world. The 'more-than-human world' is a phrase that is intended as more precise than referring to the 'natural world', and one that will be used later. The engagement with the wider environment is intrinsic to holistic education, in part to open up the possibility not only for the spiritual development, but also for the physical and emotional flourishing that is so important to holistic formation. In exploring the sphere of holistic education what begins to emerge is an interest in the more-than-human dimension that forms a distinctive thread that can be described in terms of ecological pedagogy, or eco-pedagogy. This originates from the activism of nature writers such as Wendell Berry (1977), Thomas Berry (1988) and earlier still, Waldo Emerson's work. These thinkers recognised the integrative quality of life as well as the need to protect it. This is an arena of campaigners, activists and, to coin a phrase, 'eco warriors'. As with the early writers, eco-pedagogy appears most associated with those prepared to be marginalised and regarded in some way as being 'beyond' the mainstream.

The interesting aspect of this kind of writing and practice is that it shines a light on the edges of the mainstream and in doing so reminds us that consciousness is ever subject to change and expansion. Within these writings, as with other perspectives directly addressed out of the indigenous educational experience, for example, significant caution is expressed about a Western preoccupation with intellectualism. At its most dramatic, intellectualism is regarded as a poison at the heart of disconnection with self. Holism runs contrary to such an intellectualised frame of reference and education is subsequently understood from a somewhat different perspective. The pedagogy of place, letting the land speak and engaging in sensing journeys reflects the roots out of which learning emerges and that eco-pedagogy exists.

More recently, eco-pedagogy has benefited from a range of new thinkers including Jennifer Gidley's work on postformal education (2018) by which she refers to a need for a new visioning of education beyond the legacy of an industrial model of education. Calling for a shift in consciousness, Gidley argues that nothing less than a revolution in social systems will position education as part of the solution to the planet's challenges. The Crex Crex Collective's innovative account of journeying in nature, Wild Pedagogies (Jickling, 2018) provides an example of education as if the planet mattered. Jeff Buckles' work (2018) connecting sustainability, the ecological social imaginary with the educational task demonstrates the kind of damage to the environment and the human species through disconnective models of schooling and higher education.

The prevailing theme in what I am describing as eco-pedagogy is activism. LeFay (2006), for example, in offering a critique of education and arguing in opposition to its deadening rationalism, calls for 'a quantum leap in consciousness' and an approach to education that leads 'to a deep awareness of our interdependent place within the dynamic web of life, and a re-enchantment of the world as a powerful mystery'. She hopes that we might see the 'world holistically and act to protect, respect and restore the Earth, our living home' (LeFay, 2006, p. 36). In this arena, it is not sufficient to admire nature, or simply 'engage' with it. The task is to hear it, both externally and internally. To understand that what is 'out there' is the same as 'in here' and that, furthermore both 'it' and 'I' are under threat in terms of survivability. Here we find a rejection of a kind of education that is deeply entrenched in constructing the very features which create the threat, and an activism for establishing a practice of education which is about being well in, and with, the world. My hope is that my own work contributes to this field of educational discourse and possibly motivates readers to consider how practice outdoors might widen the possibilities for how students choose to exist in the world.

During the time in which I have been developing these ideas, I have also been attending to a particular project in my involvement as a teacher in the transactional analysis (TA) professional community. This has involved presenting a specific development described as ecological TA (Barrow and Marshall, 2020) and a part of that work has been exploring the notion of the 'outdoor mind', which is offered in contrast to the more prevalent 'indoor mind'. Whilst the wider body of TA theory and practice is outside of the remit of the book, it might be useful to offer some observations about this differentiation of 'mind' that reflect the character of eco-pedagogy. For instance, whereas the indoor mind perceives the world from a static position, the outdoor mind encounters the world through movement and I think that this accentuates the phenomenological potential of education, a topic I come back to shortly in relation to methodology. Also, and perhaps rather obviously, the indoor mind tends to locate the individual within the human world and turns attention 'inwards', whilst a shift to the outdoor mind involves engagement with the more-than-human world and is outward facing, avoiding the 'cut' at the skin level. This refers to how an indoor mind tends to sharpen the sense of the skin boundarying the individual from its contact with the world (for more thought on this observation, see Shepard and McKinley, 1969).

The reference to eco-pedagogy in some respects leads to a third adjoining field, which is the sphere of indigenous educational philosophy and practice. This is a topic that is dealt in more detail in the fourth chapter and focuses particularly on the work of Gregory Cajete (1994). However, it is also worthwhile at this point explaining a little more about how this sphere helps in locating my work. In critiquing the limitations of product-orientated education, I am aware that this rather sets my vision of education in an especially alternative position because it is unusual not to have a perspective that is not in some way orientated towards outcome. I have already set out how this preoccupation results in education being an exercise in certainty and accentuates the cause and effect of the teacher's objective on the student's output. However, because this is such a prevalent educational frame of reference, it can be challenging to imagining how education might otherwise exist. To do so, I have been interested in turning attention to examples of where the notion of outcome is more oblique or held lightly in the educational task. This interest leads to what might be described metaphorically as a 'far flung' field, one that is furthest from the farmhouse and is perhaps less visited, or managed. Consequently, it is the field where the wild things have begun to have their way with the land. More prosaically, this has meant my exploring educational traditions which are less featured in mainstream and formal education contexts.

To talk of indigenous education philosophy is arguably an impossibility given that much of the writing on the topic describes what is essentially a non-philosophical experience. Nevertheless, anthropologists, almost exclusively located from Western societies, have offered extensive commentaries to frame the thinking about traditional practices in education. However, I have also been aware of the activism in the work by writers who come from indigenous communities. Simpson (2014), for example, presents her argument that much of formal state education is designed to promulgate and uphold settler colonialism. Having been involved in local initiatives to integrate her own indigenous peoples within the higher education college, she is exacerbated and declares that we 'must stop looking for legitimacy within the coloniser's education system and return to valuing and recognising our individual and collective intelligence on its own merits and on our own terms'. Withdrawing our considerable collective effort to 'Indigenize the academy' in favour of a resurgence of Indigenous intellectual systems ... (Simpson, 2014, p. 22). Clearly, when education is undertaken with the land in mind, there can be an energetic shift to action and indigenous educators have an extensive history of land-based practice.

One of the ideas taken from this material that I have found useful to have in mind is sovereignty. Used generally to denote the independent state, from an indigenous perspective, the term is used to affirm 'status and a way of being that respects connection with place, community, family, self and the natural world' (Landry, in Petrovic and Mitchell, 2018, p. 26). I have been interested in considering sovereignty, in this use of the term, with 'immanence', a reference to the completeness of the frame of reference of the individual, and out of which the choice is made to exist anew in the world. To complicate what is already a challenge to those accustomed to existence equating with the here and now experience of the atomised individual, an indigenous perspective also requires maintaining a broader concept of time; 'indigeneity is the state of being and becoming that is faithful spatially, socially and spiritually to the indigenous group's past, present and future' (Landry, 2018, p. 29). This reference to the ancestors is one that I found helpful when developing my own thinking about eldership and the concept of 'grown-up-ness' (Biesta, 2017) which are featured in Chapter 5.

In connection with this general understanding of indigenous education is the more specific domain of story and myth. The oral tradition of passing down experience, knowledge and understanding cannot be overestimated in indigenous education and I have been particularly interested in seeking ways in which this can inform the development of my ideas. I have needed to take care at times not to have this take over the direction of the project, in effect needing to manage some of my own field boundaries in order to maintain the shape and balance of my work! Whilst much of Western education discourse is conducted in written form, it too once relied on its origins in oral history (Regan, 2005). However, at times the impact of story and in particularly the notion of the storied life, surfaces in the book, both later in this chapter, and again, in Chapter 4 in relation to liminality. It is important to emphasise here – as indeed later – that I am not interested in the use of stories as vehicles for moral education, or as psychoanalytic or metaphorical material. Instead, I am referring to them as powerful, untamed and mysterious and which tell the truth crookedly; 'Myth, in its most ecologically discreet form, among people who live by hunting and fishing and gathering, seems to be the song of the place to itself, which humans overhear' (Kane, 1998). What I regard as an indirect quality, or implicitness, is, in my view, very much in line with the view of education that I am exploring. It is this sideways, low key approach that I suggest is the way in for wildness – remembering that the wild encroaches literally from the side. I am referring to stories and myth as wild creatures, alive in ways that the mythologist Martin Shaw explains:

> To be in touch with wildness is to have stepped past the proud cattle of the field and wandered far from the twinkle of the Inn's fire .... Wildness is a form of sophistication, because it carries within it true knowledge of our lace in the world. It doesn't exclude civilisation but prowls through it, knowing when to attend to the needs of the committee and when to drink from a moonlit lake .... Wildness carries sobriety as well as exuberance, and has allowed loss to mark its face'.
>
> (Shaw, 2011, p. 8)

To provoke, re-direct and incite the attention of the student is one aspect in the role of the teacher and stories do this too, hence my interest in testing how this might be pertinent in the context of an education orientated towards soil, soul and society.

Introducing the Methodology

Having scoped out where my work is located in relation to other discourses, I return now to the central focus of this chapter, which is my methodological approach. Having established a critique of product-orientated education, I argue that a distinct alternative empirical approach to methodology is required, and that this generates particular challenges for research where 'encounter' is at the heart of the educational task. I am also aware that the reader will have just read a section of stylised writing and that this is the first in a series of anecdotal, or vocative writings (van Manen, 2014). These form the empirical contribution to the book, and I will be referring to this type of writing throughout the chapter to illustrate my thinking about the methodology I have developed for the work ahead.

In Chapter 1, I have already given an indication of the limitations of research in the context of product-orientated education. To briefly re-cap, there is an underlying premise that there is causality between what is taught and what is learned. In a world view that regards education as a 'strong' concept leading towards fixed outcome, the emphasis on identifying causal links might possibly be legitimate. Furthermore, focusing on 'what works' becomes a high priority in a system that prizes performance. The 'evidence-based practice' movement, allied to the GERM programme, has arguably dominated education policy and inhibited teachers' capacity for establishing their own professional judgements (Bennett, 2016). I suggest that such a 'cause and effect' methodology is unhelpful and inappropriate when considered from the view of education orientated towards (re)connection. This is primarily because the working practice of such research involves the streamlining of what constitutes a worthwhile educational outcome. By implication, this approach to research minimises the interconnectedness in which educational experience occurs. The justification for evidence-based practice is accountability, and in particularly where schooling is funded via public expenditure. As Bennett declares,

> Who would say that evidence should not be used in education, however? Such a claim is irrational. If evidence exists, it must be accounted for and, if necessary, disputed, modified or embraced. If there are limits to the evidence base, that must be understood. Where evidence is overwhelming, it should be adopted, or rejected on better grounds.
>
> (Bennett, 2016, p. 256)

Bennett continues by suggesting that teaching should be an evidence-augmented profession and argues for greater teacher engagement in generating practice-based research. Whilst I am drawn to Bennett's adjustment, and the general encouragement of professional activism, I think that this is insufficiently robust in challenging the frame of reference about educational research. Product-orientated education is deeply embedded in the professional psyche and a more radical shift in methodology is needed if an educational encounter is to be better understood. Without such a shift, research methodologies are at risk of further embedding practice and policies which advocate education that fails to acknowledge connection with soil, soul and society. What is lacking in the quest for increased accountability is a response to the question; accountability for what, and for whom is accountability intended? Referring to O'Neill's Reith lectures in 2002, Biesta highlights two problems with the growth of accountability in the public sector. First, its tendency to focus on a proxy public interest through, for example, regulatory bodies, government departments and statutory requirements (as opposed being in direct relation to the public). Second, that performance indicators are chosen which are most efficient to measure (instead of focused on good performance); '... the predicament is whether we have ended up in a situation where we are valuing what is being measured; that is, a situation where measurement has turned into an end in itself' (Biesta, 2016, p. 88).

Congruent Methodology and Parallel Process

In this section, I intend to move away from discussing research methodologies associated with a product-orientated education and introduce two features central to what I offer as a distinctive and possibly new methodological approach in my interest to develop a way of researching educational work rooted in the notion of encounter. In doing so, I have resisted slipping into adopting methods which are designed primarily to generate, or 'capture' data for analysis and instead consider a methodology that catches the experience of encounter, whilst avoiding explaining it. I am mindful that if I was to do so and 'explain' the encounter, it might become concretised and subsequently will undermine, or negate, the naturally elusive quality of what encounter entails. By implication, the encountered experience is unpredictable, un-'anticipate-able', fleeting and subjective.

I suggest that there is also an ethical consideration alongside the matter of managing the indeterminate character of encounter. This relates to the appropriateness of the research methodology to the content of the perspective. I mean by this something different than simply the suitability of a chosen approach, but that there is an integrity between method and the focus of this work. This is best understood in terms of congruence, its etymology emphasising 'agreement' and 'harmony between things'. So, in developing a methodological congruence, I have wanted to find a way of establishing an 'agreement', as such, between the 'what' and the 'how', in terms of addressing the work's empirical dimension.

In pursuing a congruent methodology, I am setting out to create a parallel process among the fieldwork, the presentation of ideas and the experience of the reader as they engage with the material. Parallel process (see, for example, Proctor, 2000) is a concept originating in the supervision of psychotherapy, counselling and coaching interventions. It refers to how the dynamic experienced, for example, between a counsellor and client is then 'paralleled' in the process between the counsellor and their professional supervisor. There is a recognition that aspects of work 'in the field' are unconsciously carried into the supervisory process. This is in addition to the conscious material shared by the practitioner, and it exerts an influence, frequently unspoken, on what occurs in the supervision session. There is, in effect, a fractal of the client's process held in subsequent relationships that reflect the original experience. In this professional domain, identifying and working with the parallel process is critical in more fully understanding the predicament of the client and it provides a powerful resource for identifying helpful interventions. Where the parallel process goes un-named, or ignored, it tends to influence the supervisory work and results in a cycle of 'stuckness', confusion or some other counter-productive experience.

In turning to my methodological intentions, I am aware that there are a series of parallels in the process which run through different layers of the book and which can be tracked from the fieldwork itself, through to those reading it. To be more explicit, and at risk of moving too soon in outlining much of what is at work here, encounter is featured not only as a theme in the theoretical treatment of education, but it is also the focus of what is encountered within the fieldwork. More importantly, in the reporting of the fieldwork, I am tentatively offering the 'data' in such a way as to possibly provoke an encounter with its readership. It is in the interplay of the direct experience in the field, with the writing that comes out of that experience, which in turn impacts you, as reader, that the encountering is paralleled. Furthermore, that the character of such layered encounters is orientated towards the significance of soil, soul and society, as envisioned in the educative task.

Having described in broad terms the concept of parallel process as a feature of my methodological intention, I am equally aware that I am not able to 'control' it in such a way as to deliver a specific outcome. I may set out to ensure that the book reports on, and explores, education encounters, and that I also hope to engender such an experience for the reader, but I cannot, nor wish to, guarantee that this will be the case. Given my comments in the opening chapter, you, the reader, and in other paralleled relationships – the student – is 'free' in terms of how, or even if, they respond to the experience created by reading the book. In this respect, education as encounter involves an act of faith,[1] and this in turn is what this work entails. The mention of education as an act of faith brings my discussion back to the matter of risk in education referred to in the opening chapter, and by extension, the risk involved in presenting this vision of education.

The Educational 'Object'

Before turning to the methodological approach in more detail, and the particular technique adopted in creating the empirical component of the book, I want to introduce a meta-model for framing how this all operates. Having established the concept of parallel process, and the associated idea of the 'fractal', I suggest that this is useful in holding the different layers of how the book is structured. In doing so, I want to introduce an idea that I refer to as the 'educational object'. By this I mean that aside from the positions of teacher and student in the educational dynamic, there is a third object to which both teacher and student have a relational connection. This third object, unlike the teacher and student, is passive. I mean by this that the object 'just is'; it has no direct voice in the sense that it is capable of dialogue. I am referring to this third object as the 'educational' object because as I will explain, it becomes integral to the educational task of the teacher and the student.

In the general arena of formal education, an example of the third object can be found in this triad; teacher – curriculum – student. In this instance, the curriculum for the immediate purpose of student and teacher simply is what it is; a syllabus, a scheme of work, a set of associated resources. Whilst it has clearly been previously constructed, once it is in the relational dyad of teacher and student, it is to all extent and purpose, subject solely to the meaning that each make of it. As the 'third', educational object, it exists in 'stasis', unable to answer for itself, yet its presence generates possible interaction between it, and across, the teacher-student dynamic.

The example of an education triad model outlined above might be considered further in relation to the situation in product-orientated education systems. There is the potential for a series of 'enmeshments', in which one of the three elements is compromised to the detrimental value of education. For instance, if the alliance between student and teacher becomes significant to the extent that the curriculum is discounted, then the danger is that a symbiosis is established which takes the form of either seduction, indoctrination or therapy, by the teacher of the student, through the misuse of positional power. Alternatively an enmeshment can develop where the student and curriculum become more closely aligned at the expense of the teacher. 'Learnification' (Biesta, 2014) is the danger in this dynamic, where the teacher exists only as 'facilitator' and where the teacher is of little relevance beyond that of a technical operative. Finally, a third enmeshment is possible in which the collusion is between the teacher and the curriculum, at which point education becomes highly technocratic and the student becomes an object of the process.

This triadic model is a central idea to the way in which the book 'works', and there are several layers of such triads built into its architecture. As will be presented later in this chapter, at the heart of the empirical component there is an account of a series of educational encounters featuring my own experience as a novice farmer. This narrative centres on a relationship among myself as student, an old farmer as teacher, and the farm itself, as the educational object. This can be regarded as the initial fractal layer. This narrative becomes the focus for the book which, in turn, becomes an educational object. This book, like the farm in the original fractal, is not capable of developing a voice, or entering dialogue, but clearly is influential in informing what occurs between myself and you, the reader, and this is the second layer, or fractal of my work. Furthermore, the themes of the book concern the interplay among the teacher, the student and the context in which the educational work takes place, and that this a third layer. Finally, a fourth meta-level fractal centres on the themes of soul, soil and society.

My reason for introducing this model for thinking about the book is that I want to emphasise that whilst this text acts as an educational object, it is not a 'dead' object. There are key elements of it that are designed to speak direct to you, the reader; they are 'addressive' sections which invite or call out to the reader. This is characteristic of the purpose of my educational concern, which is that in educational encounters, one orientated towards soil, soul and society, the student – or reader – is called upon to act, to 'show up'. There is, of course, the possibility to decline, but to do so nevertheless implies a response, albeit a kind of 'non-response response', to the addressive quality of the work. In other words, the act of reading of this book becomes in itself an enactment of the kind of education that I am setting out to explore in its pages.

Introducing the Vocative

In my developing a vision of education there have been several influences drawn from the broad fields of narrative enquiry and phenomenology. I have been especially influenced by the work of Max van Manen, and specifically his central work on phenomenological research, Phenomenology of Practice (2014). This forms the central focus of this chapter and I will set out how aspects of his ideas about the 'vocative' are closely aligned with the approach I have developed in exploring the experience of encounter in education. In particularly, I will be focusing on his use of 'anecdote' and aligning this with an additional perspective, 'embodied writing' taken from the field of transpersonal psychotherapy (Anderson and Braud, 2011).

An educational encounter involves the student being 'called' and this, by implication, involves a phenomenological process of both being called forth and the declaration of arrival. In both of these aspects, or in Ardentian terms, these 'actions', the voice is central. I will deal more precisely with the implications of this in reference to van Manen's concept of the 'vocative'. Etymologically the term vocative includes 'to call', or 'to be addressed', and refers to the voice itself; 'to bring to speech'. It implies a call and response dynamic in the sense that if one is addressed it is anticipated, but not mandated, that there will be a reply; it has been listened to. When rendered into the written form the vocative text seeks to replicate a similar dynamic with the reader,

> There exists a relation between the writing structure of a text and the voking effects that it may have on the reader. The more vocative a text, the more strongly the meaning is embedded within it.
>
> (van Manen, 2014, p. 241)

This kind of writing contrasts with more conventional research writing 'whereby results can be severed from the means by which the results were obtained' (van Manen, p. 241). Here, where connection is key to a vision of education, it is imperative to seek out methodological approaches that promote connection. To do otherwise would reduce the integrity of the work, creating an unhelpful parallel process through its incongruity. There is a quality to such writing that is elusive and perhaps challenging in the context of 'severed' professional writing,

> Phenomenological research is unlike such research in that the link with the results cannot be broken.... To summarise a poem in order to present the result would destroy the result because the poem itself is the result. The poem is the thing. Similarly phenomenology, not unlike poetry, is a vocative project; it tries an incantation, evocative speaking; it is a primal telling... Poetizing is thinking on original experience and is speaking in a more primal sense. Language that authentically speaks the world rather than abstractly speaking of it is a language that reverberates the world.
>
> (van Manen, p. 241)

I will return to van Manen's use of the term 'primal' later, but for now the emphasis on writing from the 'inside' of the experience is particularly important. Writing from the field of research in transpersonal psychotherapy, Anderson and Braud use this particular turn of phrase in their presentation of 'embodied writing',

> Human experience is relayed from the inside out. Entwining human sensibilities with the sensibilities of the world, embodied writing is itself an act of embodiment that nourishes an enlivened sense of presence in and of the world. In an attempt to describe human experiences – and especially profound human experiences – as they are truly lived, embodied writing tries to give the body voice in ways typically not honoured, especially in research praxis.
>
> (Anderson and Braud, 2011, pp. 267–268)

In developing my methodology, I am integrating both van Manen's general idea of the 'vocative' and the specific mode of 'embodied writing', in order to give voice to the encountered educational experience. Both sets of materials support the importance of congruity between experience and its 'expression' throughout my research methodology. I find it useful to think of this in terms of an 'expressive research' method. The term 'express' can refer to 'state explicitly, not implied, clearly made known', in addition to 'taking the form of an image' through the exerting of pressure. I think both of these qualities have relevance to the kind of text that I am presenting.

Unlike the familiar pre-determined and qualitatively designed outcomes of product-orientated education, there is an elusive, indeterminate quality to the encountered experience and it is one that remains, for the most part, at an implicit level, held in the interior experience of the individuals involved. My intention has been to create writing that makes this as explicit as possible within the limitations of (English) language. In doing so, I am aware that there is a lyricism, or poetic quality, that comes with such writing and in that respect requires a concentration – or an exerting of pressure – on the language. I am suggesting that the intensity of the language in embodied writing, as an example of the vocative method, is particularly congruent with that of the encountered experience.

Embodied Writing

I will turn now to setting out in more detail the features of embodied writing and in doing so also make reference to van Manen's perspective on the vocative method. By drawing on these ideas, as part of an expressive research method I am also, by implication, establishing this book, and the reading of it, as potentially embodying experiences. I am not able to 'make' this happen, in the sense that I can force it to become an experience that I might wish for, or design for, the reader. How a reader might engage in the text is clearly not in my control, but my intention is to create the possibility, or an invitational kind of text that might evoke such an experience,

> The human science researcher is a scholar-author who must be able to maintain an almost unreasonable faith in the power of language to make intelligible and understandable what always seems to lie beyond language.
>
> (van Manen, 2014, p. 242)

The vision of education that I am developing in itself requires such an act of faith, and it is this that I suggest Biesta refers to when declaring 'that education always involves a risk' (2014, p. 1). To regard education, and by extension research of education, as an act of faith, or as 'risky', involves a frame of reference quite distinct from that of product-orientated education where, I suggest, it becomes the object of the researcher. Whereas through the lens of my idea of expressive research methodology, embodied writing and the vocative domain, 'subjectification' (Biesta, 2014) becomes the focus, and by definition the direct experience of being in, and of, the world in both sociological and ecological terms.

Embodied writing offers a technique for gathering a sense of the experience of educational encounter in a way that 'least intrudes by extrapolation or interpretation its occurrence' (Anderson and Braud, 2011, p. 269). To re-iterate, it is an attempt to record experience, in written form, from the inside out. In presenting this kind of writing, Anderson and Braud identify seven distinctive features summarised below:

1 True-to-life, vivid depictions intended to invite sympathetic resonance in the reader
2 Inclusive of internal and external data as essential to relaying the experience
3 Written specifically from the inside out
4 Richly concrete and specific, descriptive of all sensory modalities, and often slowed down to capture nuance
5 Attuned to the living body
6 Narratives embedded in experience, often first-person narratives
7 Poetic images, literary style and cadence serve embodied depictions and not the other way around

(Anderson and Braud, 2011, p. 269)

The authors further explain how embodied writing has been incorporated in research of the outdoor and wilderness experiences, they offer examples of embodied writing and exercises through which to develop competence and confidence in creating this type of text. More importantly for my purposes, embodied writing is advocated as having the capacity:

> ... to call forth the writer's unique voice or way of writing. Writers gain voice, a particular voice. Far from making everyone sound alike by employing a specific style of writing, embodied writing seems to call forth the unique qualities of a writer... In the act of writing, slowing down and looking for resonance within one's own body seems to reveal the tangibly unique – and sometimes ineffable – qualities of the writer's experience and way of being in the world.
> (Anderson and Braud, p. 268)

What I think is significant about this description is that there is a parallel process with the educational encounter, which can be created by substituting 'writer' with 'student' in this passage. Doing so acknowledges the conformist limitations of 'making everyone sound alike' through a product-orientated education. Instead this supports offering an alternative vision of education that encourages the student to experience a way of being in the world.

Anecdotal Writing

In developing an expressive research method, I will consider a supplementary approach featured in van Manen's discussion of the vocative method; anecdotal writing. I see this as closely related to embodied writing,

> Stories or anecdotes are so powerful, so effective and so consequential in that they can explain things that resist straightforward explanation or

conceptualisation. Anecdotes bring things into nearness by contributing to the vividness and presence of an experience.

(van Manen, 2014, p. 251)

The anecdotal voice is regarded by van Manen as a means by which the individual sets out to 'evoke' or call forth to the listener about a particular experience. By doing so the speaker creates a sense of 'nearness' to the listener; '... the aim of evocative inquiry is to listen to the things that are before us, that have a hold on us, through the mediating function of the evocative text' (ibid, p. 250). Not only is the use of anecdote intended to bring the reader closer to the experience, but it is also a way in which the singularity of the experience is expressed. There is an understanding that through anecdote an account is shared which can neither be extrapolated nor generalised. In this respect, I am suggesting that this parallels with the unique experience of the education encounter which lends itself to being featured in anecdotal writing,

The 'anecdotal example' does not express what one knows through argument or conceptual explication, but, in an evocative manner, an 'anecdotal example' lets one experience what one does not know (in an intellectual or cognitive sense). So, both the anecdote and the example (which may be the same textual unit) can make the singular knowable. They can do this because the exemplary anecdote, like literary fiction always orients to the singular. Indeed, any literary story or novel is always some unique story that brings out the particular or singularity of a certain phenomenon or event.

(van Manen, p. 256)

Throughout the following chapters, I am emphasising the exclusive and elusive quality of the education encounter. 'Exclusive' in the sense that it occurs solely within the domain of its protagonists; there is an intimacy in the process which I associate with van Manen's emphasis on singularity. It is also 'elusive' in the sense that the encounter cannot be mandated or its form prescribed, so in this respect it is also not 'knowable' to use van Manen's term.

Anecdotal writing can be used to illuminate the essence of an experience and to do this effectively van Manen suggests there is a narrative structure that he describes as follows:

1   An anecdote is a very short and simple story.
2   An anecdote usually describes a single incident.
3   An anecdote begins close to the central moment of the experience.
4   An anecdote includes important concrete details.
5   An anecdote often contains several quotes (what was said, done and so on)
6   An anecdote closes quickly after the climax or when the incident has passed.
7   An anecdote often has an effective or 'punchy' last line: it creates punctum.

(NB: 'Punctum', in this last element, refers to the 'sting' in the tale; it is the detail that disrupts or disturbs.)

(van Manen, p. 252)

van Manen further develops the use of anecdotal writing as a research technique by offering guidelines for editing draft material. These have been useful in my drafting of the series of vocative texts and include:

- Remain constantly orientated to the lived experience of the phenomenon.
- Edit the factual content but do not change the phenomenological content.
- Enhance the eidetic or phenomenological theme by strengthening it.
- Aim for the text to acquire strongly embedded meaning.
- When a text is written in the present tense, it can make an anecdote more vocative.
- Use of personal pronouns tends to pull the reader in.
- Extraneous material should be omitted.
- Search for words that are 'just right' in exchange for awkward words.
- Avoid generalising statements.
- Avoid theoretical terminology.
- Do not rewrite or edit more than absolutely necessary.

(van Manen, p. 256)

In setting out to share writing that combines qualities from embodied and anecdotal approaches, my intention is to create for the reader a series of interludes that interrupt the anticipated flow of argument, anticipated in the sense that the content develops concepts and also breaks into the expected and commonly accepted academic writing 'register'. These interrupting interludes parallel something of the disruptive quality that is in a vision of education that centres on encounter. It is in these interludes that the reader might become aware of a shift in expectation about how to exist in relation to this text. There is the possibility of a 'natal moment', when the reader catches themselves no longer in their familiar self, or immanence,

The special effect that phenomenological tone aims for is epiphanic; it is meant to touch our understanding of life's meaning that we experience as meaning in life.

(van Manen, p. 267)

By introducing the notion of epiphany, van Manen extends the potential of the vocative towards the transformative,

Epiphany means that a text has a provocative quality, so that its deeper meaning may exercise and provoke a transformative effect of the self of the reader. Epiphany refers to the sudden perception or intuitive grasp of the life meaning of something. This experience is so strong or striking that it may stir us at the core of our being.

(van Manen, p. 293)

Whilst I have a caution about the general idea of transformation in the context of the vision of education I am presenting, the sentiment in van Manen's statement aligns with how I will explore the existential quality of the educational encounter and is intended to deepen the congruence of my approach. I will turn now to consider an example of writing which I suggest combines features of the embodied and anecdotal techniques.

Natality as Embodied and Anecdotal Writing

I will be following this section with the passage entitled, Natality. In doing so, I will introduce the reader to how this kind of writing is threaded through the book with the objective of illuminating a vision of education that accounts for soil, soul and society. The practical context of the piece is that it describes the experience of lambing as part of my life as a small-scale farmer. As will become clearer in this vocative dimension, I was not familiar with farming, having been born and raised in the city. These sections of text track my educational experience, a series of encounters, through which I discover a way of 'arriving' into the world anew, through relationship with an old farmer who I was taught by. I will resist at this point revealing more of the educational journey and focus on the function of the writing itself. Natality is not solely a description about the task of lambing on a smallholding. Whilst it is obviously concerned with birth at the most literal level, the passage is primarily intended to be something different than an instructional account of sheep-rearing. The piece is also not a straightforward metaphorical account in which I am ostensibly discussing lambs being born but 'really' I am understood to be writing of education as a 'kind of' birth. Neither of these sufficiently captures what I am dealing with in this, and subsequent, embodied writings. What I am setting out to do here is to amplify the conceptual and intellectual experience of natality, which is a key feature in the distinct vision of education I am developing.

As will become evident in the chapter that follows this passage of evocative text, natality, a central idea is presented in the convention of academic writing. Natality is treated in its abstract form by several authors, each of who emphasise features associated with the concept. My intention is to move into providing 'data' that illuminates for the reader a more visceral or phenomenological insight, as to what natality involves, and, furthermore, expand on the concept from within the experience of it. This results in a kind of writing that is neither quite factual nor figurative, but explicit and compacted, so that it becomes expressionistic, hence my preference for terming this method 'expressive' research.

By presenting these sections of anecdotal and embodied writing, I hope to resist the tendency to 'explain' or prescribe the concepts which are being illuminated. I am offering a tentative account of the experience of being immersed in the specific concept, as for example in the opening piece on natality. To be clear, I am not suggesting that the experience itself is tentative, but that the writing of it is a tentative representation of the experience. And, rather obviously, it is a deeply subjective rendition, so another person might write something completely different within the experience of lambing, from that of my own. I am offering accounts of an encountered education that reveal something of my own experience of subjectification, so as to illustrate, present and suggest that a vision of education orientated towards soil, soul and society is imaginable.

Expressive Research Methodology: Some Critical Considerations

In this short section, I will offer a critique that considers two aspects of my approach which I see as potentially problematic; first, the possibility of seduction in the methodology, which I will argue is also a feature of educational encounter; and second, empiricism as fiction, in contrast to truth.

Seduction

I am aware that in adopting a style of writing which is by definition lyrical and highly expressive there is a seductive quality which can transport the reader's focus away from where they intended. Seducing involves an enticement, which is morally suspect, and Manen acknowledges that this can be the effect of the vocative, 'It lets the text speak to us in an addressive manner so that its reverberative meanings seduce us to attentive recognition' (p. 249). The mention again of 'address' reminds us that the vocative approach is intended to establish a calling out to the reader. The objective is to arrest the reader in such a way as to invite them taking account of what is being expressed both at the textual and experiential levels. There is a degree of seduction in the invitational quality of the writing, designed to evoke the reader, as indeed the teacher similarly provokes the experience of the student in the educational encounter.

The combination of address and seduction is an important consideration here and the work of Kierkegaard in relation to seduction is valuable in this regard. I turn to focus on a discussion by Saeverot (2012) and his treatment of Kierkegaard's original writing that deals with the themes of seduction and existential education. Saeverot contends that Kierkegaard identifies two types of seduction, one of which is termed as 'vulgar' and relates to the more familiar use of the term, involving erotic manipulation and enticement. However, there is a second type of seduction, aimed more at an intellectual and spiritual enticement that has closer relevance to the educational task. Aware of the potential for mis-use of power, deceit and, ultimately, indoctrination, Saeverot considers the legitimate role of seduction in education. In fact, he suggests that there is a connection with seduction and Biesta's notion of sub-jectification, arguing that the skilful presencing of the teacher can open up possibilities from which the student chooses a path that would not otherwise have been available. This is subtle territory I suggest, and Saeverot is acutely careful in the way he constructs a nuanced position – creating almost a seduc-tive intervention in its own right! The important balance in this practice, as Saeverot sees it, lies in the integrity of the teacher, the teacher's motivation and their understanding of the quest or curiosity of the student. He identifies five 'conditions' that must be considered when using seduction in education:

- Respecting Pupils
- Tact and Introspection
- The Value of Secrecy and Trust
- Seduction Versus Indoctrination
- Open for Choice.

(Saeverot, 2012, p. 571)

I am aware that there is the possibility that in creating a series of expres-sive writings, using a combination of embodied and anecdotal techniques, the reader becomes enticed, drawn away from the intended purpose. I set out with this possibility in mind, although have no control as to whether this actually occurs, in the same way that in advocating for encounter in the educational task I am not able to make it happen. Nevertheless, in setting out with such a hope, I am mindful that the reader – or student – is drawn out of a familiar position and towards an unintended experience of oneself. However, unlike the characters in Kierkegaard's writing where they had a particular alternative end point for the unsuspecting seduce, I have no pre-defined outcome or destination in mind. The purpose of this book is to create the conditions by which the student/reader arrives at a place in which they are free to decide how to act in relation to self, others and the world.

> The individual can only become himself free, or, independent by taking the existential choice on his own, and then inscribe the existential or sub-jective truth in his own life. The point is that the individual can not live someone else's truth about existence.
>
> (Saeverot, 2012, p. 563)

Whilst my focus is on highlighting the seductive potential of the vocative writings, I am also pointing to how the integrity of the methodology is en-twined with the themes in the content of the book. A second aspect I want to consider is the issue of 'truth' and the empirical dimension of my writing.

Truth and Empiricism

I want to acknowledge that whilst my methodology sets out to deepen and make more explicit the phenomenology of experience, this approach does not seek to establish what is 'true'. That there is a 'fictionalisation' of experience is not in dispute,

> This realisation may strike some qualitative researchers as problematic. But the important reminder is that even though phenomenology employs empirical material, it does not make empirical claims. Phenomenology does not generalise from an empirical sample to a certain population, nor draw factual conclusions about certain states of affairs.
>
> (van Manen, p. 249)

The resistance to generalise 'truth' beyond the subjective account is intentional. I will be advocating that an educational encounter, by its nature, is incapable of holding an objective meaning other than that experienced by those engaged in the process. A substantial point of the argument is that this kind of education, one that is primarily existential in character, runs contrary to the kind recognised as product-orientated. In the latter form, education is designed precisely along lines whereby objective measure, certainty and standardisation are established with increasing efficiently. In this context, empirical research is aimed at contributing to evidence from a specific exercise that can be extrapolated and applied for more general effect. Such a strategy is predicated on the notion that education can be understood, in my view reductively, to input and outcome, cause and effect; that education is essentially transactional.

I offer an exploration for envisaging education that arises in the unique interplay among student, teacher and a third, educational object. The phenomenon itself is elusive, resists prior design and is dependent on the intersubjectivity of its protagonists. Furthermore, as will be argued in subsequent chapters dealing with place, this is a kind of education that is inextricably connected to the space out of which the encounter occurs. To pursue generalised conclusions, suitable for wider application is neither appropriate nor relevant to this approach. Instead the empirical material here is intended to inform the kind of questions that thoughtful educators may want to ask about their practice, and the purpose of education. In offering what might be regarded as a challenge to normative ideas about the research of education, I think I have been already clear that I will be drawing on the power of story and I will turn now to why and how story is important to both its process and content.

From Telling the Story to Being Storied

At the opening of the section introducing van Manen's work, I referred to a quotation in which he refers to the 'primal' potential of phenomenological narrative. His use of the term is quite specific and I want to draw an important connection between van Manen's position as an advocate of phenomenological research and a particular understanding of story and myth, most notably developed in the work of Shaw (2017). In paying attention to these two sources, I intend to bring the methodological approach closer to the existential domain, which in turn parallels the thematic concerns with reference to soil and soul specifically.

van Manen sets out to explain how phenomenological research – including the use of vocative methods – are especially problematic in endeavouring to account for the experience after it has taken place; 'A fundamental issue of phenomenological method is that even in naming an experience we have already lifted it up, so to speak, from the seeming raw reality of human existence' (van Manen, p. 52). Drawing on the earlier writing of Husserl, van Manen refers to this pre-reflective dimension as primal impressional consciousness. This incorporates not simply the immediate material reality, but the 'matter at issue', or, 'the roots of everything' in the transcendental structures of consciousness …. It may be helpful to regard experiences as the living of life. To experience something is to 'live through something' (p. 53). In comparison to non-phenomenological methodology, 'phenomenology wants to investigate the original emergences of human experience and meaning …. It's method aims at uncovering and seeing through the presumptions and suppositions that shape our understanding of the world and understanding of life' (pp. 54–55). van Manen's discussion offers a perspective on the power of the report on original experience which I suggest is close to how story telling can be understood as functioning in a similar way.

Shaw is arguably the leading living mythologist current working on matters that address the relationship among people, story and ecology. Most contemporary approaches to story tend to emphasise the psychoanalytic potential of the material. Furthermore, that the story is somehow allegorical in the sense that it is understood as meaning something other than what it presents. In addition, individuals can be regarded as the author of 'their own story', with encouragement to change how they want the story to unfold. Shaw takes a quite different perspective, referring to the mundus imaginalis – the imaginal world – where human imagination is open to the more-than-human world,

> So with myth you are working not just with imagination but with the imaginal …. In other words, as we turn ideas around in our head, we're not just thinking but we are getting thought.
>
> (Shaw, 2017, p. 188)

This intimates the conceptual shift in mindset from regarding stories as accounts that individuals create, to one where the story already exists, like a wild creature with an agency of its own. Effort to reduce story to allegory or a psychoanalytic instrument is an attempt to 'tame' or trap a story. In doing so, the individual misses how being 'storied' involves the heightening of direct experience of life itself, and crucially the encounter with the ecological context. Shaw refers to metis, an ancient Greek term for a kind of 'divine cunning in service to wisdom',

> A story is not just an allegory, or a metaphorical point. It is a love affair, and one of the most wonderful ways of breaking the trance states being put on us at this point in time, is to figure out what you love. Figure out what you're going to defend. And develop the metis, develop the artfulness, to bring it out into the world.
>
> (Shaw, p. 197)

The reference here to 'breaking the trance' has a particular significance in relation to education as I am describing it. I am suggesting that the prevalence of product-orientated educational discourse acts as a kind of trance state that closes down the possibilities for expanding the educational imagination. This might be further paralleled for teachers and students in that there is a risk of being seduced by the attractions that come with product-orientated education despite its reductionist, homogeneity. The methodological approach I am developing, and in particular the notion of being storied, is in part intended to interrupt a trance state. In other words, stories are not about casting a spell, but breaking them. My caution to the reader, as with the teacher and student, is that if you want to be seduced, you are not paying attention. Doing so risks getting lost in the story, lost in what is being taught and, in existential terms, remaining 'lost' in oneself.

I will be referring to Shaw's ecological activism in relation to storying later on when I turn my attention to the importance of indigenous education. For now, I wanted to introduce a glimpse into how the importance of narrative in my research methodology extends beyond its association with van Manen's approach to phenomenological methodology. To be storied involves a surrender of sorts to what lies beyond the immediate boundary of the individual's 'completeness', it is to be reminded that the world cannot be entirely co-constructed, nor indeed have the individual at its centre. That something already existed, by implication, means that there is a place – a soil – from, and in which, experience emerges, and that encounters with others occurs.

Summary

In bring this chapter to a close, I offer a series of observations to summarise what has been set up in the sections of writing so far. The intention has been to invite the reader into the world of the book, opening with a story that will form the basis of the shape of the vision of education that I have in mind. This personal account not only carries the essence of the themes and content of what follows but also constitutes an empirical component of the work and is traversed across six individual episodes in the overall educational narrative. In some respects, this first piece, Arrival, is in itself trying to arrive.

Arrival is also how I have prefaced the opening rationale, making it clear that in doing so my interest lies some place other than in the familiar context of product-orientated education. My rationale explains why I am setting this vision apart from what might be recognised as a more mainstream preoccupation with teaching and learning and instead suggests what might be at stake when attention is so intently focused on education as outcome-based and the teacher-student relationship as being one of cause and effect. My intention in the opening chapter has been to advocate the possible purpose of an education that is orientated towards soil, soul and society and which also takes place through an encountered experience.

However, I recognise that by setting out in a direction away from the familiar it might be helpful to locate the ideas, so as to better navigate its intentions, themes and motivations. I have introduced a second example of an evocative text which pays attention to the marginal spaces that lie between the main fields of cultivation, the places where wildness thrives. I have done so in order to cultivate not so much a particular 'product', but a curiosity, and hope that the reader finds it useful to think of the book as having its roots in these 'edge-rows'. Having situated this work as being distinct from the familiar, and yet not adrift from any moorings, I have dropped into a more detailed consideration of the methodology by which I have set about my exploration of its themes.

The interleaving of evocative-embodied writing with theoretical discussion is presented as the weft and warp of the fabric of the book. The theoretical trajectory will follow a journey that has begun with arrival and will lead into natality in the next chapter and ends with departure and harvest. Meanwhile, the empirical accounts provide the experiential illumination of what otherwise would be a purely academic commentary, and that will not do in the context of a vision of education that is born out of the land, involves an arrival to a world and the challenge to live well in relationship to others.

What follows from this point is the main body of work. We have entered the marginal space, hunkered down into the edges with one view out to the open field and another view along the hedgerow. So, I turn now to the experience of arrival and what it means to enter the world and why this is so important to a view of education orientated towards soil, soul and society.

Note

1 I define faith as a complete trust and confidence in what might be possible, whilst not being immediately realised. This can be illustrated by the notion of the 'tragic gap' (Palmer, 2004) in which the individual learns 'to hold the tension between the reality of the moment and the possibility that something better might emerge' (p. 175).

References

Anderson, R. and Braud, W. (2011) Transforming Self and Others through Research: Transpersonal Research Methods and Skills for the Human Sciences and Humanities, New York: State University New York Press.

Barrow, G. and Marshall, H. (2020) Ecological Transactional Analysis – Principles for a New Movement, The Transactional Analyst, Vol. 10, No. 2, Spring, pp. 5–9.

Bennett, T. (2016) The Polite Revolution in Research and Education, in Evers, J., Kneyber, R., eds., Flip the System: Changing Education from the Ground Up, London: Routledge.

Berry, T. (1988) The Dream of the Earth, San Francisco: Sierra Club Books.

Berry, W. (1977) The Unsettling of America: Culture & Agriculture, Berkeley: Counterpoint.

Biesta, G.J.J. (2014) The Beautiful Risk of Education, Boulder: Paradigm.

Biesta, G.J.J. (2016) Good Education and the Teacher: Reclaiming Educational Professionalism, in Evers, J., Kneyber, R., eds., Flip the System: Changing Education from the Ground Up, London: Routledge.

Biesta, G.J.J. (2017) The Rediscovery of Teaching, London: Routledge.

Buckles, J. (2018) Education, Sustainability and the Ecological Social Imaginary: Connective Education and Global Change, Switzerland: Palgrave Macmillan.

Cajete, G. (1994) Look to the Mountain: An Ecology of Indigenous Education, Colorado: Kivaki Press.

Gidley, J. (2018) Postformal Education: A Philosophy for Complex Futures, Switzerland: Springer.

Gordon, M. (2016) Existential Philosophy and the Promise of Education: Learning from Myths and Metaphors, New York: Peter Lang.

Jantzen, G. (1998) Becoming Divine: Towards a Feminist Philosophy of Religion, Manchester: Manchester University Press.

Jickling, B., ed. (2018) Wild Pedagogies, Switzerland: Palgrave Press Macmillian.

Kane, S. (1998) Wisdom of the Mythtellers, Ontario: Broadview Press.

LeFay, R. (2006) An Ecological Critique of Education, International Journal of Children's Spirituality, Vol. 11, No. 1, pp. 35–45. DOI: 10.1080/13644360500503290

Miller, J. (2000) Education and the Soul: Toward a Spiritual Curriculum, Albany: State University of New York Press.

Miller, J., et al,eds. (2005) Holistic Learning and Spirituality in Education, Albany: State University of New York Press.

Miller, J.P., Nigh, K., Binder, M.J., Novak, B. and Crowel, S., eds. (2019) International Handbook of Holistic Education, London: Routledge.

Noddings, N. (1984) Caring: A Feminine Approach to Ethics and Moral Education, London: University of California Press.

Orr, D. (2004) Earth in Mind: On Education, Environment and the Human Prospect, Washington: First Island.

Palmer, P. (2004) A Hidden Wholeness: The Journey Toward an Undivided Life, San Francisco: Jossey-Bass.

Petrovic, J.E. and Mitchell, R.M. (2018) Indigenous Philosophies of Education Around the World, Oxford: Routledge.

Proctor, B. (2000) Supervision: A Guide to Creative Practice, London: SAGE Publishing.

Regan, T. (2005) Non-Western Educational Traditions: Indigenous Approaches to Educational Thought and Practice, New York: Routledge.

Rogers, C. (1968) Freedom to Learn, Columbus: Charles Merrill Publishing Company.

Saeverot, H. (2012) Indirect Pedagogy: Some Lessons in Existential Education, Rotterdam: Sense Publishers.

Shaw, M. (2011) A Branch from the Lightning Tree: Ecstatic Myth and the Grace in Wildness, Oregon: White Cloud Press.

Shaw, M. (2017) Scatterlings: Getting Claimed in the Age of Amnesia, Oregon: White Cloud Press.

Shepard, P. and McKinley, D. (1969) The Subversive Science: Essays toward an Ecology of Man, Boston: Houghton Mifflin Company.

Simpson, L.B. (2014) Land as Pedagogy: Nishnaabeg Intelligence and Rebellious Transformation, Decolonization: Indigeneity, Education & Society, Vol. 3, No. 3, pp. 1–2525.

Todd, S. (2012) Learning from the Other: Levinas, Psychoanalysis, and Ethical Possibilities in Education, New York: SUNY Press.

van Manen, M. (2014) Phenomenology of Practice: Meaning-Giving Methods in Phenomenological Research and Writing, London: Routledge.

Chapter 3

Natality, subjectification and the function of physis in education

Arrival

Natality

Setting the Scene

'Fluid' is the word that comes immediately to mind when I feel my way into the experience of natality. It is such a wonderfully fluid word; an ideal starting point from which to enter an exploration of becoming. Although, when I turn to the material fact of birth, the quality of fluidity emerges only after an initial anchoring. To be specific, I will be exploring the idea of natality in relation to lambing, an enduring, seasonal event which has connected people to the land across millennia. I will do my best to resist slipping into a more prosaic agricultural appreciation of the process and focus on my lived experience of what it is 'to lamb'. Yet, it's worth a moment to consider the background to lambing, because there is something utterly remarkable, integrated and powerfully cyclic in what culminates in a harvest of new life.

Most of us who have disconnected from seasons and soil will be unaware that in the northern hemisphere, just before daylight hours reduce, there is a rush of new growth in grass yield, in the northern hemisphere, in the months of September and October. This gives the adult ewes an opportunity to pick up 'condition' and become especially healthy and fertile. As the daylight hours diminish in early autumn, this triggers a hormonal change in the females, and they come into 'heat'. Ovulation is absent earlier in the summer; nature has made it so, and for good reason. As the females come into 'season,' they are ready for the rams; the ewes will now 'stand for it', and ewes mated in the autumn will lamb in the spring just as the first grass of the new year emerges. It is possible to intervene and artificially influence the breeding cycle, but this

DOI: 10.4324/9781003407751-4

invariably involves a more extensive re-configuring of feeding regimes and flock management. My point here is that left to the force of nature, ewes will only become pregnant at a time which will best guarantee rich feed at the arrival of the new lambs, which is around April. The grass grows steadily from this point, increasing in yield through to mid-June, at which stage most flocks have lambed and they graze off the remaining pasture through high summer, typically a time of weaning, shearing and setting apart the breeding and fattening stock.

As someone returning to the seasons and soil, I have found raising sheep the most direct way into connection with the seasonal cycle. Other stock – apart from goats – can now easily be bred around the calendar, but sheep remain best raised aligned with the ebb and flow of the sun-light and vitality of the meadow. For us, it has tended to be early March when I look out several times day and night for signs of lambing. I notice how reference to lambing interchanges between me and the ewes; 'Are you lambing this spring?' I am asked. 'I had a ewe having trouble lamb-ing this year', I exclaim. 'We lambed well, we're done lambing for the season' so my neighbour tells me. This natal experience is a shared busi-ness. Farmer and stock are in it together, and often quite literally.

Lambing

I mentioned that natality begins with anchoring. It never fails to fasci-nate me that the first reliable sign of imminent birth is the ewe pawing the ground. The ewe selects a place. This might be determined by a smell, a slight undulation that appeals, a preferred patch of grazing. There is rarely an obvious rationale for the choosing, but once decided upon the place is set steadfast. There is something sacrosanct about this discernment, for once declared there is no moving the ewe - she is there to stay until the task is done. The sharp-eyed shepherd can pre-empt this by ensuring that the ewe is close enough to a sheltered yard or field hut, but so often this moment is missed and the ewe screws herself into the spot of earth that will serve the birthing. She paws and turns in cir-cles, cycling around, smelling at the soil, perhaps licking it for minerals until the first contractions begin and she starts lambing proper.

'Arrival' is a complicated concept when applied to lambing. I am not sure when the 'event' actually begins. Is it when I notice that we have started? Or is it somehow announced by the unseen, mysterious move-ment of the unborn. Nevertheless, a powerful shift occurs in myself when I realise the time is coming. I know it is best to be grounded, easy in my body, observant and alert, yet more frequently I worry about the distance to the shelter, the circumstances of the previous lambing by the ewe, the reserve of energy I have available if help is needed and the wondering about another new life to come. How many? What markings? Ram or ewe? Have I 'arrived' at this point, I wonder? Yes, perhaps this is the point at which I enter into the life of another, bringing on the one hand a kind of authority in terms of responsibility for welfare, whilst on the other hand, no power to determine the nature of what I am due to meet. But there is a determination to meet; I will become a part of this, and that might matter. In doing so, I, and we, and what is birthed, will have done so as a result of our meeting; my decision to arrive, and the ewe's, or more precisely the unborn lamb's compelling claim, to become.

Soon fluid shapes what happens next and takes on the character of natality. The ewe, her lamb and I become immersed in fluidity. Waters break and the amniotic flow splashes to the sacred spot and in some instances on my boots or wrist. We are now each in the liminal space that is fundamental to the natal process. We are neither pregnant nor born, but this fluid place of in-betweenness, where time passing is crucial but the clock does not matter; natality could be at any time, it occurs when it must. Of course, it is more often the case that the process unfolds swiftly, the contractions strengthen, the feet and nose appear and, after a particularly powerful surge, the head is out and the rest slips on to the floor. But it is not always like this.

Each year there will be a birth where fluidity describes a different in-between place; to live or to not live. Whilst there is the visceral, hot, slipperiness of birth, there is also in parallel an existential task being played out right in front of me. The risk of natality is that it is too feeble an urge, that it's desire is out of time, or before it's time. Simply wanting to live is sometimes not enough; a peaking surge may lack sufficiency. When I began breeding sheep I failed to act, to 'arrive' in good time, believing that nature would 'sort things' out. Maybe it was because of this naive dependence, or unavoidable deficiencies inherent in the ewe, but lambs die, and ewes too. It would seem that mortality has to be possible for natality to thrive. There is an opening when life has its best opportunity to reveal itself, to shift from immediate survival to an onward flourishing, but this is rarely promised, instead it is fought for, accomplished, deserved. Even where no assistance is required there is struggle, dis-ease and the kind of bodily disturbance that must accompany transformation.

I am quicker now to spot the signs of distress, of some kind of lack, where supporting the ewe may hasten the act, or extend the opening for life to emerge. If we are lucky the ewe and I may be in the field shelter where there will be straw on the ground, walls to protect from the wind and equipment to hand. And sometimes we are caught in the open field, on dark and damp earth, a strengthening wind and rainfall. Perhaps there is still light snow or new frost on the ground. The task now is more involving. First I check the presentation; normally a lamb enters the world head first with its front two feet upfront, almost as if it is diving out of its mother. Sometimes all is well, but the mother is simply tired, or the lamb is especially large, and the help is straightforward. I run my fingers around the rim of the opening, curl them over the back of the lamb's head and on catching the next contraction will just ease it out, saving the ewe valuable energy.

On other occasions the situation is more complex. An initial inspection indicates an awkward presentation. Maybe a leg showing belongs to a twin which is lodged towards the back of the birth passage and is obstructing the forward sibling. This demands a more substantial commitment. I might be enmeshed with the ewe and her lambs for ten minutes, or over an hour. There will be times when I feel lost – that the space between visualising what my hand is navigating and a capacity to translate that into action becomes too great. I am in what came before the birth – a chamber that is constantly shape-shifting yet ultimately containing. Like a thick-skinned internal heated sack, this birth canal flexes to my pull and touch. As I bring a leg forward so the boundary of the space changes too. It is a living khora, a pre-formed, maternal space, subject to impregnation, whilst remaining impossible to fix and define. This is fluidity at its most perceptual and visceral. The amniotic fluid is vital to help lubricate, but in time will begin to decrease and become absorbed making the passage increasingly subject to friction. Other fluids combine, perhaps some blood appears, under the strain, shit happens, some veterinary lubricant becomes necessary, my own sweat gradually mingles in as the sustained searching for limbs in the dark, runs down my arms into the slippery work.

Etymologically 'fluid' is associated with the Latin root, 'flowing', and this in turn catches a sense of the interplay between myself, the ewe and the lamb in this birthing process. It becomes evidently clear that there is a physical dynamic to the task. There is a natural momentum building, comprising ebb and flow as contractions come and go, as breathing, mine and hers, falls in tandem. The ewe strains and pushes, I pull back and her will is allied to my strength as we bring the lamb forward. Many times the side of my head, my face is pressed into the belly of the mother, my nostrils full of lanolin, the proofing oil that gives the sheep its distinctive smell. There is an intensity to the 'flow' in this aspect of fluidity, and I can recall those occasions where I lose sight of where I begin and end, apart from the literal boundary of skins, we meld into a single, co-creative experience. It is not always like this. There have been times where I have fought against the natural intention, those infrequent situations where the lamb must be pushed back inside to re-arrange a limb or return a prolapsed uterus; in each instance, this results in such peculiar hard effort and strain and always must end in exhaustion for both, and sometimes worse for lamb or ewe.

This is also a hot place to be. My hand, wrist and forearm will be deep in the internal space of the ewe, wrapped around legs, necks and bodies of lamb. I feel the sharp contrast of the often freezing condition outside, with the mother's blood hot heat. It brings to mind just how intimate natality can be. I am inside the other, touching where no other has been, sometimes caressing the inner walls, gently pulling at a soft plump torso or warm delicate feet. The most remarkable, spectacular act is to check if there is life in the lamb which is yet to be born. I find the hard roundness of the head and carefully work a finger to the muzzle and tease open its mouth. Shifting the tip of the finger between its tongue and roof of the mouth I wait for the critical sucking motion that tells me this life wants living. I work quickly but with care to re-direct limbs, bodies and heads – sometimes pushing back into the mother a wrongly aligned face – so that the birth passage can be vacated. Often it is enough to be able to pull the feet downwards – never horizontally – and outwards. Just occasionally a more robust intervention is needed and a soft, slim rope is looped around the feet and a steady heave will have the lamb curling out, and the newborn can now claim that title. We are almost across that defining threshold.

Lying its full length on the ground it can take several moments for the lamb to take its first breath and shepherds will wipe the mucus from the muzzle, often with straw or grass in order to stimulate breathing and clear the air passage. When this is not enough, tickling the nose with a strand of straw, clearing the mouth with a finger and, if need be, swinging the lamb to and fro, are ways in which taking in air is encouraged. Eventually the lamb will splutter, shake its head with a gentle slapping of wet ears and be fully alive in the world; this is arrival. I lean back on my heels, take my own breath and relax a little. The ewe will have immediately begun to lick down the lamb, nibbling the birth membrane off the shining, translucent yellowed fleece. Gradually its true colour comes through and the lamb, suitably encouraged and beginning to re-attach to its mother this side of its natal task, begins to rise to its feet. It has a job to do; find its first feed and it does so as the mother continues to lick and call it. These early minutes become critical to completing the natal experience, partly because it is during this time that the mother is learning the distinctive smell of her youngster and that the lamb is understanding the call of its mother. It is also the time in which the lamb continues to activate what happens next. As it finds the udder, and begins to suck – or 'latchin on' as it's called, this triggers a new series of contractions. Either a second lamb is born, or the placenta is passed, ensuring that the ewe 'cleans out', as a consequence of the new upsurge in hormones. Once the lamb has taken a first feed – not milk, but a potent combination of nutrients and antibodies known as colostrum – we are all in the safer territory of having been born.

There's another, more obscure thought arising from this experience, and it relates to the difference between livestock, wild animals and the role of the shepherd. I am often asked; 'What happens if the ewe doesn't get the help? What happens in nature?' The answer is straightforward enough - the ewe would often die, and sheep, as we know them, don't really live in the 'wild'. They have been domesticated over the centuries so that there is an ancient co-dependency between the animal and the farmer. The shepherd must be there because he has 'made' the sheep such that he has to be available to them. Their position as owner and provider is pretty much self-ordained. Despite how it appears even in the more remote areas where sheep are farmed, lambing is undertaken in lower pasture, or indoors. It is only the most primitive of breeds that have the remaining capacity to self-manage.

My mind wanders to what this all means educationally. Has schooling, synonymous for some with 'education', domesticated the wildness of what education might otherwise be? Have we devised it as such that students are only required as far as they meet how the teachers expect them to be? That teachers exist because learners must be taught? Where might natality occur in such circumstances? My mind wanders and I reach around in the dark, choretic space searching for an education beyond captivity.

Introduction

To arrive into the world, and to be experienced by others in doing so, is the existential challenge at the heart of this book and the following chapter. I will be unpicking the existential aspect of my educational vision, and introducing ideas that are core to the role of the teacher and the task of the student. I will suggest that this educational episode centred on arrival is a process akin to 'birthing', and attends to the 'subjectification' of the student (Biesta, 2014). Importantly though, education is not presented here as if the student's arrival is an objective of the educational task. Instead, I am exploring how such an education occurs in relationship in terms of the social and ecological domains. The student's experience of arrival is contingent on the presence of the teacher and is mediated through the place in which it emerges. To explore this further, I will be considering the concept of natality in this chapter. I will discuss its importance from two perspectives, namely the original writing of Arendt (1954, 1958) and later works by Jantzen (1998, 2009, 2010), and consider associated ideas, including chora, and life force, as understood through the concept of physis. Finally, I will introduce the subject of interruption and consider an educational perspective on the experience of 'being addressed', which will point towards the following chapter, 'Liminality, place-based education and the role of myth and story'.

What is arguably distinctive about my treatment of natality here is that I am seeking to locate it in the field of educational praxis. In other words, I want to render the concept into the context of educational experience so that, in figurative terms, it comes alive itself. My concern is that such a vital educational idea can tend to be remain an intellectual proposition, whereas I am interested in it as inextricably linked into the 'what' and 'how' of the teacher-student dynamic. As is illustrated through the preceding sections of vocative writing, my intention has been to speak of natality and arrival from within the experience of these ideas. In the following discussion, my intention is to highlight the importance of natality in orientating the educational encounter towards soil, soul and society.

This chapter is intended to be 'arrivalistic' in its style and purpose. This is perhaps an unusual term and one that might be regarded by some as ungainly, but it does a good job of capturing what is going on in the following discussion. It is not so much that an account of arrival in relation to education is the 'outcome' of this discussion, but that through being attentive to ideas about arrival, the nature of what emerges educationally might become gradually revealed. The discussion functions as a metaphorical 'birth canal' through which the 'subject' of the student might occur. So, the focus of this section is to create a sense of what arrives in educational work whilst resisting the tendency to over-define it. My hope is that in adapting an arrivalistic perspective, something becomes more clearly understood about the experience of arrival, yet the subject of the arrival remains beyond concrete definition.

To begin with the concept of birth is perhaps an obvious idea for a discussion of education. In the context of a benign, product-oriented view of education, a process of birth draws attention to a journey of cultivation and maturation by the student, supported by the educator who might be characterised as a cultivator or midwife. This metaphor is arguably found most commonly in humanistic and holistic pedagogies, where realising the full potential of the student is regarded as the central objective of the educator (see, for example, Miller et al, 2019). However, in the context of my present argument, and in relation to an interest in the existential dimension of education, my approach to the concept of birth is more particular, and I will set this out by describing a distinctive perspective on natality. The trajectory of realising the potential of an individual is not what I am interested in here, but more that the natal moment is one in which the student is addressed and 'appears' as a subject, which is to say, as someone confronted by the question of how to exist in the world.

Student as 'Subject' and the Event of 'Subjectification'

Before moving into the discussion of natality, it may be helpful to say something first about the notion of the student as subject and the concept of subjectification. If this chapter is 'arrivalistic' in the sense that it explores the experience of the individual occurring in the world, I think it is important to offer an initial explanation of how I am referring to the 'what' is appearing. In doing so, I am drawing on the work of Biesta and in particularly a domain, of education which he refers to as subjectification (2014). This term is one of three domains, the other two being qualification and socialisation which refer, respectively, to the means by which the student accomplishes a level of understanding about knowledge and skills that are recognised and validated, and also, often implicitly, their experience of a process of induction into the cultural norms and values of society.

However, subjectification is what is of most interest to me when considering the experience of arrival. The term has been prone to misunderstanding, something that Biesta recognises in a paper offering clarification (2020), and yet nevertheless, it offers a useful starting point for describing the subject of this account of arrival. In explaining why subjectification is educationally significant, Biesta associates this domain with a particular kind of freedom, which is revealed in how the individual 'shows up'; 'Put simply what is at stake in the idea of subjectification is our freedom as human beings and, more specifically, our freedom to act or to refrain from action' (2020, p. 93). Whilst I want to avoid an extended discussion of the relationship between education and freedom at this point, I think it is necessary to offer some brief observations as they relate to freedom and the student as subject. First, I find helpful Arendt's observation that freedom is limited when it is understood in relation to an individual's state of mind. She argues, as does Biesta, for a kind of political freedom in which the individual has capacity to address matters of living in a pluralistic world that include equality, justice and power: 'This freedom... is the very opposite of "inner freedom", the inward space into which men (sic) may escape from external coercion and feel free. This inner feeling remains with outer manifestations and hence is by definition politically irrelevant' (1954, p. 146). Significantly, given the interest in (dis)connection, Arendt continues;

> Whatever its ["inner freedom"] legitimacy may be... it was originally the result of an estrangement from the world in which worldly experiences were transformed into experiences within one's own self. The experiences of inner freedom are derivative in that they always suppose a retreat from the world, where freedom was denied, into an inwardness to which no other has access.
>
> (1954, p. 146)

To remain inwards, therefore, is to resist the call outwards, into arrival, and by implication, to be neither free, nor experience one's 'subject-ness'. For both Arendt and Biesta, to exercise freedom involves first appearing in the world and then second, experiencing its pluralistic nature with a view to making a decision about how to act within it, or not. This experiencing of oneself in relation to a world that is dynamic, and outside of one's 'control' is an important feature of subjectification, as I am understanding the term. The interplay, or more specifically, the capacity of the individual to calibrate between their desires and those of others, is the exercise of freedom, and this is predicated on the individual moving from an inward position, to that of newcomer, which is why the experience of arrival is so fundamental to the event of subjectification.

A second important observation about the student as subject, and subjectification, is that I find it useful to consider this as a state of being, or experience, as opposed to a fixed destination or outcome. To be a subject, or to engage in subjectification, is not equivalent to having arrived, but to be in a state of arrival, and that this is an on-going, or at very least, a recurring, experience. The individual does not stop arriving and therefore complete 'subjectifying'. This is the means by which renewal takes place and that by definition is continually required. It is an important observation in that this hopefully explains why this chapter is arrivalistic in its nature, and that its intention imitates the features, or character, of the subject in the natal experience.

A useful final observation already implicit in the previous remark is that I want to avoid associating the use of the term 'subject' with that of a particular person as such. Of course, individuals will have a personal identity, a sense of 'who' they are. But subjectification is to discover how the 'I' experiences and appears in the world outside of any notion of who this 'I' might be internally. It is in these moments in which the individual knows whether who they are is how they exist, or conversely, that is to say, how they arrive in the world is who they are. Perhaps, as a way of illustrating more explicitly the concept of subjectification, it may be helpful to refer to an experience from my own practice, which I have written about previously (Barrow, 2018). The case involves my delivering an adult education programme in an Eastern European country and a particular situation that took place in an afternoon session. I am sharing it at this point in the chapter to provide a sense of the kind of experience of arrival which I hope begins to emerge over the coming theoretical discussion.

During the afternoon session, I became aware of how passive the group was behaving. Whilst the students made notes and nodded amicably enough I was increasingly aware of their over adaptations to my input – they were beginning to become the object of my teaching. I paused a few times and pointed this tendency out to the group but I was encouraged to continue teaching, even though whenever I asked a question the room fell silent. Eventually I stopped and made it clear that I was unhappy to continue until we had explored the process. The group insisted that I continue, but I resisted and one student began to explain that many of them had been educated during the period of communist totalitarianism where the emphasis was on the student showing obedience and certainly not to question the authority of the teacher. They felt reluctant to be with me differently. I responded by suggesting that, even so, any one of them could get up and leave if they believed that it would be more effective. Again, the group asked me to continue to teach them material, although by now I felt my own reluctance in continuing to be 'in control' for any longer. I offered to present for just a few minutes more and then I would stop and they would have to decide for themselves how to use the remaining time of the workshop. At this point, a woman in the group stood, looked about to see if any would join her – they did not. She looked at me and I repeated that the choice to leave was hers. She turned and left. After a few minutes of further presentation, I stopped and gradually all of the group left the building.

An hour later the group returned. Within minutes, five members of the group had spontaneously begun to draw over the existing models on the board, or were critiquing ideas and introducing their own views on theory, but this is not especially relevant to the topic of subjectification. It was the experience of the woman who had left alone which was most surprising and revelatory. In debriefing her experience, she reported that after leaving, she had encountered an unfamiliar understanding of herself. That in some way she had crossed a threshold she had not even realised existed. She was visibly moved and wondered if there was now a new life emerging from what she had arrived into, not only literally in terms of her having gone out into the world, but also existentially through the choice she had made by venturing beyond what had been the familiar world; she had made a choice that had been hidden from view.

Later in this chapter, I will offer another means by which to contour around what subjectification entails when I look to the idea of spontaneity and improvisation, but for now, I have offered these opening thoughts in preparation for the discussion on natality so that the reader may have an indication as to what is emerging in the general experience of arrival. I mean this not only in terms of the educational encounter, but also in relation to what happens as this chapter unfolds.

Introducing Natality

I begin my discussion of natality by considering the work of Hannah Arendt who is most associated with first defining and exploring the use of the term in her social and political writings, most notably The Human Condition (1958). For the purposes of my argument, I want to consider two ideas that Arendt introduces, the first of which is natality itself and, later in this chapter, the addressive quality that she associates with the natal experience. It might be helpful at the outset to contextualise how I understand Arendt's use of natality. The significant point that she presents is the importance of the vita activa, which is essentially a particularly political engagement by the individual within the plurality of the world. However, Arendt is emphatic in identifying pluralism as one of the several conditions that impinge on the human experience. Mortality, reason and natality are also recognised as conditions by which the individual is obliged to navigate their experience of living in the social, political and material world. For Arendt, human engagement – the vita activa – is contingent on the natal experience, the means by which humanity renews itself, and thereby the world. Natality is an aspect of the human condition and a prerequisite for everything that follows in Arendt's commentary. The reference to 'condition' is intentional, 'To avoid misunderstanding: the human condition is not the same as human nature' (Arendt, 1958, p. 10). Human conditions are those aspects of experience which have to be negotiated, whereas human nature is orientated towards the question of who are we? and the answer to which, in Arendt's view, 'surely only a god could know and define it' (ibid, p. 10). So, I am turning first to Arendt to introduce the concept of natality because of the significance of arrival in my vision of education.

To talk of natality is to engage in the experience of birth, beginning and becoming. For Arendt, natality is a general term to describe one of the existential conditions of being human and her references to birth and beginning is used specifically:

> This beginning is not the same as the beginning of the world; it is not the beginning of something but of somebody, who is a beginner himself. With the creation of man, the principle of beginning came into the world itself, which of course, is only another way of saying that the principle of freedom was created when man was created but not before. It is in the nature of beginning that something new is started which cannot be expected from whatever may have happened before. This character of startling unexpectedness is inherent in all beginnings and in all origins.
>
> (Arendt, 1958, pp. 177–178)

Furthermore, Arendt emphasises that the essence of 'who' the beginner is appears in this natal episode, having been hidden prior to this moment,

> ...it is more likely that the 'who' which appears so clearly and unmistakably to others, remains hidden from the person himself, like the daimon in Greek religion which accompanies each man throughout his life, always looking over his shoulder from behind and this visible only to those he encounters.
>
> (ibid, p. 180)

At the core of the natal experience, there is the possibility that someone is addressed, or summoned, and that in its beginning, the person is made known in the world. Arendt's concern is that the newcomer might best engage in the vita activa, a specific phrase that divides the human condition into three domains. These include labour, which Arendt equates with the utilitarian task of meeting biological needs, and work, which describes how humankind distinguishes itself from the natural world through the unnatural, or manufactured, production of things to supplement life. Finally, Arendt refers to action which is the capacity for the newcomer to engage freely in connection to others in order to renew the world,

> Action, the only activity that goes on directly between men without the intermediary of things or matter, corresponds to the human condition of plurality, to the fact that men, not Man, live on the earth and inhabit the world... Plurality is the condition of human action because we are all the same, that is, human, in such a way that nobody is ever the same as anyone else who ever lived, lives or will live.
>
> (ibid, pp. 7–8)

The emphasis on the appearance of the individual's unique expression of and capacity for action is important for the kind of experience I am exploring here. Arendt also regards speech as central to action and this, too, I connect with the addressive quality of the educational exchange in my perspective, a theme I pick up again at the end of this chapter. As important a link with Arendt's account of natality is the recognition that it reflects the cyclic movement out of which the human condition emerges,

> The miracle that saves the world, the realm of human affairs, from its normal, 'natural' ruin is ultimately the fact of natality, in which the faculty of action is ontologically rooted. It is, in other words, the birth of new men and the new beginning, the action they are capable of by virtue of being born. Only the full experience of this capacity can bestow upon human affairs faith and hope...
>
> (ibid, p. 247)

Although her commentary of Arendt on natality was part of a wider political discourse, her earlier essay, The Crisis in Education (1954) considers its implications for school teachers and policy makers, and more generally, adults and children. In a paper that essentially despairs at the deterioration of education at the expense of a child-centred pedagogical movement, Arendt appeals to educators to think again about the need to distinguish between the grown-ups world and that of the newcomer. To do so is an action by which the world might be properly known, to a new generation, through the task of teaching, by those who 'are altogether worthy' of their ancestors, (p. 194). Importantly for the purpose of my vision of education, Arendt associates this with an on-going commitment to the world,

> [Natality]: the fact that we have all come into the world by being born and that this world is constantly renewed by birth. Education is the point at

which we decide whether we love the world enough to assume responsibility for it and by the same token save it from that ruin which except for renewal, except for the coming of the new and young, would be inevitable.

(Arendt, 1954, p. 196)

In a critique that echoes my earlier commentary on product-orientated education, Arendt is concerned with the implications of a generation of teachers who on one hand do not comprehend the importance of being 'grown-up' in relation to the new generation whilst, on the other hand, fail to understand that to do so involves something quite different from the authoritarian,

> Basically we are always educating for a world that is, or is becoming, out of joint...Because the world is made by mortals it wears out; and because it continuously changes its inhabitants it runs the risk of becoming as mortal as they. To preserve the world against the mortality of its creators and inhabitants it must be constantly set right anew. ... Our hope always hangs on the new which every generation brings; but precisely because we can base our hope only on this, we destroy everything if we so try to control the new that we, the old, can dictate how it will look.
>
> (ibid, p. 192)

Product-orientated education is precisely a model of education that sets out to 'control' the way in which a new beginning, symbolised in the appearance of the student, is standardised so as to become assimilated into an 'old world' (ibid, p. 193). Additionally, and perhaps inadvertently, Arendt offers the prescient comment that the failure of education is to 'preserve this newness and introduce it as a new thing' (ibid, p. 193). In this case, the world itself is at risk of becoming mortal – of being worn out – a reference to how ecological entropy is at risk of being paralleled through product-orientated education that concretises itself. I am setting out natality here as a central concept in the educational encounter and one that is orientated towards soil, soul and society and, in Arendt's writing, I suggest that there is a sufficient justification for making this link. For the student to appear uniquely associates with the soul of the individual, whilst they simultaneously arrive in support of the renewal of the world, not only literally in terms of soil, but also politically in relation to a pluralistic society.

Freedom and Irreplaceability

Before I draw this section to a close and move to a second consideration of natality, I want to expand on the previous mention of uniqueness and pluralism in the context of Arendt's work. I am aware that in referring to particularity and uniqueness there may be a sense that I am speaking of the distinctiveness of the individual student in terms of them being a person, or referring to a sense of the 'self'. Whilst indeed the student may have a sense of themselves as a unique individual, and that cultivating such a sense of self might also be an objective for some educators, as discussed earlier in relation to holistic education, this is not what I am interested in relation to the vision of education in this work.

Instead I am talking of the uniqueness in the choice that the student might make in order to exist in response to the world. It is this challenge that locates my work in the existential domain and one that connects with a particular understanding of freedom. To describe what I mean by this idea in more detail, I will return to the encounter that I presented at the beginning of this chapter in which the student decided to leave whilst her colleagues remained in the room. Of course, the student is a unique individual in the sense that she is different from any other person, but in that respect she is actually no different from any other! We all share the common fact that we are different as persons, an observation Biesta refers to as the idea of uniqueness-as-difference (2017, p. 12, author's italics). What this student demonstrated in relation to others, whilst also encountering it for herself, was a unique response to a confrontation by which she was addressed. In turning attention to the group's passivity, the opportunity arises whereby a remarkable choice might be made to leave, by which I mean a choice that warrants a 'remark' precisely because of its uniqueness. This moment is where the individual is asked, 'When does it matter that I am I? [This question] looks for existential events where my uniqueness is at stake and where I am therefore at stake. ... These are situations where the call comes to me and where it is only I who can respond. They are, in other words, situations where we encounter a responsibility...' (Biesta, 2017, p. 12). The student-as-subject is 'at risk' because the encounter requires her to step out of her immanence, or 'in-dwelling', and arrive into a way of existing in relation to the world that is demonstrably beyond her control. This is a condition of the pluralistic world that Arendt speaks of and which is central to my understanding of education. It is what Biesta, who draws on the work of Levinas, describes as a shift in perspective,

> Here uniqueness is not a matter of difference – a third person perspective – but a matter of irreplaceability – a first-person perspective. Uniqueness, as Levinas puts it, is about doing "what nobody else can do in my place" (Levinas, 1989, p. 202). There is of course no one who can force us to take on the responsibility we encounter.
>
> (Biesta, 2017, p. 12)

The language of responsibility may initially appear incongruent with the idea of freedom, yet this is precisely what is at stake in how I envisage arrival in the educational relationship. I am working towards a view of freedom in education that recognises that rather than being possessed by the individual, freedom is demonstrated by how the individual chooses (or not), to act in the world. In other words, it is irrelevant as to whether the group of students might claim to be free; what matters is that they might choose to be so when the opportunity is encountered. Arendt writes of this more explicitly in her essay on freedom when she associates its connection with the fact of human becoming,

> Man (sic) does not possess freedom so much as he, or better his coming into the world, is equated with the appearance of freedom in the universe; man is free because he is a beginning and was so created after the universe had already come into existence.... In the birth of each man this initial beginning is reaffirmed, because in each instance something new comes into an already existing world....
>
> (Arendt, 1954, p. 167)

I have been particularly influenced by Arendt's attention to the act of the newcomer's appearance in the world. This natal moment, a breaking in to the world anew, is an educational moment precisely because it brings about a test of whether the world, both materially and figuratively, can renew itself. For now, suffice it to say, education involves arrival into the world, to know it, and be seen in one's particularity, by the world and as connected within it. Whilst Arendt's work opens up possibilities for applying natality to my interest in arrival, it is in the writing of Jantzen that I find an elaboration of the idea that brings a more vivid quality to my own thinking about its importance.

Natality: Grace Jantzen

Whilst Arendt is regarded as the first writer to develop the philosophical idea of natality others have developed it further, either philosophically (see, for example, O'Byrne, 2010) or with specific regard to education (see Gordon, 2001). However, I am especially interested in the approach of Grace Jantzen, a Western theologian who establishes a feminist application of natality, drawing on Arendt's earlier introduction of the concept. Jantzen's project is to reframe or extend a contemporary Western moral and cultural imaginary that is orientated towards mortality, going so far as to suggest that a combination of necrophilia and necrophobia are the dominant preoccupations in particularly Western political, cultural and existential domains. Her intention is to incorporate natality as the basis of an alternative theological-philosophical view in which human flourishing is central. Jantzen argues that by doing so, the lived experience is more properly accounted for and contrasts with a tendency towards intellectual, abstract and disconnected narratives.

> A symbolic focused on birth, and hence on our material basis and connection with one another... would go along way towards shifting the agenda away from intellectual justifications and toward material justice.
>
> (Jantzen, 1999, p. 146)

It is not my intention to set out a critique of Jantzen's broad theological position, but I do recognise points of alignment with her position, and the educational perspective that I am developing. For example, Jantzen argues that natality is regarded as a component part to creating an antidote to counter the disconnecting excesses of a neo-liberal culture, the kind of culture which, I argue, generates the product-orientated education of which I am highly critical. This observation appeals to my educational vision that appreciates that arrival is an action, which occurs in a place, and with others who also exist in a shared, located and pluralistic world.

Jantzen's perspective on natality is not wholly aligned with that of Arendt, and I am aware that I am forging an application of the concept that neither Arendt nor Janzten intended. In particular, I will draw out what I see are the distinctive features of Jantzen's account of natality and consider them in relation to the educational task, which is beyond the theological domain in which she was developing her ideas. Jantzen addresses the theme of natality in two substantial texts, On Becoming Divine (1999) and Place of Springs (2010). While neither text is intentionally educational, Jantzen is setting out a critique of conformist religious tradition and presents a vision of a theology based in connectedness in spiritual, ecological and social terms. In On Becoming Divine Jantzen is setting out a feminist theological position that challenges what she regards as a limited Christian frame of reference which, she argues, is profoundly distorted by a particular idea of mortality. In her later writing, Place of Springs, Jantzen explores a more general critique of a Western cultural tradition in which the rise of a patriarchal social, political and religious order diminishes the boundaries of the moral imaginary. Jantzen weaves links between what she suggests is a preoccupation with consumption and exploitation with a general sense of disconnection from the material world and a subsequent fear and fascination with death and dying. There are echoes of Jantzen's general critique with my own concerns of a product-orientated education and, perhaps not surprisingly, I have been curious as to how her particular ideas about natality illuminate the development of my ideas about the educational task.

In Place of Springs, Jantzen presents a perspective on natality that is designed to turn attention away from disconnection of the individual from society, self and ecology and, instead, turn towards the nature of a world where natality is a more central. It is this feature of her work – the quality of a world as experienced through the natal lens – that is especially pertinent to the educational imaginary that I am exploring,

> Now, a moral imaginary of natality would necessarily be very different from a moral imaginary of death. Natals require care and protection to flourish. They rely on interdependence; and unless they are welcomed into the world they will not survive. A moral imaginary that proceeds in terms of atomistic individualism simply could not get off the ground if we were

thinking in terms of natality. Moreover, it is precisely the fact of natality that makes for possibility; natality is the condition of new life entering the world. It is therefore the condition of hope and of future. A moral imaginary of natality is one that takes up the tough fragility of life. Its hopefulness and its possibilities, its interconnectedness and the dependence of its flourishing on the whole web of life around it, not excluding the earth.

(Jantzen, 2010, p. 180)

There is much in this explanation that I see as useful to the direction of education vision I have in mind, which challenges a culture of product-orientated education. The emphasis on acknowledging interconnectedness is in direct contrast to the threefold separation which is embedded in contemporary education. Jantzen begins here to indicate the character of what I see an educational experience might entail were it centred on natality. Importantly, she recognises that a natal perspective is not idealistic, in the sense that it suggests that the world is complete, certain or safe. The 'tough fragility of life' acknowledges that occasionally the world does not match with what we want it to be. It reminds us that the individual – the student – is not at the centre of the world, but part of it nevertheless. This theme of interconnection, as implied by the fact of our birth, and the implications of this are addressed in Jantzen's earlier work,

Moreover, by the fact of our natality we are connected with other bodies, firstly with our mother and ultimately with the whole web of life on earth… without a supportive interconnected network we would not have survived. The fact of our natality thus has ethical and political consequences as surely as does the fact that we will die. For every Plato who ponders death as the release from the prison-house of the body, and for every Heidegger who sees confrontation with mortality as a freeing us for authenticity, there is a gap in the tradition for a philosopher who ponders our gendered, interconnected embodiment and all its creative potential.

(Jantzen, 2009, p. 198)

Certainly, in a comment made elsewhere, Jantzen emphasises the potential for natality to counter the kind of reductionist practices that I have suggested are inherent in some iterations of product-orientated education, 'Where natality is celebrated, totalitarianism becomes impossible', (Jantzen, 2010, p. 148). There is an echo here of Arendt's earlier concern that by understanding the educational potential of natality it is possible to stem a move towards cultural infantilism, by which totalitarianism can prosper. In response to what Arendt regards as governmental preoccupied with policies advocating child-led learning in schools, there is, in her view, a corresponding diminishment of the natal experience because adults step back from occupying a position by which a necessary cross-generation transaction takes place. 'Authority has been discarded by the adults, and this can mean only one thing: that the adults refuse to assume responsibility for the world into which they have brought the children' (Arendt, 1954, p. 190). In Arendt's view, the outcome of this refusal is a society susceptible to totalitarianism.

It is in Jantzen's extension of Arendt's earlier presentation of natality that brings the experience of natality more clearly into focus. As an aside, in considering Jantzen's treatment of Arendt's work, I am drawn to a further remark concerning the function of story in relation to natality. Arendt recognises that through speech the newcomer announces the quality of who they are and that this takes the form of story. Speaking of the meaning of the word 'life', and specifically in relation to natality, Arendt explains,

> The chief characteristic of this specifically human life, whose appearance and disappearance constitute worldly events, is that it is itself always full of events which ultimately can be told as a story, establish a biography... For action and speech...are indeed two activities whose end result will always be a story with enough coherence to be told, no matter how accidental or haphazard the single events and causation may appear to be.
>
> (Arendt, 1958, p. 97)

In the context of my own methodological approach, the connection between natality and story is notable because it emphasises that it is primarily through the expression of personal narrative that the experience of arrival and appearance is made known. Jantzen, in recognising this, adds to the quality of such storytelling,

> This story is not the story of a soul, but of an embodied life, situated in material conditions which shape experience and subjectivity and are also shaped by them. It is thus ultimately from natality, constituting as it does the fundamental condition of narrativity, that human stories arise: the concrete events are set into a narrative to form a meaningful whole.
>
> (Jantzen, 2010, p. 148)

In further exploring Jantzen's position, several features of natality begin to emerge, including relationship, embodiment, gender, and beauty, each of which have further implications for how I am framing the educational task and which I discuss in the next section.

To summarise at this point, I am proposing that natality is the primary experience out of which the student as subject emerges, which is central to the vision of education that I am seeking to establish. Natality provides a conceptual backdrop, or existential framework, with which to understand the experience of the student's arrival and will in due course link to the particular, addressive role of the teacher, to be discussed later in this chapter. Arendt's earlier work on natality is helpful in recognising its significance as a necessary condition of human experience. To navigate arrival is seen as essential by Arendt, both in relation to activating individual engagement with the plurality of the world and in order to ensure the renewal of the world. I see each of these dimensions of natality as important to a view of education that emphasises connections with soil, by which I mean the world of nature, landscape, elements, climate and natural cycles and rhythms, and society. Jantzen's somewhat different view of natality offers a theological dimension which aligns with my interest in how arrival has implications for envisaging the connection with soul. Furthermore, Jantzen's rationale for why a natal lens is so important, and her critique of a mortality-orientated culture, echoes my own concerns with product-orientated education as discussed earlier in my opening chapter.

Relationship, Embodiment, Gender and Beauty

From Jantzen's writing, it is possible for me to identify additional features of the natal experience which, I suggest, integrates natality with the themes of soil, soul and society.

Jantzen argues that if our experience of birth and the inevitability of death are two existential reference points, then it is the fact of our natality, as opposed to our mortality, that determines human relatedness. All persons are born out of, and into relationship. No-one is born without the existence of a prior relationship, and no-one is born alone, even if only the mother is present. There is also a relationship between persons and with place; we are all born somewhere.

If we then translate this in educational terms, the student arrives in the presence of the teacher. Furthermore, that this partnership also incorporates the interplay with the educational object, as discussed in my previous chapter on methodology, and that this is undertaken in a specific location. The point I am making here is that in the vision of education that I am creating relationship matters in a particular way when the educational task is envisaged as interconnected, as opposed to being a transactional exchange. To regard the student as a 'natal', in Jantzen's terms, or a 'beginner', or 'newcomer', in Arendt's writing, is quite different from the objectification which occurs in a product-orientated process. The implications of this for the teacher are similarly different, shifting from a role of technical operative to one which calls for grown-up-ness (Biesta, 2019) and which is discussed in Chapter 5. For now, to engage with a student from this particular teacherly position can be a radical departure for the teacher more familiar with exercising technical competence at the expense of developing professional wisdom.

Jantzen is clear that if we are to embrace natality as the basis of a new moral and theological imaginary, then in addition to the primacy of relationship, the themes of embodiment and gender become especially significant. To arrive is not an abstraction; someone, with a body, occurs in a place. Of course, in most circumstances, the arrival of a newborn baby generates an immediate concern that they are physically intact. The 'newcomer' in this instance presents entirely as embodied. For Jantzen, her concern is with how, within a cultural Western imaginary, there is a separation of mind and soul from the body, discounting the importance of embodiment and its implications for remaining interconnected with both others and the natural world.

> Taking the idea of natality seriously has direct and immediate consequences for a shift in the imaginary. It affirms the concreteness and embodied nature of human lives and experience, the material and discursive conditions within which subjects are formed... There could thus be no truck with the view ...of disembodied and unsituated minds denying their foundation.
>
> (Jantzen, 1999, p. 146)

Embodiment, in other words, is essential to the human condition, and pretensions of transcending this ontological condition contribute to a disconnecting frame of reference. This is in some respects an oversight in Arendt's work that is accounted for in Jantzen's approach. Just as mortality, reason and natality are necessary conditions that the individual must navigate, so I would argue, is the fact of our embodiment and it might be helpful at this point to clarify my use of the term and why I am using it. Ellingson (2017) offers a valuable account of the role of embodiment in research generally and cites Perry and Medina's (2011) term of embodiment referring to:

> Bodies as whole experiential beings in motion, both inscribed and inscribing subjectivities. That is, the experiential body is both a representation of self (a 'text') as well as a mode of creation in progress (a 'tool'). In addition, embodiment is a state that is contingent upon the environment and the context of the body.
>
> (Medina and Perry, 2011, p. 63)

It is not only such bodies that experience the natal moment, but it is also from within this embodied state that subjectification is located. The student is encountered precisely because of, and out of, a physical place, and freedom, which is necessarily incorporated with becoming a subject, is also framed in the dynamic among individual embodiment, socio-political constructs and the environment.

I want to digress a little at this point to address how I understand Jantzen's references to 'embodiment' and the 'material' world. It is important to understand that Jantzen is arguing for a re-connected vision of human experience, recognising that theological and philosophical discourses have been dominated by the 'masculinist philosophy of the west' that have led to the 'unedifying spectacle of male appropriation of birth, taking it away from mothers and bodies and gender and making it bloodless and lifeless' (1999, p. 141). In other words, typically there is a tendency to separate out the components of mind, body and spirit for distinct considerations, resulting in a (philosophically) fragmented view of existence. For Jantzen, embodiment is an attempt to re-insert, or re-connect, the soul back into the territory of life, in the here-and-now physical, or material, world. Natality is the genesis for this,

> Birth is the basis of every person's existence, which by that very fact is always already material, embodied, gendered and connected with other human beings and with human history...If anyone will become divine, it will be as an embodied, gendered, situated self: there can be no other selves than selves of woman born.
>
> (1999, p. 141)

Jantzen's treatment of natality is closely aligned to how I am framing its use here in the educational perspective. As a means of amplifying this emphasis on the physicality of the natal event I want to also introduce the work of Abram, an ecological philosopher to whom I will return to more fully later in Chapter 4. At this point though, I want to draw on his critique of the use of the word 'material', which might indicate the absence of vitality, a tendency that he suggests is associated with the rise of rationalism by which 'material reality came to be commonly spoken of as a strictly mechanical realm' and that led to 'purging material reality of subjective experience' (Abram, 2017, p. 32). Instead, Abram seeks to rehabilitate the material world as both the soil in which all our sciences are rooted and the rich humus into which their results ultimately return (p. 34), and he sets out to emphasise this point by turning to the concept of 'flesh'. He considers the later writing of the phenomenologist Merleau-Ponty (1968), in which he coins the phrase the 'flesh of the world' that in turn refers to,

> a sort of incarnate principle that brings a style of being wherever there is a fragment of being. The flesh is in this sense and 'element' of Being. Not a fact or sum of facts, and yet adherent to location and to the now.
>
> (Merleau-Ponty, 1968, pp. 139–140)

With this in mind, Abram explores the idea of im/materiality and offers what I find a helpful clarification of the corporeal quality of natality as I am using it within my view of education. Discussing the reciprocity in touching, for example, the bark of a tree, Abram suggests that not only is the person to see the tree, but is to have been seen by the world through direct contact with it,

> Clearly, a wholly immaterial mind could neither see things nor touch things – indeed could not experience anything at all. We can experience things – can touch, hear and taste things – only because we, as bodies, we are ourselves included in the sensible field...We might as well say that we are organs of this world, flesh of its flesh, and that the world is perceiving itself through us.
>
> (Abram, 2017, p. 68)

As I hope was evident in my vocative text in which I was describing lambing, the arrival I am speaking of is a visceral experience, as is, I suggest that of the student. The woman I referred to in my earlier account of the workshop did not simply engage in an intellectual or abstract consideration of the possibilities of a new imaginary; she found herself uncomfortably thrust out into the world anew. The experience of cognitive dissonance, emotional upset and body reaction indicated the material, or flesh level, quality that accompanied such an existential event.

It is perhaps already clear how important embodied relationship is becoming to my vision of an education based on soil, soul and society. However, Jantzen adds that not only does natality emphasise the significance of the physical body, but it is also gendered,

> Moreover, it can hardly be doubted that birth is inextricably involved with gender; every body who is born is gendered, and gender shapes the trajectory of natals... everyone who has ever been born until now has been born of woman.
>
> (Jantzen, 2010. p. 180)

It is beyond the remit of this book to be drawn into a wider discussion of gender, although I do want to consider important links between Jantzen's critique and my own concerns about the limitations of product-orientated education. One of the prime concerns raised in Janzten's critique is an association she makes between the death-seeking and destructive tendencies of a cultural and political imaginary based on mortality. Jantzen argues that the combined fascination and fear of death is demonstrative of a masculine frame of reference, whereas natality is more aligned with what she regards as a feminine orientation. (Jantzen is clear at this point that this is her own elaboration of Arendt's earlier writing and not a position with which she, Arendt, would likely endorse).

A final distinctive feature of natality introduced by Jantzen is the importance of beauty. I want to explore this is in detail here because whilst it is absent in the context of a product-orientated approach to education (because it is irrelevant), I suggest that beauty is integral to an education rooted in soil, soul and society. Jantzen opens her discussion of beauty accepting that it has been beset with problems of definition and a never-ending to and fro debate centred on objective and subjective perceptions. Jantzen's interest is in identifying some of the features of beauty and considers the implications of this in establishing an alternative imaginary rooted in natality. Embodiment and gender are regarded as important to beauty and that we are drawn to the beautiful, 'Beauty attracts', Janzten writes, 'we can say that if we find something beautiful we are drawn towards it' (2010, p. 15). Furthermore, that there is pleasure to be had in such attraction, the senses are stimulated and this provokes desire, and this becomes key to understanding Jantzen's particular interest in beauty. Traditionally, or at least in a culture founded in patriarchy, desire has signalled a 'lack of', or to 'want for'. Consequently beauty so defined has been prone to exploitation and pursued as something to be possessed and I suggest a parallel in this with product-orientated education and the pursuit for attainment with students' performance designed to be ultimately owned, personally and exclusively.

I will return to Jantzen and how her discussion shifts from beauty towards creativity shortly, but at this point I want to draw on Biesta, from The Beautiful Risk of Education (2014), and a slightly different, yet aligned, perspective on beauty. In his writing, the rationale for the educational risk being described as beautiful is that the encounter involves the appearance of the student as subject. This arrival – the natal experience – is one that is viewed by another, and is therefore, in the domain of perception which in turn is a matter of aesthetics. 'The reason to refer to these risks with an aesthetic term – beauty – is because the reason for "allowing" these risks in education has everything to do with the possibility for the student to appear, and to appear as subject' (Biesta, 2020, p. 103).

In other words, to regard subjectification, as a matter pertaining to beauty, is to fully appreciate its quality by the fact of their appearance. I will return again to Biesta as I turn now to a related theme, that of creativity, in Jantzen's developing dialogue relating to beauty.

Jantzen suggests that in being drawn towards beauty there is 'this desire to create beauty in response to beauty' (2010, p. 163). If there is a longing, it is to replicate, not simply copy directly, but to create nevertheless,

> The desire to create however, is a desire to simultaneously to preserve and to bring newness into the world, something original that will be a thing of beauty in its own right even while in some sense imitating what already exists and inspires it.
>
> (ibid, p. 164)

I am curious about the implications of this in the context of an educational encounter where beauty and creativity are incorporated as features of natality. In a consideration of the theological ramifications of this, Jantzen continues her exploration, and I find it illuminating to substitute religious terminology with those of education in the following,

> A theology [an education] that shows little interest in the exuberance and excessiveness of divine creativity, the joy of divine desire in the outpouring of plentitude, will hardly have the resources to foster human creative desire.
>
> (ibid, p. 168)

Here is an underlying assumption, about the fecundity of the world, and I suggest that an education focused on connection is an activity that contributes to the renewal of such abundance. I am not meaning though that either creativity or desire is without any parameters, and I want to turn to Biesta's perspective in describing the 'beautiful risk',

> I am interested in education as itself a creative 'act' or, to be more precise, in education as an act of creation, that is, as an act of bringing something new into the world, something that did not exist before.
>
> (Biesta, 2014, p. 11)

However, Biesta is not describing creation in 'strong terms, that is, as the production of something' (ibid, p. 11). Instead the creative act is that which is contained in the occurrence of the natal moment; the creation of a possibility. That it is a creative act, in the terms of reference set out by Jantzen, asserts it is also beautiful, and that by implication evokes desire. Biesta clarifies this point,

> The educational concern...lies in the transformation of what is desired into what is desirable. It lies in the transformation of what is de facto desired into what can be justifiably be desired - a transformation that can never be driven from the perspective of the self and its desires, but always requires engagement with what our who is other...It is therefore, again, a dialogical process.
>
> (Biesta, 2014, p. 3)

Both Jantzen and Biesta highlight that natality involves presenting a paradoxical situation whereby the newcomer at once excites desire, and beauty, by virtue of their arrival, and yet despite the novelty of appearing cannot remain central to the world, even though, by such an act, it – the world – is renewed.

> This makes the educational way the slow way, the difficult way, the frustrating way, and, so we might say, the weak way, as the outcome of this process can neither be guaranteed no secured.
>
> (Biesta, 2014, p. 3)

The risk of education is beautiful because it is concerned with both the appearance of the student as subject and of its perception, which is a creative act. I find Jantzen's distinctive treatment of natality supports this perspective, primarily through her attention to what might be described as the more material features of the natal experience, namely embodiment, relationship and gender. Furthermore, I suggest that Jantzen's work creates a conceptual bridge between Arendt's presentation of natality, Biesta's concepts of subjectification and the student as subject, with how I regard arrival as central in the educational encounter orientated towards connection with soil, soul and society.

From Where Natality, and Why? Introducing Chora and Physis

In the followings section, I want to consider two questions which I believe are associated with natality but can be overlooked in terms of their educational implications. The first relates to the question; from where does the student arrive and a second, which is why is the event of subjectification possible? Whilst the value of natality is acknowledged and the student's experience of subjectification is regarded as being especially important to an existential view of education, these two questions are less frequently considered. In exploring the 'where from' and 'why' of natality, I will turn attention to two classical concepts which I believe will not only provide some answers to the questions but also illustrate how education, or at least the re-wilded view of education I have in mind, is to be understood as close to an expression of 'Life's longing for itself', a term taken from Gibran (2014). I am drawn to this poetic turn of phrase because it elegantly catches the essence of an enduring compulsion to 'show up' that can be seen amongst not only the human domain but also in all natural life. It is to some extent what makes the question of the choice about how to exist even possible. The concepts of chora and physis, I suggest, can be associated with the cyclic renewal character of how I envisage the education, and I will begin by exploring the territory out of which the natal event occurs.

Chora

When reading Jantzen on the theme of natality, I am struck by her commentary on the classical view of the birth of man, which she centres on Plato and the way in which the individual is thrown out into the world, thrust into existence as if from nothingness or nowhere, and expelled in many respects into a life that is orientated towards death and its meaning defined by mortality. However, this is possibly only a partial view of how this is understood by Plato and I want to offer an additional perspective. For instance, the ancient Greeks referred to the place outside of the city walls as the chora (also referred to as khora) and is a term which Plato used to refer to as a space, or receptacle and as such, one without form,

> Wherefore the Mother and Receptacle of all created and visible and in any way sensible things is... an invisible and formless being which receives all things and in some mysterious way partakes of the intelligible and is most incomprehensible.
>
> (Timaeus, 51a)

My interest, as I have already discussed in terms of the location of my work, is in what lies out at the edge of the mainstream. So, I am intrigued by the association of chora as not only being beyond the margins, but also having a maternal character, which might be regarded as being oceanic in quality, subject to its own current, ebb and flow. I referred to the choretic space in the previous account of lambing in which the indeterminate, ever-shifting membrane from which the unborn lamb arrives is both unintelligible and yet has the capacity for a radical becoming. Radical in the sense that such an event is unique and impossible to define. As the farmer in relation to lambing, or the teacher in my example of the group process, I cannot perceive, let alone govern the nature of what is to arrive, and yet can hope that it occurs nevertheless.

I want to move a little closer into considering the educational equivalent of the choretic space, which is the state of the student prior to the event of subjectification. In my own experience, described in the vocative text that explored arrival in the opening of this book, I described a sense of myself prior to the move from London to the countryside as having a sense of completeness in relation to the world, as I understood it. I do not mean by this that it was predictable, or uneventful, nor even that I knew it entirely. What I am referring to by 'completeness', is that it was the world as I understood it in relation to myself. Furthermore, it was a world that was knowable and also one in which the possibilities for how I might exist in such a world were imaginable. I was in most respects in a state of 'indwelling', or immanence. To be immanent means to be 'remaining within' a given state of being in the world. I suggest that prior to the educational moment, such immanence has a choretic quality to it. There is a formlessness to it, despite it also being simultaneously familiar to the student.

I want to resist creating what might be regarded as a simplistic dichotomy, in which the state prior to the interruption is by definition inferior to that which arises afterwards. There is a richness in the region of chora in terms of its resource, its potential, and that despite its elusive identity, is a prerequisite for the student being capable of arrival. In my vision of education, it might be more useful to think of chora as where the student has a sense of being, but not of existing as student-as-subject in their uniqueness in the world, which is what might be accomplished, or risked, through their arrival into it. (I also think it might be important to consider whether it is always clear as to who has arrived, student or teacher? As will become clear in the story being told through the vocative passages, whilst 'student' and 'teacher' are ascribed roles, there are possibilities for uncoupling these from the person). I will later explore the notion of interruption and discuss how this is dependent on the addressive impact of the teacher on the student's subjectification. For now my point is to acknowledge a tension in conceptualising the choretic space which is that, like a literal membrane, the chora demarcates a state that is only partially definable, and yet also provides a state of completeness – immanence – that provides the condition for natality.

The concept of the 'immanent' only requires the letter 'i' to be substituted for it to become 'imminent', and this shifts the meaning etymologically to 'be at hand', 'be about to happen', 'be near to', and 'overhanging; impending'. I find this a particularly fascinating development in the educational task, to be attending to the point between the choretic state just before the natal moment. Herein lies what I experience as the mystery of the educational movement, which precedes the 'beautiful risk of education' (Biesta, 2014). It is the point I describe in the previous section of vocative text about lambing, where the unborn lamb can be felt, blindly by hand, to be expectantly suckling, shifting its limbs and eventually pulling towards the birthing place. Whilst I have referred to it as having a mysterious quality, I know that is not entirely the case, and I turn next to the second question I raised at the outset of this section; why is natality possible?

Physis

If the chora is the pre-natal space out of which arrival is possible, it would be reasonable to wonder at why arrival has any impetus. In the following discussion I am suggesting that an arrivalistic experience is to usher into the world an expression of life. In other words, in the context of my vision, education is a 'pulse point' which gives rise to the choice to exist, a sign of life. To elaborate on this comment I want to focus on the concept of physis, one which has received little attention in educational discourse, and return to Arendt's explanation of the term as a way of introduction,

> It is characteristic of all natural processes that they come into being without the help of man, and those things are natural which are not 'made' but grow by themselves into whatever they become.
>
> (Arendt, 1958, p. 150)

With this Arendt introduces the concept of physis and refers to it as a way of distinguishing a natural process from that of manufacture, which involves an intended process including design and production. Whilst the Latin root *nasci* refers to being born, physis originally comes from phyelin, to grow out of, or appear by itself. Arendt does not continue her discussion of the term, but it is an idea that caught the interest of Eric Berne, who founded transactional analysis. He considered this reference to 'life force' as a way of understanding why, despite the challenges of poor mental health his patients seemed determined to return to health; '...a neurosis has many advantages for the individual. If he is better off in many respects with his neurosis, what is the force which makes him want to get 'better'?' (Berne, 1957, p. 98). He turns to physis as a possible explanation, although with some ambivalence,

> Perhaps physis does not exist at all, but in spite of our inability to be definite about this subject, there are so many things which happen as if there were such a force, that it is easier to understand human beings if we suppose that it does exist.
>
> (Berne, 1957, p. 99)

Later in the development of transactional analysis, Petruska Clarkson (1992) wrote more affirmatively about the importance of physis, further contextualising its classical origins and highlighting the ever-changing character of nature,

> …we are born from it and re-enter upon death. Change as Physis comes spontaneously from within as part of a greater and general "fire". Change must occur because change is life. Physis, then is the all powerful force for both physical growing and ageing and mental/emotional change with his characterised as that which gives is life…It has no telos, there is nothing normative about the concept, it is simply change as flux or stage of being….Physis is nature, coming from the deepest biological roots of the human being and striving towards the greatest realisation of the good.
>
> (Clarkson, 1992, pp. 11–12)

Clarkson here begins to account for what I suggest is the source from which a decision to choose how to exist is rooted, it is the source of the desire that is the focus of discernment and it is the root of the unique expression of life that is possible in the educational task. As will also become clear in my next chapter, such an impetus does not arrive out of nowhere or nothingness. One of the limitations of both Berne's and Clarkson's treatment of physis is that it is understood essentially in terms of human experience. To fully appreciate how I am referring to the concept, it is necessary to go to the origins of the term.

The earliest reference to physis is a fragment of text attributed to Heraclitus: Nature loves to conceal itself – Things keep their secret (Fragment 10, trans. Haxton, 2003). From the outset, physis has had a mysterious quality to it and to reduce it to the contemporary Greek translation to refer simply to 'nature' is to miss the significant point implied in Heraclitus' use of the term. Physis, in other words, is more precisely understood as the life force that is manifested in nature. It is the energetic pulse that is displayed in the capacity of a flower to blossom, the spring in the step of a new lamb or the determination of grass to shoot up through a concrete path. It is also in the movement that we experience in the cool breeze, or the warmth of sun on our face. And, in the terms of this book, it is the education moment that shifts the student from their state of immanence to a state of being imminent. It is also what becomes revealed at the natal moment; the arrival of the student which is witnessed by the teacher.

I think that it is important to explain that I regard physis as different from the notion of 'will' or motivation, which have featured in discourses on education. This can be found in the general field of character development of students, whereby the aim of education is seen as an act of cultivation with an intended outcome by the teacher on behalf of the student. Whilst there may be merit in such a process, it falls outside of my concern here, resonating too much with the function of a type of product-orientated education. The difference I see in physis from individual 'will' is that it – physis – is a natural energetic impulse that exists at a biological level and which flows through and in between student and teacher. 'Will', or motivation might be a distinctive expression of physis, dependent on the concept of a 'self', or identifiable character – a 'who', but such a manifestation is not, in my view, synonymous with physis.

In my view not enough attention has been given to the role of physis in educational work. I suspect that aside from the obscurity of the term itself, the idea that there is an inherent, concealed agency in the student, which neither conforms with the notion that they are a 'bucket to fill', nor that they are a 'fire waiting to be lit', confounds conventional educational theorising. Physis, revealing itself through ever-changing experiences, including the educational, continually bears witness to how interconnected the human experience is with an entire web of existence that incorporates the more-than-human ecology. To envisage education in this way is to also put in perspective the futility, or at least the impermanence, the ambitions of a product-orientated approach. To do this also exposes the 'manufactured-ness' of the teacher and student functions, whereas to hold the educational partnership as one that bears the desire of 'Life's longing for itself', is quite different.

The difference in this idea of education, from the product-orientated, lies in the premise that the soil out of which the teacher and student engage is understood as alive in its own right. It's a view of education that sees the life-seeking impetus breaking out from immanence to subjectification, and that by doing so offers the possibility of renewing the vitality of the civic realm and ecological terrain. In other words, whilst the arrival of the student is an important event within my educational vision, physis provides the 'why' education is possible. However, it is not inevitable because there is the possibility that instead what might occur is a pseudo-education, referred to as learning, or even further reducible to 'schooling'. Product-orientated education is precarious in that it 'risks', or tends towards taming education in these ways. An educational vision that acknowledges physis is primarily orientated towards interconnectedness and is by implication vital, volatile and constantly subject to variability, qualities that are counter to the stability, security and surety required of product-product-orientated education.

Speech and Arrival

I turn now to the final aspects of the natal experience and consider the significance of speech and on the action of 'being addressed'. I return again to Arendt as a useful starting point for considering the function of speech in the arrivalistic experience. In her presentation of natality and its relation to action, she pays particular attention to speech. For Arendt, the capacity to speak is an important way by which the individual makes themselves known in the world and the means by which the world recognises their arrival as a newcomer.

> With word and deed we insert ourselves into the human world and this insertion is like a second birth…This insertion is not forced on us by necessity…It may be stimulated by the presence of others who company we may wish to join, but it is never conditioned by them; its impulse springs from the beginning which came Ito the world when we were born and to which we respond by beginning something new on our own initiative.
>
> (Arendt, 1958, pp. 176–177)

I have already written about the importance of the vocative, or addressive writing which forms an important feature of my methodological approach and which reflects how instrumental a specific kind speech can be to the vision of education that I am proposing. It is a kind of speech that, as Arendt describes, is compelling and yet not conditional. This is a form of speech that announces the subjectification that Biesta refers to, and is associated with the arrival of the student as subject. Such speech is part of both the experience of arrival and that of the teacher. Arendt's comment above focuses on the speech of the beginner, the student's, but there is also that of the teacher, which Biesta suggests is addressive, and that the student's speaking is in the context of having been addressed:

> While listening and recognition can be configured as acts of benevolence, 'being addressed' works in the opposite direction. Here it is not for me to recognise the other, but rather to recognise that the other is addressing me – that I am being addressed by another human being – and for me to act upon this recognition. This suggests that if any recognition is involved, it is recognition that is directed toward the self, not towards the other.
>
> (Biesta, 2019, p. 89)

By summoning the subjectness of the student, the teacher's impact provides the conditions out of which the educational encounter might emerge. I do not mean here the kind of interjection that teacher might make in order to clarify, define or judge the work of the student. This is not about explaining the student's experience to themselves. Nor is it about explaining how the world exists in relation to the student. A more educational interruption is one in which the student experiences an awareness of their capacity to exercise their own responsibility, their authority in relation to self, with all their desire, inclinations and motivation and to discern being in the world in relationship to others' needs and such a desire.

> The educational principle here is that of suspension – a suspension in time and space, so that we might say – that provides opportunities for relationships with our desires to make them visible, perceivable, so that we can work on them.
>
> (Biesta, 2017, p. 18)

There is a hint here of what is to come in the next chapter, which is concerned in part with the potential for what happens in the space in-between the student and teacher, although it is perhaps enough for now for me to have emphasised the importance of being addressed in the natal experience.

Summary

I opened this chapter by proposing that arrival and interruption is the opening move in an educational experience that sets out an alternative to one of product-orientated education. I have been discussing arrival explained through the lens of natality because it appeals to the ecological interest in the vision I have for education, and also because, in Arendtian terms, it makes explicit the political direction of such an educational purpose. It also serves the connection to self – or soul – that I am interested in as a third theme of connection. Furthermore, the concept of natality deepens the significance of the experience of arrival in the educational task, and it resonates with my decision to using a methodological approach that incorporates addressive and vocative features. By introducing Jantzen's elaboration of Arendt's earlier work I am accentuating the material, embodied qualities of natality which are also relevant to the threefold vision of education I am presenting in this work.

By attending to Jantzen's framing of natality I have begun to highlight not only the phenomenological qualities inherent in natality, but also the theme of creativity and beauty, supported by the writing of Biesta, which I suggest are important aspects of my perspective and which are specifically associated to my understanding of the experience of natality, but which are regarded as generally irrelevant to product-orientated education. Even so, for my purpose, this falls just short of what I have sought out as a more complete understanding of the phenomenon of natality. Through introducing first the idea of chora, I account for what comes before the natal moment and have made a distinction between immanence, a state of existence prior to an educational one, and one which is imminently to become so. In staying with the ecological thread of this chapter, I have introduced physis – a way of understanding the natural life force – as the primary driver for why any of this is happening at all.

I have begun to close this chapter with an observation that whilst arrival and interruption suggest a fixed moment in time, it ushers in a process that is both vital and volatile. In some respects, it is from this point that the capacity for variability increases, and an experience that may have been previously determined by what was concealed and incomprehensible, is quite suddenly rendered more uncertain. It is to this phase in the educational task that I turn next in the following chapter in which I will explore the place 'betwixt and between', the concept of liminality and the implications for the student and teacher dynamic.

References

Abram, D. (2017) The Spell of the Sensuous: Perception and Language in the More-Than-Human World, New York: Vintage Books.

Arendt, H. (1954) Between Past and Future, London: Faber and Faber.

Arendt, H. (1958) The Human Condition, Chicago: Chicago Press.

Barrow, G. (2018) For Whom Is the Teacher and for What Is the Teaching? An Educational Re-Frame of the Parent Ego State, Transactional Analysis Journal, Vol. 48, No. 4, pp. 322–334. DOI: 10.1080/03621537.2018.1505113

Berne, E. (1957) A Layman's Guide to Psychiatry and Psychoanalysis, London: Penguin.

Biesta, G.J.J. (2020) Risking Ourselves in Education: Qualification, Socialisation, and Subjectification Revisited, Educational Theory, Vol. 70, No. 1, pp. 89–104.

Biesta, G.J.J. (2014) The Beautiful Risk of Education, Boulder: Paradigm.

Biesta, G.J.J. (2017) The Rediscovery of Teaching, London: Routledge.

Clarkson, P. (1992) Transactional Analysis Psychotherapy: An Integrated Approach, London: Routledge.

Ellingson, L.L. (2017) Embodiment in Qualitative Research, London: Routledge.

Gibran, K. (2014) The Prophet, London: Oneworld Publications.

Gordon, M. (2001) Hannah Arendt and Education: Renewing Our Common World, Colorado: Westview Press.

Haxton, B. (trans.) (2003) Heraclitus: Fragments, New York: Penguin Books.

Jantzen, G. (1998) Becoming Divine: Towards a Feminist Philosophy of Religion, Manchester: Manchester University Press.

Jantzen, G. (2009) Violence to Eternity: Death and the Displacement of Beauty, Vol. 2, London: Routledge.

Jantzen, G. (2010) Place of Springs: Death and the Displacement of Beauty, Vol. 3, London: Routledge.

Miller, J.P., Nigh, K., Binder, M.J., Novak, B. and Crowel, S., eds. (2019) International Handbook of Holistic Education, London: Routledge.

O'Byrne, A. (2010) Natality and Finitude, Bloomington, IN: Indiana University Press.

Chapter 4

Liminality, place-based education and the role of myth and story

Beyond Arrival

Beyond Arrival

I still find the arrival of a newborn calf a most special occasion; it's like the birth of a princeling. The size of a leggy dog, glistening in summer sunshine, the wet muzzle and sleek dark coat against the richness of the green in the grass; there's newness here. The story begins with the arrival of our first calf and my attention is on what happens next and in doing so engages with reluctance, resistance, shame and, eventually, pride. I want to move beyond arrival because whilst this is important it is not sufficient.

In turning to my journal of the time, the date is notable, 15 June 2007; my daughter's birthday. It had been with some trepidation that I had agreed to buy a cow. In fact, I am reminded as I write this that it was only because of the relationship with David, the old farmer, that I even considered the idea of keeping a cow. This strikes me as more significant given my purpose for writing about this; deciding to keep cattle was due to the belief in me by my teacher (what a curious instinct, to claim a teacher as 'mine'! What implications lie there, I wonder?) Molly was a Dexter, a shorter legged and generally smaller breed of cow, and she was black as night and came to us in-calf with a calf at foot, which meant that she was pregnant when we bought her and came accompanied with the previous year's calf. At the outset, I was fearful of her, but David thought nothing of it to enter the stable and run his hand over her back, around her neck, and then, after a time, to stroke her face. Soon, with his encouragement, I also grew confident enough to do the same and eventually she and her calf were let out to the field, and before I knew it, I was keeping cows.

We were unsure of the anticipated calving date and, not knowing what I now know, I was agitated for weeks beforehand, continually on

DOI: 10.4324/9781003407751-5

the look-out and fretting about why we had no calf in the field. Then, as I returned from dropping my daughter off to school on her birthday, I saw that there, right up there, at the furthest corner of the field, Molly was circling the ground (why do they birth always so far away?). I raced to the scene, saw, with utter exhilaration the curled shiny black form of a calf, turned and ran to my teacher to tell him the important news. He gathered his stick and coat and we wandered, painfully slowly given his infirmity, to the site of the birth. Together we enjoyed the sight; my first calf and for him, the return of cattle to his field after many years. A perfect combination – this new arrival, the satisfied mentor and his happy apprentice. In retrospect, I see now that in that moment when David and I were standing in front of the mother and calf on that sunny morning, at the beginning of the end of an encountered arrival and the start of my engaging in the world 'as subject'. This moment beyond arrival when the decision to choose has been taken and the responsibility from doing so confronts and tests whether the choice is sufficient. I tell stories here of moments when a student experiences the freedom to exist as subject, exquisite episodes accounting for an inflection point, an existential crossroads where an unexpected path opened up, an opportunity taken, but what does this then go onto mean? What experientially is required in the risk undertaken and how does that tumble out for teacher and student? Ah, the story beckons ....

It was, as I have already mentioned, my daughter's birthday and the plan had been for the grandparents to visit and spend the weekend with us on the farm, and I was the more delighted at the prospect of being able to show off our new arrival. As the parents arrived, I accompanied them proudly to the site of the birth, noticing that David had returned and was making his way too. But this time, perhaps because of the excitement of newcomers, the cow stirred and warned her calf which startled, bounded off, darted through a hole in a hedge and collapsed in the deep boundary ditch on the other side of the field. David came and told me that such a new calf would not be able climb back out and that it would need to be fetched. Reluctantly (see, here, that word first surfaces), I made my way to the hedge. The ditch was full of ripened nettles – my journal mentions that I wore shorts that day – and the blackness of the calf was barely visible. I ventured through the hawthorn, down into the overgrown ditch and pulled up the calf, tucking my arms under its front legs, dragging it back up, into the field to rejoin its anxious mother. Until that time I had not been so close to a calf, nor realised how heavy such a creature might be. We watched whilst the cow coaxed her calf and David commented on how it had yet to suckle and that it would need to do so soon. For my part, I was relieved to be out of the ditch and not a little disappointed that he had not noticed my hardship in retrieving the calf.

The day progressed, more visitors arrive, and each time we view the newborn, so David, irritatingly, reminds me that it has yet to suckle. By the afternoon, my children return from school, we admire the cow and calf and return inside for birthday cake. The local garage calls to tell me my vehicle is ready for collection and as I leave to go, David is waiting outside. He lets me know that the calf is now ailing and in response I tell him I have to collect my car. 'You leave now, and you lose this calf – you'll be no farmer, if you go now', he replies. Reluctantly, I agree to stay. This word – reluctantly – has an interesting etymology in that it includes the quality of 'bend' and 'twist', as well as to 'wrestle'. It can mean to do so in relation to others, or with oneself. My reluctance was ostensibly against David's instruction; who was he, telling me what to do! But I also experienced it at an internal level in that I was twisting, or bending between a growing fear of what was being demanded of me, and a desire to be more fully capable, in this instance, to be that farmer David spoke of. I wanted and yet could not, with fear fuelling my sense of reluctance. I did not yet know what was being asked of me, what new experience lay ahead, but I was convinced that it was beyond me. Retreating to the familiar – fetching the repaired car – seemed the better strategy. What actually happened next was that I carried the calf the length of the 3-acre field, followed by the cow, and we gathered them in a small paddock. David held the cow standing with a pair of nose pincers to prevent her from moving off. From the journal;

> The calf was clearly suffering, she couldn't stand and her tongue was beginning to swell, thereby making it increasingly difficult to breathe, let alone swallow. Right then, you'll need to get some of its mother's milk – go and milk the cow', David explained. I couldn't believe David was serious. I had never milked a cow before. 'I can't', I cried.

> 'You'll do it!' [Even as I copy this out, I feel moved by the belief instilled in me by his command.]

> He took the pincers, plugged them on to the mother's snout and she bellowed and pulled back, trying to get loose. To make it easier, David tied the pincers closed and tugged hard. 'Right, get the bottle and milk the cow, just like you did with ewes at lambing time'. So I went to the udder. I had expected her to kick me, but she waited whilst I took almost a full bottle of hot, creamy milk. David continued to hold her steady. I offered the milk to the calf and almost immediately

it began to suckle... Very quickly the bottle was empty – I was chuffed to pieces, and thought we were done.

'Good' said David, 'now offer the calf up to the udder'.

I could not believe he was telling me do this. 'How do I do that?' I asked.

'Just as you did the lambs – come on, now!' So I took the calf, which was even now rousing. As I grabbed her head and guided the mouth to the udder, the calf began to nuzzle and within moments was suckling hard. 'It's feeding!' I called. David let the cow free and then without a word simply wandered off home.

Writing this again brings me in contact with the power of what became a pivotal episode in our relationship. The inherent tension of the process, the urgency of the situation, the potential life and death of the calf, and also metaphorically, of myself, in terms of whether I would make it, or not. I can recall the heat of the mother as I drew in close to her belly, me sweating through a stinging rash of nettles in the high afternoon sun and the physicality involved in the reviving beast in my arms. This was new territory and I was emerging alive, fear now behind me. But David had disappeared.

I had encountered the opposition of David, the sense of the Other, and he, perhaps, felt the disappointment at my reluctance to act. I had both experienced a kind of confrontation with the world, a place of doubt and disillusionment. There was a sense of uncertainty having broken into this new space. There was the shock of discovering that making such a choice is continually called upon, that whilst 'arrival' has a singular quality, the need to do so, and to exercise my responsibility which is exclusively mine to hold, keeps coming into view. I knew that the relationship with David as my teacher could no longer be as it had been previously; he and I had both witnessed some type of fallibility or limitation in encountering the call to choose. This was a point of reckoning in that we were to bear some sense of incompleteness, despite the hope it might have been otherwise.

A different story, this time where I was in the role of teacher. A few years ago I wrote an article on the theme of adolescence (Barrow, 2014). It included a case study of a young man, Alex, who was part of a school group camping at the farm. It concerned an incident that resonates with what I am exploring here and is revisited later in Chapter 5, but for now it is useful in emphasising the themes of doubt and reluctance. A group of students and their teachers arranged to camp at the farm and came from a secondary school in central London. The school was based in one of the most deprived areas in the city, and the students had been identified as being especially vulnerable within the context of their school.

Upon their arrival, the level of need amongst the group of students was clear to see. Some were physically under-developed or showing signs of poor nutrition; most were ill-equipped for a farm stay and some had language or general developmental delay. I had been keenly anticipating the arrival of this group and now they were here I wondered if they might be overwhelmed by the dramatic change in their environment. However, as they tipped out of the mini-bus and into the camping field they showed little sign of distress. They whooped and started scattering about the site, barely able to put words to their excitement and let out their pent-up energy. When I think now of my own process with David, the parallels are striking. As he must have seen in me the inexperience, the 'lack of' and unpreparedness, so I was quick to notice something similar in the initial arrival of the school group; the incongruence of their garish city gear and pallid complexions, arriving into a ripening rural landscape in full summer bloom.

The teacher suggested a brief walk around to exercise after the long journey and we made towards the main field where livestock graze. As we walked, the teacher began to tell me a little about the students, letting me know their names and finally mentioned Alex. Of the group, this was the student who could prove most difficult and the one for whom there had been reservations about coming on the trip. Just as she told me this, a group of boys – including Alex – began to run across the field, yelling as they did so. The teacher was worried at this and called the boys back but they could not hear. Towards the end of the field, the sheep were grazing and although the teacher was immediately apologetic that the boys were scaring the flock, there was nothing she could do.

At this point, I thought I had a good idea. I let out my sheep dog and sent him off to gather the sheep, which were by now beginning to be alarmed by the boys. The dog ran quickly to the end of the field, overtook the boys and circled behind the sheep and began to bring them to me. The boys were in the way, and as the sheep ran to them they divided and rushed past the boys. The boys, in turn, had stopped and now the dog was running towards them to keep up with the sheep. It was at this point that something happened. Alex began to get distressed. He fell to the ground and began to cry – he was soon screaming. The other boys left him, the dog ran past to meet me, and the teacher ran to comfort Alex, who was obviously traumatized.

As I approached the teacher and Alex, his anxiety increased. He could see the dog at my side and looked terror-stricken. The teacher now remembered that when he was an infant Alex had been attacked by a dog and this incident had clearly triggered a re-enactment of that earlier trauma. I remember in that moment how dispirited I felt. The anticipation of a positive camp experience for the group was beginning to evaporate and yet they had been on site for just 20 minutes. My internal process was one of self-reproach; how could I be so stupid not have thought about this possibility? My instinct was to immediately send the dog back to his yard and keep him locked away and begin trying to make up for my error of judgement. And here it is, the collapse of idealised roles and grandiose possibilities, as paralled in my earlier process with David. At this moment I am obliged to consider that with all of my certainty at being ready, that nevertheless, I might not be enough. And, conversely the student – Alex in this instance, myself earlier – is confronted with the likelihood that they might not be sufficient in the face of what is asked of them at that moment in relation to the world.

I was just about to return the dog to its pen, full of displaced anger at the dog, instead of myself, when for some unclear reason I turned and walked towards Alex, my dog at my side, unleashed. Much of my conscious self was warning me against bringing the dog to Alex. I had already begun framing my action in terms of a mistake; I should not have let the dog out in the first place. It certainly felt like a mistake and I experienced some shame in myself for not having been more thoughtful (mark that reference to the teacher's shame, reader, it's important). As I got near him, the boy's anxiety rose and I was aware of his fear at the dog at my side. I let him know that the dog had done what it is trained to do; to protect the sheep and to bring them to me. Alex refused to hear this and cried that he was sure the dog would bite him. I assured him this would not be the case and that the dog knew not to bite; that the dog's task is to gather the sheep and to protect from harm. The dog remained quietly at my side and we stayed like this whilst the boy took deep breaths and steadied himself. He told me about how dogs can attack and bite and be scary and I, and the teacher who was holding him, agreed that that had happened in the past – that it had been true. And that it wouldn't happen here and now. After a while, the other students had gathered round and were stroking the dog and wondering about how one animal can make another animal move on command and not attack or harm. Whilst staying close to Alex, I called the dog to round up the sheep again and the dog circled and brought them to us. Gradually Alex became grounded again and I tested him, by asking if he'd like to stroke the dog. 'Not yet', he replied.

This is the equivalent moment at which David commands me to milk the cow; 'You'll do it!' I cannot claim that this was a conscious strategy on my behalf in confronting the boy with the dog, but there's an audacity in this action that astonishes me nevertheless. It is as if the teacher carries a determination, or hopefulness, for the student at the point where they – the student – most need it, where it is most elusive. Why does this matter so much? Why did it matter to David that I stooped to do what I was most afraid of, and why was it important to me, to turn towards the boy with what he feared most? I connect with the authority in David's presence at that moment, a moment where I have the opportunity in deciding who should have authority in my life and to be in dialogue with such authoritativeness, a discussion for later in Chapter 5. For my part, I also think it has something to do with love and, in turn, is connected with soul and the task of 'finding face' (Cajete, 1994). In both instances, the intention of the educator is to direct the student to choose to exist in such a way as to be at home in the world in such a way as to bring about its renewal. Whether it is in the life-giving milk and the capacity to revive, or the resolution of earlier traumas, or the potential freedom that comes from being taught something else about the world, the role of the teacher is essentially about life-affirming, being in relationship, to oneself, others and the world, encouraged by educational love, or educational caritas (Noddings and Shore, 1984). I found this out for myself in the latter stage of the school visit to the farm. On the last day of their camp, early in the morning before the day had started, Alex and I walked into the field and I asked if he would use the dog to move the sheep. With some caution, he began to call the dog, moved it around the sheep and successfully had them gathered in the shelter. He declared it the best bit of the trip. I think I was pleased too. We had both stepped into the same uncertainty, a territory that revealed something more of ourselves than we had initially known or were prepared for. A year later when I visited his school, Alex saw me in the foyer and immediately asked about the dog.

To turn back now to my own experience with David, I knew that his swift departure at the end of the day was not the end of the encounter. I awoke especially early the following morning, anxious that the calf was still alive. She was there, full bellied, safe and part of life again. With relief I decided to see if David might be up so that I could let him know all was well. His light was on, I entered and told him that the calf was alive. 'I know that', he said plainly. I realised then that he had been up for hours, keeping watch; of course, he knew. My awkwardness of the previous day returned and I chose to apologise. And I was sorry, far more so than I let on; I had been like a small boy, ashamed of my inadequacy. David cut in and replied that he had indeed been angry, but that he had been most angry with himself. I was puzzled and he explained that he had forgotten that I had come from the town, that there was so much he took for granted about the way of farming and which I did not yet know. He had let me down, in effect, by not being truly alongside me, and, in my notes, he continues to explain;

> Yes, I was angry. I thought you wanted to be a proper farmer. I was angry because you don't leave your animals like that – the calf was dying. So yes, I was angry, he paused. 'But I have never been so proud of you. You did exactly what you needed to, I didn't know whether you could do it, well done!'...Two weeks later he bought me my first set of farm overalls. 'You're a farmer now, so stop wearing those old clothes – take some pride, wear these!'

This struck me as an unexpected and potent exchange. David's admission of anger and shame somehow meant I was free to understand the experience, as opposed to remaining caught within it. I have seen this since, in other settings, where the teacher acknowledges their fallibility which offers the student a way of meeting how to exist in the world when its 'otherness' runs contrary to how it was anticipated.

Beyond arrival trouble awaits and let's hope it's the right kind of trouble, as Irish storytellers say. When the lamb is born, its first task is to stand up – there's a responsibility for those who arrive and choose to live. The mother calls and coos, the farmer might even hold the muzzle to the udder and the milk may well be ready, but it is all in vain if the lamb will not rise nor suckle. And by doing so its existence perhaps has only just begun, life, and its renewal, requires continual attention and is constantly a re-negotiation of what is and might be. It is the territory of the unfamiliar, but is the world we exist in nevertheless, and the choice has been made to live in it, not regardless of the uncertainty, but because of it.

Introduction

In this chapter, I will be exploring what comes after the point of arrival. If the previous chapter was concerned with the question of how the student arrives into existence, the following discussion attends to the question, into what, and as importantly, into where does the student as subject arrive and exist? Discussion of education relating to the question of existence tends to focus primarily on the experience of the student, becoming engaged with the cultural, social and political world so that it might possibly be enlivened and sustained. However, in this chapter, I suggest that the experience of 'becoming' occurs in a place, and that by being specifically located, such a place matters. Furthermore, I suggest that it is in part because of a specific location that the natal encounter occurs. The educational encounter is not occurring in abstraction, but is experienced as doing so somewhere – not just anywhere. The idea that place matters is important in this chapter for two reasons. First, because educational encounters are located on Earth, a place in common, which is the arena in which all education has been and currently continues to be undertaken. By virtue of this fact, and in the interest of my vision of education, a 'pedagogy of place' warrants consideration. Second, my contention is that it is through the event of subjectification, through arrival, that there is a possibility for how the student might contribute to the renewal of the world, in social, political and ecological terms.

Associated with the interest in place, liminality is another theme which I will address in this chapter. I am suggesting that having arrived as subject, the student experiences a degree of discombobulation, a rupture of sorts, from the completeness or immanence that preceded the moment of interruption. I will discuss this experience in relation to liminality, a concept understood in relation to rites of passage (van Gennep, 1909); Turner (1969) and which I see as integral to encountered education. A central feature of liminality is that whatever has been once familiar to the individual becomes less relevant, whilst simultaneously the liminal phase breaks open new experiences and possibilities by which to re-engage in the world. Liminality is an episode in which the notion of time changes, where improvisation becomes paramount in responding to the experience for both student and teacher, a factor that is illustrated again in the vocative text preceding this chapter. In some respects, I set out to parallel the disruptive features of liminality in the way in which the chapter develops. If the previous chapter had an 'arrivalistic' quality, then this one might be described as 'liminalistic'. In other words, I will be taking the opportunity to break into my discussion with ideas that come from outside a frame of reference which is orientated towards a more familiar, product-orientated educational perspective. I suggest that if we remain within the limits of this perspective idea such as interconnectedness, homonomy and freedom can be compromised by an intellectualisation of what is primarily a bodily experience. To overcome this limitation, I am going to draw from material which is grounded in the particularity of place, suggesting that it is through such a 'placed-ness' that educational experience can be properly orientated to soil, soul and society.

Liminality

In some respects, liminality can be described as the place 'betwixt and between'. Its etymology is Latin for 'threshold' and refers to the mid-point between two points of certainty. The concept is used variously in relation to spaces and places, experiences, cultural reference points and periods of time. Originally developed by Arnold van Gennep, a folklorist, it was the later work of the anthropologist, Victor Turner (1969) that established liminality as a significant idea in understanding aspects of cultural experience. Both writers based their initial writing on the practice of rites of passage and identified liminality as a mid-phase in which the individual is passing from one state, for example, of being a child, to the next phase, that of adulthood. Adolescence, therefore, might be treated as a liminal phase. Liminality remains an interesting concept for considering where change is taking place and that includes those educational approaches that prioritise change, or growth, as a primary objective. However, in the context of this chapter specifically, I am introducing liminality to emphasise the experience following the arrival of the student as subject. In doing so, I have been influenced by the work of James Conroy (2004) who has developed an extensive perspective on how education – and schooling in particularly – can be understood through liminality. For Conroy an important aspect of the liminal is that it draws attention to borders, including the border between different stages of student development, different ideas about the world, ascribed roles and physical and social spaces, such as that of the school and society.

My interest in referring to liminality in the work of Conroy is in the notion of the border encountered in the event of subjectification and how that is experienced by the student. In the account of the Eastern European student in the previous chapter, that of Alex and myself in the text prior to this chapter, a border is crossed between two ways of existing in the world. The first of which provides a familiar and certain experience and the second of which is an engagement with the unanticipated and unknown. In this chapter, my focus is on the indeterminable moment in between these two existences. This 'no-man's land' territory is where wildness roams and thrives, and is a reminder of how I have positioned the idea of this book, set out in Chapter 2, as being born out of the marginal tract of land that runs the borders of the open field. Educationally, it is the point during which the student is confronted with the consequence and responsibility of choosing, or not, how to exist. The emphasis on choice, as opposed to obligation, is important to make here because fluidity is a quality of both the experience of arrival and that of liminality. The loosening of what once constituted a fixed position, for example the student's immanent state, can also be associated with what Conroy describes as encounters at different 'contact zones'. This can be in relation to the student, to the private place of their home and family, or that of the civic space represented by the school. But it can also refer to the nature of the contact zone which is created between teacher and student. A different quality of space is experienced in which, in Conroy's perspective, and reflecting Turner's earlier understanding, involves a re-adjustment of socially accepted status.

Accordingly, all traditional denominations of status disappear and those in the liminal state are equal in a manner unimaginable in that structured life, which on either side ends in the liminal... In such circumstances the liminal is conceived as eruptive, emerging out of those interstices that exist inside bounded spaces... the liminal moment may arise within the bounda-ries spaces of a given society while at the same time not being of it.

(Conroy, 2004, p. 55)

As an aside, I understand the references to 'denomination' and 'status' as referring to an ascribed role, dictated by social norms (as opposed to referring less formally to the quality of an individual's presence). If arrival is out of one of the 'interstices' and departure from the other boundaried position, then what I am framing as the 'beyond arrival' experience focuses attention on what goes on in-between, and where the liminal begins to offer a range of possibilities,

What the transitional figures in the liminal period or space have in common is their explicit estrangement from the normatively structured environment of everyday life... In this liminal space there arises the possibility that I might be able to acknowledge that I am always, to some extent, a stranger even to my-self. If I am, so to speak, a pilgrim – a stranger in a strange land – then there is always a bit left over, either that of which I am not aware, or to which, in the normal course of my everyday transactions, I do not have access.

(ibid, p. 57)

In this I hear an echo of what I previously discussed with regard to the emergence of the student's experience of subjectification, and what I will re-turn to in the following chapter in considering dissensus. Here though, my interest is in exploring the potential for the student to discover how to engage in the world through a liminal experience.

Conroy offers one of the few considerations of liminality in respect of edu-cation. As part of his argument, he also draws on Arendt's work, suggesting that schools in particular offer a liminal space in which the cross-generational encounter of which Arendt writes in her treatise on education might occur (1954). Conroy is clear in his view that the necessary liminal experience, which is so central for educational work, must exist within a bordered arena. Whilst there are aspects of his treatment of liminality that resonate with my own perspective, I find Conroy falls short of fully accounting for the level of disruption that accompanies the liminal. In my experience, when I have worked with students, the experience of disturbance is at a more visceral level than that of solely upturning social roles,

The nature of liminality involves an experience which is akin to immersion and that ranges beyond cognition. It is not so much a case of not being able to think straight, but of being in bewilderment. The etymology of this term means to be 'lured into the wild', or 'led astray' into the wild, and in our experience this is captures a function of a liminal process.

(Barrow, 2020, p. 60)

I have written elsewhere (Barrow and Newton, 2015) about how liminality disrupts the existence of the individual, creating a complex state of vulnerability. Educationally, having traversed a threshold, which I have described in terms of an arrival, the student experiences a departure from the choretic realm, the state of immanence. There is a severance of sorts, which brings the individual into an experience that is essentially one of uncertainty. This, I suggest, activates several factors which accentuate a state of vulnerability. First, whatever the student once knew in terms of information about the world becomes unreliable, or redundant. Second, that familiar ways of self-management are no longer effective and that, third, previous ways of co-constructing the world prove equally unhelpful. A fourth factor is that options once available disappear and finally that there is a change in the notion and location of power between the student and the world. These five factors – experienced in varying degrees by individual students – heighten the liminal quality of encounter and by doing so give rise to possibilities. This opening up into the world, despite its discombobulating effect, is precisely what enables the possibility for the renewal of the world that is important to my vision of education. Each factor associated with the student's vulnerability indicates a way in which their subjectification might be encountered. To be more specific, the student might experience their arrival into the world by the difference in terms of their power and agency, or a widening of options and range of information with which they might choose to exist.

It is the sense of vulnerability and bewilderment that confront the student beyond the point of arrival which I want to focus on and, to some extent, re-create, within this chapter. In doing so, I will set out to shift from the familiar frame of reference of product-orientated education and be referring to ideas that are unusual in the context of such discourse and are from less familiar educational contexts. Importantly, these alternative reference points are based on the premise that human beings are a part of nature. This position contrasts with one that regards the student – and the educational endeavour – as being apart from nature and, furthermore, that the human experience is understood as unique, in the sense that it is separated from that of other living organisms. I suggest this separating out is significant in bringing about the kind of rupture that creates the disconnective educational approach typified by product-orientated education. It is arguably an inherent trait for those whose experience has been forged in a culture that valorises individuality, autonomy and a sense of personal freedom predicated on being apart from the more-than-human world; this will always involve us in working our language 'backwards' to articulate what has already been lost. Whereas in this chapter, I am drawing on sources that are closer to understanding education on the basis of being part of nature, and that, in general terms, means focusing on educational practices rooted in place.

Liminality and Lebenswelt (Life-World)

In preparing the path towards a consideration of placed-based education, I want to consider liminality a little further and suggest that the educational encounter is part of nature, as opposed to being apart from nature. I am interested in exploring the potential framing of education as having its vitality because it emerges from, and is informed by, the place where it is undertaken and that such a place is alive. Furthermore, that the disruptive liminal quality of the encounter is such precisely because of where it occurs. I will be exploring some examples of place-based educational encounters, but first I want to re-state, or emphasise, what I mean when I refer to the aliveness of place. To do so I will return briefly to the importance of the phenomenological theme, which I discussed earlier in Chapter 2 in describing my methodological approach, and draw on the work of ecologist and philosopher, David Abram (2017), who in effect, picks up the interest in phenomenology from earlier writers, including Husserl and Merleau-Ponty. Abram is primarily interested in making sense of the direct experience when encountering the entirety of the world, and I too am similarly interested in describing what this means in relation to the event of subjectification. He suggests that 'phenomenology would seek not to explain the world, but to describe it as closely as possible the way the world makes itself evident to awareness, the way things first arise in our direct, sensorial experience' (Abram, 2017, p. 35). This notion that 'the world makes itself evident' has me curious as to what this means in terms of the educational encounter and raises the question as to what arises in the sensorial experience of the student? There is an acknowledgement here that the world is already alive, and I will return to what I began to explore in the previous chapter regarding the materiality of the world. I have already emphasised the importance of interconnectedness as a key feature in my understanding of the 'soil' and I will next I set out an elaboration of my earlier discussion.

I referred to the work of Angyal (1941) in my opening rationale and in particularly to his term 'homonomy' to describe the tendency for living organisms to seek out connection and relationship. Angyal is also attributed to the ordination of the term 'biosphere' to denote the realm in which the trend towards homonomy occurs. He offers the following definition,

> I propose to call the realm in which the biological total process takes place the 'biosphere', that is, the realm or sphere of life. The biosphere includes both the individual and the environment, not as interacting parts, not as constituents which have independent existence, but as aspects of a single reality which can be separated only by abstraction.
>
> (Angyal, 1941, p. 100)

The concern that underpins the rationale for my work here is that education has typically served to undermine the possibility of understanding existence as interconnected, according to Angyal's explanation of the 'total process' of life. I am interested in redressing this disconnective impact and look to a kind of educational encounter that arises because it is directly informed by the biosphere. Abram offers a further idea, elaborating on an earlier term introduced by Husserl, Lebenswelt – life-world – as a way of describing the vitality of the world. It reflects how I have been using the term 'material world' here, which I refer to, in full, below:

> The life-world is the world of our immediately lived experience as we live it, prior to all our thoughts about it. It is in that which is present to us in our everyday tasks and enjoyments – reality as it engages us before being analysed by our theories and our science. The life world is the world that we count on without necessarily paying it much attention, the world of the clouds overhead and the ground underfoot, of getting out of bed and preparing food and turning on the tap for water. Easily overlooked, this primordial world is always already there when we begin to reflect or philosophise. It is not a private but collective, dimension – the common field of our lives and the other lives with which ours are entwined - and yet it is profoundly ambiguous and indeterminate, since our experience of this field is always relative to our situation within it. The life-world is thus the world as we organically experience it in its enigmatic multiplicity and open-mindedness, prior to conceptually freezing it into a static space of 'facts' – prior indeed, to conceptualising it in any complete fashion.
>
> (Abram, 2017, p. 40)

Abram's concern, which is reflected in the emerging vision of education here, is that there is a possibility of being able to return to an integrated experience of ourselves, which incorporates being part of nature. I am suggesting that education might provide such a possibility, if it can be understood as incorporating an arrival that occurring within this sense of a material, or life-world.

By turning towards the ecological reality of the educational encounter, I think it is also important to emphasise what happens in terms of authority and power. If the educational task involves teacher and student in their relationship with place, then I suggest we must acknowledge a more-than-human agency that features in the dynamic. This kind of agency, which perhaps can be called ecological agency, is outside of the immediate control or direction of the teacher, or student. It might be helpful to think of this as nature 'having its way' with the educational encounter and as such is 'at loose' in the liminal space. The tendency can be for the student to avoid, or in some other way escape the liminal disturbance, as seen for example in the passivity of the rest of the group members in my earlier account of the training programme, or my own excuse to pick up my car from the garage to step back from the challenge of acting as farmer. Staying with the liminal experience is an integral component in the kind of educational encounter I am exploring and it is one that is inextricably connected to the energetic impact of where it takes place. In fact, I would argue that it is because of this undirectable factor, this unreliable agency (in the sense that it cannot be trusted to 'perform' on command) that is fundamental to the liminality central to the educational encounter. I am speaking of an education situated in the particularity of the material world, one in which liminality opens up an upturning the student's experience of the world so that it might be understood again.

To establish this vision of education in a culture that valorises product-orientated approaches is challenging because there is an emphasis to promote education as being 'certain' of itself, to deliver outcomes, and be efficient in the process. In opening up education to this kind of ecological view, I see a distinctive shift emerging from autonomy, which might be more readily associated with an ego-centric view, to one of homonomy, as discussed in my opening rationale. The emphasis on interconnectedness is again at the heart of my vision of education in which connective experience includes the human and more-than-human world.

> It is, indeed nothing other than the biosphere – the matrix of earthly life in which we ourselves are embedded. Yet this is not the biosphere as it is conceived by an abstract and objectifying science… it is, rather, the biosphere as it is experienced and lived from within by the intelligent body – by the attentive human animal who is entirely a part of the world that he, or she, experiences.
>
> (Abram, p. 65, author's italics)

We have arrived at the point at which I want to turn to accounts of education as 'lived from within' a place and consider what I will begin to describe as a located education encounter.

Located Education Encounter

The significance of a place-based education (PBE) is that it pays attention to the particularity of the 'life-world' and how this is activated within the liminality experienced by the student. To overlook or reduce the impact of place in this experience is to simultaneously limit the potential for an encounter of subjectification. The attention to location is important to advocate because one of the consequences of the globalised, product-orientated education described in my opening chapter is that the importance of place is often rendered irrelevant. In fact, perversely the place-lessness of such education is instrumental in ensuring the homogeneity required for its 'success'. This leads to a subtle deception in that this kind of education appears to be everywhere, can be franchised anywhere, whilst apparently coming from nowhere - not dissimilar from the 'local' Starbucks or McDonalds outlet. The distinctive feature of a particular place are appropriated, assimilated or eliminated, in order to construe a sense of the familiar; as we walk into the global branded coffee shop it is as if one has not travelled, or encountered the material, life-world. The 'product' has a reliability for the customer who gets what they want, but the disconnection from the local is on-going. If place no longer matters, or is regarded as immaterial, then it is more likely to be objectified, exploited and consumed. It becomes subject to the 'control over' tendencies that are apparent in education. One of the implications of this place-less-ness is that the ubiquitous global education movement eliminates, or pushes to the margins, a way of understanding education that pays attention to where it occurs. Other, more indigenous and rooted educational realities are made invisible through such a dislocated global education model. Whereas if the specific place is recognised as being alive, that it is differently alive than elsewhere, and that we are alive within it, then there is a possible question; how might I choose to exist here?

I am aware that I have just introduced a reference to indigenous and this is a term I have found important in developing my thinking about located education. My referring to indigenous might risk setting up a distracting discussion from my focus on what is a complex anthropological concept and so I shall start out with a brief explanation of how I am using the term here.[1] To be indigenous refers to those who are born out of, and remain close to, the place where they were born, the word being understood literally as to be 'originating', or 'occurring naturally in a particular place'. Etymologically the word also carries the notion of 'in-born' or to be 'birthed within', and consequently, the obvious significance of location is a reason for why I am introducing indigenous into my work. By doing so I am acknowledging that the student arrives somewhere, and that there is a quality, or presence, associated with the student's experience precisely because of the specific 'where'. Whilst all of us, naturally, arise out of somewhere, I am suggesting that most of us typically find ourselves 'anywhere', and in doing so experience a disconnection, from the particularity of a place. It is important at this point to distinguish such a chronic state of disconnection from the sense of dislocation associated with that of liminality which I introduced earlier. Whilst both states imply an existential challenge for the individual, the former disconnection of 'sameness' in effect anaesthetises the individual from exercising existential choice because it neuters the impact of the life-world, whereas the latter orientates the individual towards an existential activism.

I will stay with the idea of indigenous experience in general terms before moving into a more detailed account of this way of framing the educational encounter. In doing so I want to hold at a distance a potential for establishing a Western vs. indigenous dichotomy in my exploration, which I am aware has been a tendency in writing on the topic and my caution is twofold. First, it can be too easy to position the indigenous as being of some place other than cultures typically associated with Western values and by doing so discount the distinctively indigenous groups who reside within those areas. Second, it becomes apparent that the language of 'perspective' is commonly used as a way of describing a different 'filter' on what can then be assumed as a universal experience, or 'truth' about human experiences. I have a reservation about this because it risks eliminating, or limiting, the possibility of recognising different realities. I am suggesting that the challenge of located education is for the encounter to be fully open to, and activated by, the particularity of the place in which it occurs. Consequently, what is encountered cannot be understood through an abstract 'perspective' which then generalises and 'flattens out' the reality of what is distinctly located. Instead, I am interested in using the term indigenous in a more literal fashion to describe education that is encountered in relationship with place. Such an indigenous education is predicated on the principle that the world is alive and that it speaks to the student's condition and provokes the student to choose in what way to exist in relation to it. Indigenous education recognises that place matters not only because it is alive but that it gives rise to possibilities and limitations. In other words, the agency of location shapes the discernment of the student in deciding what is desirable.

In developing an indigenous reality of education, the emphasis on the more-than-human environment raises a further challenge when considering the significance of place. A question arises about the limitations of humanistic philosophy and how it has impacted on culture, including education. Declaring that humanism is in crisis, following a series of atrocities, including, and since, the world wars of the last century, Le Grange, in his contribution, suggests that what he sees as a 'perennial education crisis' is also 'a crisis of humanism' (Le Grange, 2018, p. 43). In his critique, Le Grange reflects some of my earlier concerns about the tendency to abstraction in Western educational discourse, for example through the 'humanist assumptions of critical pedagogy' which are constructed on the 'notion of a human being that is disconnected from the realities experienced by humans in their daily lives' (ibid, p. 44). This reference to what Le Grange identifies as a limitation of critical pedagogy is echoed in what I regard as a significant paper by Gruenewald, who suggests a convincing integration of critical pedagogy with PBE (Gruenewald, 2003). In his view, critical theory targets issues of oppression, power and authority and in the educational domain challenges the assumptions and practices that sustain inequalities in the dominant culture, whereas PBE, with a focus on cultivating an ecological sensibility, has been more closely associated with an appreciation that social dynamics are 'always nested in ecological systems' (ibid, p. 4). For Gruenewald, a necessary task is to understand the interrelationship between the two approaches, suggesting an amalgamation which serves the broader purpose of my own perspective by synthesising two of its themes – soil and society. In referring to how educators have been associating PBE with ecological activism, Gruenewald offers the following insight,

> One result of these primarily ecological and rural associations has been that place-based education is frequently discussed at a distance from the urban, multi-cultural arena, territory most often claimed by critical

pedagogues. If place-based education emphasises ecological and rural contexts, critical pedagogy – in a near mirror image – emphasises social and urban contexts and often neglects the ecological and rural scene entirely.

(Gruenewald, 2003, p. 3)

In the light of this comment, I want to return to Le Grange who goes on to describe an interconnected experience of arrival into a world, echoing Arendt, which is more than politically pluralistic, and profoundly ecological,

We cannot know of what affects we are capable in advance but can engage in a life of experimentation and also to engage in an active life, one that enhances rather than thwarts life. The impetus for living an active life does not lay outside of life itself – it does not transcend life – but is a power within, the power that connects all things in the cosmos, produced by the materials flows and intensities of life.

(Le Grange, 2018 p. 45)

To illustrate how this is framed indigenously, Le Grange points to two African terms – Ubuntu and Ukama. The former refers to a commitment, the 'deepest obligation to become more fully human and to achieve this requires one to enter more deeply into community with others', whilst the latter refers to an experience of 'relatedness to the entire cosmos' (ibid, p. 46) and embraces ubuntu. In the context of these terms, Le Grange cites Ramose (2009) in the distinction of humanness from humanism, echoing the idea of natality, 'Humanness suggests both a condition of being and the state of becoming, of opening or ceaseless unfolding. It is thus opposed to any, "-ism", including humanism, for this tends to suggest a condition of finality, a closedness or a kind of absolute either incapable of, or resistant to, any further movement' (ibid, p. 47).

Principles of the kind of indigenous approach of which I am interested includes interconnectedness and the importance of place. A third aspect is concerned with mystery and myth. To experience education out of the land and in ecological relationship means also to experience all that came before and all of what is beyond us. This can mean comprehending that a crop is not simply something to eat, but that it occurs from a specific place, within a particular cycle of which the individual is embedded. By implication, it means that subjectification occurs located within a broader rhythm by which the world, or more specifically, physis, is sustained and renewed. Such an education is peppered with references to ancestral influences, thoughtfulness for future generations and mindful of animistic energies. These, in my view, significantly expand on what has been meant by early ideas of phenomenology in a Euro-centric sense, which moves more boldly into the territory that Abram begins to scope out in his contemporary writing. It is to this literature, that of place-based educators, that I will now turn in order to illustrate how education might be envisaged when soil, soul and society are incorporated into the located educational encounter. To do so I am going to feature three examples to illustrate how education can be understood as 'situated' and in doing so pay attention to how this connects with the arrival of the student as subject. I am suggesting that each of these three 'case studies' stays with the experience of liminality, understanding its educational potential for the expression of subjectification (although in each case this idea is understood differently). The material includes Cajete's Look to the Mountain (1994); the tension held in the contemporary Bhutanese education system between traditionalism and modernism; eco-activism through story and myth as presented in the work of Shaw (2011, 2017).

Look to the Mountain (Cajete, 1994)

Look to the Mountain by Gregory Cajete (1994) is exceptional in that it is one of the few scholarly investigations into the experience of place-based education carried out by an academic who describes himself as indigenous. The aim of Cajete's work is to provide a comprehensive account of education that reflects a broad tradition found in indigenous communities from across aboriginal, north and south American and Asian regions. Cajete's motivation for presenting the common themes, principles and philosophy is primarily to inform and encourage indigenous educators to reclaim their respective heritage and re-vitalise indigenous education practices. In doing so, I find that Cajete provides substantial insights and a detailed account of what it means to educate from out of a specific place, which illuminate what I have in mind when envisaging education in connection with soil, soul and society.

Cajete is primarily focused on describing important tenets within the field of indigenous education and what this means in practical terms is that little time is given in his work to defining who, or what, is 'indigenous'. References are made to 'tribal' or Indian, and there is an underlying assumption that 'primitive', 'nature-centred', 'early', 'ancient', or 'traditional society' are all terms which are associated in Cajete's understanding of indigenous. At the outset of the work, he explains that both 'Tribal' and 'Indigenous' describe 'The many traditional and Tribally orientated groups of people who are identified with a specific place or region and whose cultural traditions continue to reflect an inherent environmental orientation and sense of sacred ecology' (Cajete, 1994, p. 15). Cajete provides a substantial account of the philosophy, terms of reference, underpinning principles and some technical aspects of understanding, planning and delivering the kind of education which is located in a specific landscape. The work occasionally positions indigenous education in relation to its Western counterpart, but mostly Cajete maintains a focus on describing a philosophy that underpins a distinctive land-based education policy and practice.

A key principle of education, for Cajete, reflects the earlier general theme I have already discussed which is that of relatedness. The underlying assumption of interconnectedness is absolutely paramount to his work, and much of what develops in terms of outlook is predicated on an ecologically relational understanding of the educational experience. Cajete initially uses the Lakota term, mitakuye oyasin, – 'we are all related' – and continues by explaining that in educational terms this implicates both teacher and student in a first-hand encounter, between not just themselves but also in relation to the natural and spiritual domains. This, he argues, is in sharp contrast to other education models which have tended to emphasise an observational position, typical in objective-orientated education, which in turn I see as similar to product-orientated education as described in my opening rationale. With reference to the modern American context, Cajete suggests there is a tendency 'to empha-size objective content and experience detachment from primary sources and community. This conditioning, to exist as a marginal participant and per-petual observer, is a foundational element of the crisis... and the alienation of modern man from his own being and the natural world' (ibid, p. 25), which again echoes my own critique of product-orientated education.

Cajete continues by identifying the Inyan, a series of 'living stones'. These form the 'foundational characteristics' of a PBE experience. In addition to emphasising the importance of interconnection and relatedness, these include principles of life-long education; education as cyclic processes connecting to levels of maturity; education benefitting individual and community; the cen-trality of story and myth; the power of education to navigate one's life in action and in spiritual direction; accounting for plurality; education rooted in living and doing, through body and spirit, as well as mind. Frequently, Cajete intro-duces metaphors and one introduced early in his work is hahoh, 'to breathe in'. This is explained as an emphasis on the integration of living and education. Tribal education involves a combination of experiential education, ritual/cer-emony – initiation, dreaming – utilising the unconscious – storytelling, appren-ticeship and artistic creation. 'Through these methods the integration of inner and outer realities of learners and teachers was fully honoured...' (ibid, p. 33). Cajete describes the hope of this approach to education as an experience to 'find one's face, to find one's heart'. Drawing on the Aztec poet-philosopher-teacher figure, tlamatinime, Cajete explains how students:

> ... find their face (develop and express their innate character and poten-tial); to find their heart (search out and express their inner passion); and to explore foundations of life and work (find the vocation that allowed the student the fullest expression of self and truth)... [this] quest for express-ing each student's gift in service to their community made them capable of creating divine things and being a complete man or woman.
>
> (Cajete, 1994, p. 34)

This reference to the divine is a recurrent one throughout Cajete's work and one with which to associate the vision of my own work here as a more appropriate account of soul than, perhaps, the more familiar Christian-Judaic notion in which the soul is seen as being located deep within the individual. The focus in a PBE is on four inter-related concepts; seeking life and becoming complete; achieving highest thought; orientation; and pathway. It is in Cajete's discussion of these concepts that some interesting insights emerge. For instance, the idea of 'place' in tribal terms relates to a people, in addition to a physical location; the concept of the spirit is both deep but also at the surface, skin (or perhaps 'flesh') level; 'Spirit is real. It is physically expressed in everything that exists in the world' (ibid, p. 47).

It is in this experience of 'finding one's own face' that I think Cajete touches into the theme of encountered arrival, whilst also begins to dissect the components of how this comes about when undertaken as located in a particular place. For instance, the use of tracking – combined with the language of hunting – is a distinct component in indigenous education as described by Cajete; 'tracking is intimately involved in the process of seeking wisdom, vision and coming to the source of spirit' (ibid, p. 55). I see a link here with the challenge for the student in moving beyond the more familiar process of being schooled and out towards one of encounter. Cajete continues with the metaphor, clarifying, 'The hunter is an archetypal form that resides in each of us... who searches for the completion that each of us in our own way, strives to find... So it is in our times that we continue to hunt for ourselves, in our families, in our communities, in our careers, in our schools, in our institutions and our relationships' (ibid, p. 57). This idea of the student 'hunting for themselves', in relation to their environment, is one which I connect with those encounters I have described earlier. It also resonates with the concept of physis being 'tracked' in the student's experience in the encounter.

In turning to the specific significance of the environment to the experience of finding one's face, Cajete shares again some of what was reflected in Abram's critique,

> Indians perceived multiple realities in Nature – that experienced by our five senses was only one of many possibilities. In such a perceived 'multiverse', knowledge could be received directly from animals, plants and other living and non-living entities... All life and Nature have a 'personhood', a sense of purpose and inherent meaning that is expressed in many ways and at all times'.
>
> (Cajete, 1994, p. 74)

The implications of this for the student-teacher dynamic is, in my view, profound, and as Cajete continues it becomes clear that he is in similar territory to that of Biesta (2017) in terms of the beautiful risk that exists in the teacher and student dynamic, in relation to subjectification,

> Native American people, through their ecological educational processes, evolved a natural response to the other – that other being, the natural

world – and allowed the other to define itself to them, rather than impos-
ing a preconceived intellectual meaning.... They allowed the land to be...
remembering that it was given to them as a gift.

(ibid, p. 75)

I suggest that Cajete captures here something of the difficult to elucidate
moment of 'risk'. The point at which the teacher is open to the impact by
the subjectification of the student, and to regard it as a gift. It is perhaps this
additional quality of 'gifting' by the student, and the wider environment, that
intrigues me. It links to the discussion in my final chapter and a curiosity;
for whom is the harvest? And it certainly challenges the notion that the student is there for the teacher to define educationally, or that the environment
is passive in the process.

In one of the most important areas of his work, Cajete introduces the idea of
'ensoulment' which involves the projection of human archetypes, and a sense
of soul, into the natural world. Cajete argues that the term best captures the
essence of how indigenous people express their relationship with the natural
world, sometimes also referred to as 'participation mystique', explaining that,

Ensoulment leads into what might be best described as a psychological
framework that fuses spiritual engagement with personhood in relationship with Nature. Because the indigenous understanding is that individuals have been literally 'born out of the Earth of their Place', indigenous
peoples experience Nature as part of themselves... people make a place as
much as a place makes them'.

(Cajete, 1994, p. 83)

What strikes me in this description about ensoulment is the association with
some of what I explored in my discussion regarding natality. In particular,
how these words resonate with the new beginning that the student presents to
the world and in doing so reaffirms the interplay of their existence to the renewal of the (natural) world, and there is also the reminder that the individual
does not simply appear 'out of nowhere', but of this world, this place.

In bringing my consideration of Cajete to a close, I will focus on his chapter entitled The Communal Foundation of Indigenous Education, in which he
makes a statement that I suggest presents a significant challenge to a placeless
educational frame of reference; 'Indigenous community is about living a symbiotic life in the context of a symbolic culture that includes the natural world
as a necessary and vital participant and co-creator of community' (ibid,
p. 167). I think this is in sharp contrast to a view that idealises autonomy and
valorises individual growth. In such culture, 'symbiosis' – co-dependency – is
regarded as a sign of weakness and, in extremis, a pathological condition,
whereas an education that takes account of interdependency between where
it is located is recognised as necessary for living a good life.

In reading Cajete's account of indigenous education what becomes increasingly clear to me is that 'education' is not separated out from the student's wider experience of living life. There is an emphasis on integrating education with ecological engagement and spiritual observance. This heightens the question as to how education exists, and what is intended by its existence. It raises a further question, for me, about further efforts to possibly demarcate education, which serves to disconnect the student from the 'life-world'. Whilst Cajete writes generally about the importance of this integration within education that is clearly located, I now move now to how such an approach to education might be envisaged at a national level and consider Bhutanese education.

Bhutan: Land of Thunder Dragon

For readers unfamiliar with Bhutan a few general remarks might be helpful in contextualising the following section. Set entirely in the Himalayas, Bhutan is a tiny kingdom flanked by Nepal, China and India, with a population of 770,000. The capital, Thimpu, is one of just a handful of towns across the country, with most people living in rural settlements scattered across the generally mountainous landscape. Rooted in its own distinctive Buddhist tradition, the country was until the early 1990s well secluded from modernity. The country was led by a longstanding monarchy until His Majesty Jigme Singye Wangchuck voluntarily abdicated in 2009 giving rise to a fledgling democracy. Aside from a highly lucrative tourist industry, Bhutan is also known for initiating the unique concept of Gross National Happiness (GNH). Initiated by its prime minister in 1998, following a symbolic fact-finding journey by the monarch across the kingdom, GNH was devised as an alternative approach to gross national product (GNP) for assessing the health of the nation. The GNH framework was designed to establish the conditions by which the nation might experience happiness, as defined as a deepening connection with self, the community and the natural environment. Each year studies and surveys are undertaken to monitor the levels of happiness whilst government departments set out to reflect GNH in policy development. Consequently the Ministry for Education sets out in its mission to establish an 'educated and enlightened society of gross national happiness'. My interest in featuring Bhutanese education is twofold. First, a personal reason, because an educational visit to Bhutan was instrumental in orientating an early framing of the vision of education on which this work is based. Second, for the purpose of this chapter, it is an exceptional example, illustrating the 'interface' between traditional indigenous education and global educational approaches at a national level. In doing so it reveals the complexity of what I refer to as the 'soil' and its implications for the education encounter.

In my discussion of Bhutanese education I have been drawn to the work of Robles (2016) whose study focused on the interruptive impact of modernity on traditional education in the country's education system. Robles sets out the history of education that begins in the religious tradition of ancient Buddhism, located in the local monastic network and which provided the only educational opportunity in Bhutan until the 1950s when the first non-monastic schools were introduced. The later introduction of GNH into the state education system was 'centred on the development of spiritual and cultural aspects of society and the rejection of a development paradigm that puts a primary emphasis on economic indicators' (Robles, 2016, p. 27). It's also important to emphasise that the educational framework reflected a wider national resistance to the contamination of its indigenous tradition by factors external to Bhutanese society and culture. For example, at the time of writing the country has resisted joining the World Trade Organisation, and thereby remains at liberty to protect its markets from the impact of globalisation; there are no Starbucks, McDonalds or IKEA, for example, trading in Bhutan. Likewise, in the spirit of GNH objectives, Bhutanese education is equally less susceptible to the global education reform movement (GERM) which I discussed in my opening chapter. This is not to say that Bhutanese education in some way censures the experience of students from engaging with a contemporary modern curriculum. The key point to be made here is that the Bhutanese approach is founded on the premise that educational experience arises out of a specific location, that this matters and requires protection.

Lhomon Education

To illustrate further how Bhutanese education demonstrates a sense of place I will turn briefly to the initiative by which the localised becomes integrated, or pushes back on the globalising tendency of modern contemporary education policy. Lhomon refers to the specific region of where the work arises from, to emphasise that people are unified not only by civically defined borders, but by the land itself. The Lhomon Society is established to provide opportunities, examples of, and initiatives directed towards, sustainable economic development, environmental conservation, cultural promotion, authentic education and good governance. It is aligned with the national framework of GNH and recognises the challenges that come with transitioning from a monarchical to democratic state, indicated by Dzongsar Khyentse Rinpoche, a founder of the movement,

> Bhutan is a democracy now. So far things have gone well. But we citizens now have to shoulder responsibility without someone else having to tell us. It is a matter of fulfilling our responsibilities without the prodding of a cowherd.
>
> (Rinpoche, 2021)

Lhomon Education (LME) is an important area of development for the Society and taking a closer look at its philosophy and approach provides an example of how education can be localised, emerging out of the place in which it occurs. In the case of Bhutan, this involves honouring the traditions that recognise the sacredness of interconnectedness with the natural environment. This in turn reflects a culture based in the territory which became known as the land of the Druk, or 'dragon', which, when founded by the Buddhist sect from which present-day Bhutan originated, there occurred a mighty storm, in which was heard a loud voice announcing the name of the country. The culture of this land is deeply tied to its sustainability, a sense that it is sacred, that all life is integrated, interdependent and that life arises within its natural environment. Educational direction is towards the student experiencing themselves as part of this enduring interconnectedness, taking an active role to enrich and sustain it. Mitchell and Gyeltshen (2019) explain what this means in terms of the curriculum in their case study account,

> The curriculum is thus place-based, in that it values the existing ecological wisdom in the community that has been formulated over the centuries. It furthers an understanding of sustainable practices, both old and new, that support a harmonious way of living in accord with the environment.
>
> (Mitchell and Gyeltshen, 2019, p. 179)

From an LME perspective the push towards modernisation, and in particularly with the introduction of the global educational movement, is bittersweet. One of its aims is to push back on the values that arrive from the outside where 'success' is either defined purely in economic terms, or social advantage bringing with it privileged status. Again, drawing on the work of Mitchell and Gyeltshen, it is possible to get a glimpse of what is entailed in asserting the local into the global education policy framework,

> It is one of the aims of LME to reverse the value orientation that has overtaken the youth of Bhutan so that they gain a real appreciation for the traditional ways of their people, ways that go beyond wearing national dress and attending festivals. The wisdom and knowledge that has evolved through the centuries has allowed the people to survive through their understanding of the climate and land on which they live. When enhanced with new techniques and ideas, this traditional knowledge has great potential to establish personal well-being and security which then extends to the security and well being of Bhutan as a whole, through self-sufficiency in the rural areas which is where the majority of the population still live. By extending entrepreneurial education and opportunities to the villagers, LME hopes to create a climate that attracts young people back to the villages... There is an emphasis on the value of community, counteracting the increasing influence of individualism that comes out of a competitive education system and media that are focused on consumerism....because the program is approached from a holistic and integrated standpoint, they

are also developing a deeply felt appreciation for the interconnectedness of all aspects of being in the world.

(Mitchell and Gyeltshen, 2019, p. 181)

It is important to point out that LME is not a movement designed to negate, or somehow ignore the existence of, the potential benefits that might come from outside of the region. The intention is for education to be located and for incoming influences to be 'translated' into the specificity of where education occurs,

What is being practised at LME has the potential for unification and harmonisation of the two systems of education in Bhutan – one that is traditional, monastic, spiritual, and focused on students' affective development, and the other that is modern, school-based, secular, and focused on students' cognitive development'

(Mitchell and Gyeltshen, 2019, p. 182)

There is much more that might be shared about the detail of the LME curriculum framework, methodology and technique, but for the purposes here, I want to resist dropping further into practice and draw attention to these two previous quotations. What I find important is that the notion of place is at the heart of the educational encounter and that it is regarded as a powerful resource in the teacher-student dynamic. I suggest that the LME approach appreciates that the land which has been sufficient in giving rise to the existence of students and students requires sustenance, which in turn becomes part of educational purpose. This is especially important to the educational vision which I am developing in this work because I am interested in developing a view of education that has an arc of return, or renewal, a theme I consider more fully in my final chapter. In the account of Bhutanese education I see a determination to initiate, through localised agency, an education that respects the function of the land and the importance of soil. I am suggesting that this position is necessary wherever education occurs, be it in a distant country, or in our own backyard. In many respects, it is all part of the same soil, and it requires renewal, literally and symbolically, which education might better serve.

Flat-Pack Education

A located education acknowledges that educational encounters arise between student and teacher in response to the environment in which it is undertaken. However, when I am using the term 'place' I mean it from the kind of position described earlier by Cajete and which is inherent in the Bhutanese approach to education. In other words, 'place' combines a notion of space and time quite different from that which is familiar in the context of product-orientated education. Place in this regard holds the presence of the ancestors simultaneously with the current generation, whilst also recognising the interconnectedness with the more-than-human world, including natural rhythms. Such an understanding of 'place' as multi-faceted, cyclic and multi-experiential possibly confounds the typically linear, compartmentalised understanding of how the world is organised which is manufactured and sustains a disconnection from place. This is important here because the impact of a product-orientated education – most notably the GERM is antagonistic to a view of education that is connected to place. I explained earlier the five features of the GERM identified by Sahlberg (2012); standardisation in relation to outcome measures; competition leading to 'choice'; test-based accountability for schools, staff and students; streamlined curriculum; diversifying the market in terms of education provision. I offer a sixth feature which is that of its portability. The capacity of globalised education to be efficient, easily conveyed via a common language (invariably, English), readily understood (due to its reductionist curriculum and assessment), ensure that it can be straightforwardly transported and introduced anywhere. It is arguably part of a wider preoccupation with becoming a global citizen and a modernist 'celebration of mobility' (Relph, 1976). The image of flatpack furniture comes to mind and one of the attractive features of this approach to the retail industry is the ease of moving items from one place to another. Consequently, commodities and franchises become ubiquitous in people's homes and, likewise, globalised education approaches can be found in the most incongruent places around the planet, including Bhutan.

For the purpose of my work, with its emphasis on soil, I want to impress the importance of the 'importability' (if there can be such a word) of the education encounter. As I have written in the previous chapter, not only is the arrival between persons irreplaceable, likewise, the encounter cannot occur elsewhere, nor anywhere, because it emerges out of somewhere particular. What I begin to appreciate in the reading of Robles' account of Bhutanese education is an attempt, through the setting of national policy, in paying attention to the interplay between the indigenous and the global perspectives. There is, in other words, interest in accounting for what already exists within the locality and that this includes its history – both in ecological, ancestral and social terms. As Robles explains, 'Global engagement in Bhutan has not been an attempt to replace "local" with "global," "traditional" with "modern," or "Bhutanese" with "Western"; rather, the government has attempted a slow and cautious approach emphasising a balance between these different elements' (Robles, p. 30). Whilst my focus on Bhutanese education makes reference to the mechanics of schooling, I want to emphasise the existential implications of this wrestle between the indigenous and the global dynamic. At the heart of the matter is the question of how encounters in educational work pivot around placement, or dis-placement, which in turn connects or dis-connects.

The portability of global education comes at a cost; 'The price is a loss of a deep experience of attachment to a place that can sustain our sense of a meaningful life' and 'has been replaced by that of a sense of homogenous "placelessness"' (Wattchow and Brown, 2011, p. 52). In their discursive chapter, A Case for Place, Wattchow and Brown introduce the notion of place-responsive pedagogy, contrasting it with other, more established but limited ideas about outdoor education that tend to position the environment simply as a dramatic backdrop, or the focus of challenge and risk which is to be overcome. Instead, place-responsive education emerges through the interaction between teachers, students and the environment. Such an approach is a challenge made the greater because often teachers are as equally displaced as students, so the practice in this dimension of educational work is overlooked, or under-estimated. David Orr, an ecologist writing in the nascent years of eco-education, explains that 'place is nebulous to educators because to a great extent we are displaced people for whom immediate places are no longer sources of food, water, livelihood, energy, materials, friends, recreation or sacred inspiration' (Orr, 1991, p. 126). In some respects I am offering a re-frame, or amplifying, what Arendt speaks of when she writes of trying to 'be at home in the world' (Arendt, 1994, p. 308). For my purposes, I emphasise it is to 'be at home' in the live, material world – that there is no other in which to be at home!

The importance of ecological anchoring education is worth further consideration and one way I want to address this is through the notion of being inside a place – as opposed to being outside of it – and I will amplify some of what I have been describing as indigenous practice with a perspective introduced by Relph (1976), one of the first contemporary phenomenological geographers writing on the theme of place. He writes of how, within an indigenous reality, a place will be understood in terms beyond that of its measurements and features. Citing, for instance, how Ayer's Rock, in central Australia, might be seen by European eyes as a large rocky outcrop in an otherwise 'empty' landscape. However, for the Pitjantjatjara people, for whom this area is their homeland, it is known as Uluru and each individual feature of the rock has its own significance, and that it exists in connection with a rich and complex wider environment. This, suggests Relph, is an example of 'existential space' which is not merely a passive space waiting to be experienced, but is constantly being created and remade by human activities', – in which I would include educational activity – 'and in which human intention inscribes itself on the earth' (Relph, 1976, p. 12).

To make a more direct illustration of what I am discussing here, I will refer to the vocative text prefacing this chapter in which David sets about teaching me to manage the newborn calf. Clearly the episode takes place on the farm, in a small paddock. It is at the height of summer and many readers will be able to create a mind's eye view of the physical landscape. However, there is a distinctiveness about the place which runs beyond the physical, visible features. The old farmer is also part of the place as much as he is distinct from it, and this is because he is connected to what George Ewart Evans refers to the 'prior culture' (2013). Evans writes as an oral historian with a particular interest in the culture of indigeneity in East Anglia. In line with other oral historians, Evans argues that it is in the oral reporting of older generations that it is possible to understand both social and ecological history. He makes an interesting observation about the generation of men and women he interviewed whose formative years had been before the First World War. At the time of Evan's recording, this group was in its old age, and he suggests that these people could reach back to a period prior to the industrialisation of agriculture, which took hold in the area post-war. He further observes that because of the delayed impact of social and cultural progress in areas such as East Anglia, much of the regional ancient folklore, with its pagan and Roman origins, remained alive in the day-to-day lives of local communities. Evans refers to this in terms of indigeneity and in my view, it amplifies my own experience of place as I am taught by David. I am present in the field, alongside the flank of the cow in the here and now moment. Yet I am at the same time embedded in a richly layered place in which all of the previous farmers, harvests and livestock are alive alongside me. I am aware of David's presence as teacher, but there is also what gets brought into the space through its historicity and the more-than-human connection that he and the land bring to our encounter. This is what makes it distinctive; it can no longer be anywhere, it is uniquely somewhere.

Relph explores how this idea of existential place links with 'insideness' and 'outsiderness', offering a calibration of what this means in how individuals experience place. I find this a useful approach to clarifying what I am referring to when I suggest that educational encounters might be orientated towards soil as opposed to education being reduced to an activity that is displaced and displacing. Such a diminished experience might lead to what Relph refers to as 'incidental outsideness' which describes a 'largely unselfconscious attitude in which places are experienced as little more than a background or setting for activities and quite incidental to those activities' (Relph, 1976, p. 52). He goes on to explain how the individual can become habituated over time in a particular place whilst their sensibility remains unselfconscious and the experience shifts to that of 'incidental insideness', where especially in a culture that valorises mobility, this is 'probably a feature of everyone's experience of places, for it is inevitable that what we are doing frequently overshadows where we are doing it, and pushes places into the background' (ibid, p. 52). I would suggest that this experience of incidental insideness is mirrored generally in product-orientated education, and especially where this is accentuated by the features of global education reform, which I would argue that the Bhutanese national policy is attempting to resist. Instead, Relph offers what I believe to be a more appropriate experience of insideness which he explains as existential insideness,

> To be inside a place and to experience it as completely as we can does not mean that existentially we are insiders. The most fundamental form of insideness is that in which place is experienced without deliberate and self-conscious reflection yet is full of significances... It is part of knowing implicitly that this place is where you belong – in all other places we are existential outsiders no matter how open we are to their symbols and significances.
>
> (Relph, 1976, p. 55)

This resonates with the accounts of the indigenous education of which Cajete writes, which lies at the heart of what Bhutanese Lhomon educators seek to establish in the educational experience. It may be alien to an educational culture that is essentially displaced, but it is central to the vision of education in the educational vision I have been presenting.

The Necessity of Place and the Importance of Myth

As I bring this chapter towards a close, I will turn to the importance of story when the educational encounter is rooted in place. As already indicated, the role of myth and an oral tradition of storytelling is important in the practices featured in this chapter. It is from storied traditions that the lives of individuals are illuminated and connected with all that has come before and encompassed in what becomes part of the future telling. It is understanding that the tales are not simply about the ebb and flow of human experience but encapsulate the interplay between humans and the more-than-human world, in other words, stories locate us. It is in such stories that our humanity becomes incorporated into a wider existential web.

To echo the description from Kane (1998) cited in Chapter 2, stories are not so much created by humans, but arise from what is overheard and co-created in relationship with the landscape. Understanding that stories catch earliest human efforts to make sense of the interconnected experience has profound implications for the way in which the contemporary ear listens to the telling of stories. I referred earlier to the work of Shaw, in my chapter on methodology, and the notion that stories are formed and exist beyond the human domain. They hold, in codified form, much of what is already live and urgent in the world, which, in the context of the work in hand, is present also in the natal encounter. Within indigenous reality, subjectification occurs within a storied life where the whole world is at play, both the human and the more-than-human. The kind of educational encounter of which I write is one in which the ordinary is sacralised, the flatness of homogeneity is broken open and the student, as subject, rises into the world in sharp relief, yet still in relationship with others. I want to emphasise that such encounters can occur out of the mediocrity of a reductionist educational process, or breakthrough the banal attempts to standardise experience. To be aware of story as live and present (rather than as dead and ancient) is to know that the small exchanges of teacher and student can be elevated into a broader, enduring encountered life that renews a sense of place and a world that is sufficient enough to find as home. The reference to story can invite grandiosity, suggesting that it applies to the extraordinary, but I like very much how Shaw comes to a more earthy perspective on this matter,

I want to circle back a moment. I'm chewing on this emphasis on out-of-the-ordinary and I have to admit something. Stories are never about the day that was just like the last, they are about the day when something happened. Reality got loosened, boundaries transgressed, betrayals experienced, you entered the arena of the unsteady and occulted. The sun tipped, of a moment, into pitch-black night. Into the nettles you fell. So I'm coming around to this slant of the extraordinary this tilt into 'sacred space' as they used to call it.

(Shaw, 2020, p. 269)

I see in this a lyrical way of speaking of the natal moment, the beautiful risk of education, when subjectification brings about an entry to the world in which there is agency, and into a world full of such agencies held by its stories. It is also a moment where the familiar idea of linear time becomes upturned and that it is arguably more useful to think of kiaros, the critical or opportune moment. Stories are abundant with tales of how such moments occur, providing key inflection points for the individual and I would suggest that this is an additional important quality in the educational encounter. In fact I might be bold enough to claim that encounters are always storied, that storied experiences are always encounters and that education located in place gives rise to the possibilities for this to occur.

Another feature of understanding story in relation to the educational encounter is in the relationship between tales and truth. Story is a way in which the truth might be told crooked, or, as Arendt once suggested: 'It is true that storytelling reveals meaning without committing the error of defining it, that it brings about consent and reconciliation with things as they really are' (Arendt, 1955, p. 105). Certainly in my experience of exploring story as place-orientated, the theme of liminality propels the actors in to initiatory, epiphany episodes in which calls the individuals called to exist in the world anew, in some way differently than before. These are episodes, often compelling because of our not understanding the destination, or the extent of the challenge of what is being asked of us, or how we might free ourselves of a predicament where we risk a loss of faith in our capacity to exist in the world. The choice to share my experience of an encountered education is a locational one not only in the sense that it takes place in a specific farm in East Anglia, but that it is nested within the story of the experience. It would not be possible, necessary or appropriate to create a tale otherwise, it would be simply fiction. The education encounter is alive through the combined expression of place and the student-teacher relationship which is also held in the storying of the experience. The interconnectedness of encounter is paralleled in the nature of its telling. To tell and be told such stories is to let the tale have its way with us, have it wreaked a little havoc in our lives, lets loose a wildness that comes at us from the margins, so that we might have to choose again how to exist in a particular place, with others. This is in most respects the kind of education that I have in mind, one in which the encounter might conjure a moment, or event, in which the student find themselves at a loss, on the one hand, but with the possibility of 'finding their face' and turning again to the call of the world. Finally, I am suggesting that an education, founded in place, can be storied in such a way that location finds its way into the imagination of the reader or listener. By doing so the educational impact gives a particular weight to the idea of a life beyond arrival, and the twin features of sustainability and renewal, themes discussed in my later chapters.

Summary

I have been gradually opening up the discussion in this chapter to ideas that come from beyond what might be familiar discourses about education. I have set out initially into the realm of liminality, intending to disturb the book narrative enough with alternative and perhaps marginal, or unexpected material by which new possibilities for envisioning how education might be understood. I have done so because questions of existence, and specifically, subjectification, has tended to treat the world in terms of the sociological and political, and my intention, particularly in this chapter, has been to consider the ecological aspects. I have set out to establish the importance of place, with the explicit understanding that this is conceptualised beyond a purely physical definition and includes a dynamic, phenomenological experience that incorporates the historic-ancestral and more-than-human impact of place. As I have explored this domain, I think it becomes almost impossible to investigate such an approach to education, without recognising the importance of myth and storytelling. The contemporary account of Bhutan is an example – a story – of how the land and the culture that comes from such a place, is embedded in the educational encounter. Furthermore, that this is an education that beckons both teacher and student to return, honour and renew not only their existence, in relationship to the other, but to the land itself. It is by opening up education to the liminal experience – not reducing it – that education purpose might more properly be informed by, and serve, soil, soul and society.

Note

1 In defining how the term indigenous is being used in the context of the study, I am keenly aware of the political implications of drawing on the term and the potential danger of appropriation of traditional cultural ideas, language and practices into the study. I am also mindful that, similarly with the theme of gender, in the interest of coherence, I have chosen to resist developing a wider discussion on the indigenous theme that might shift the specific focus on what is essentially an educational study.

References

Abram, D. (2017) The Spell of the Sensuous: Perception and Language in the More-Than-Human World, New York: Vintage Books.
Angyal, A. (1941) Foundations for a Science of Personality, New York: Commonwealth Fund.
Arendt, H. (1954) Between Past and Future, London: Faber and Faber.
Arendt, H. (1955) Men in Dark Times, New York: Harcourt, Brace & World.

Arendt, H. (1994) Understanding and Politics: The Difficulties of Understanding, in Kohn, J., ed., Essays in Understanding 1930 1954, New York: Harcourt, Brace and Company, pp. 307–327.

Barrow, G. (2014) Whatever! The Wonderful Possibilities of Adolescence, Transactional Analysis Journal, Vol. 44, No. 2, pp. 167–174. DOI: 10.1177/0362153714543077

Barrow, G. (2020) Experiencing Liminality: An Educational Perspective, Transactional Analysis Journal, Vol. 50, No. 1. DOI: 10.1080/03621537.2019.1690240

Barrow, G. and Newton, T. (2015) Educational Transactional Analysis: An International Guide to Theory and Practice, London: Routledge.

Biesta, G.J.J. (2017) The Rediscovery of Teaching, London: Routledge.

Cajete, G. (1994) Look to the Mountain: An Ecology of Indigenous Education, Colorado: Kivaki Press.

Conroy, J.C. (2004) Betwixt & Between: The Liminal Imagination, Education and Democracy, New York: Peter Lang.

Evans, G. (2013) Pattern under the Plough: Aspects of the Folk Life of East Anglia, Dorset: Little Toller Books.

Gruenewald, D.A. (2003) The Best of Both Worlds: A Critical Pedagogy of Place, Educational Researcher, Vol. 32, No. 4, pp. 3–12.

Kane, S. (1998) Wisdom of the Mythtellers, Ontario: Broadview Press.

Le Grange, L. (2018) The Notion of Ubuntu and the (Post) Humanist Condition, in Petrovic, J.E., Mitchell, R.M., eds., Indigenous Philosophies of Education Around the World, Oxford: Routledge.

Mitchell, J. and Gyeltshen, Y. (2019) Lhomon Education: Teaching for Well-Being in Bhutan, in Miller, J.P., Nigh, K., Binder, M.J., Novak, B., Crowel, S., eds., International Handbook of Holistic Education, London: Routledge.

Noddings, N. and Shore, P. (1984) Awakening the Inner Eye: Intuition and Education, New York: Teachers College Press.

Orr, D. (1991) Ecological Literacy: Education and the Transition to a Postmodern World, New York: SUNY.

Ramose, M.B. (2009) Ecology through Ubuntu, in Murove, M.F., ed., African Ethics: An Anthology of Comparative and Applied Ethics, Pietermaritzburg: University of KwaZulu-Natal Press, pp. 308–314.

Relph, E. (1976) Place and Placelessness, London: SAGE.

Rinpoche, D.K. (2021) retrieved from ski.bt/the-lhomon-society/on 5 May, 2021.

Sahlberg, P. (2012) Finish Lessons: What Can the World Learn from Educational Change in Finland? London: Teachers College Press.

Shaw, M. (2011) A Branch from the Lightning Tree: Ecstatic Myth and the Grace in Wildness, Oregon: White Cloud Press.

Shaw, M. (2017) Scatterlings: Getting Claimed in the Age of Amnesia, Oregon: White Cloud Press.

Shaw, M. (2020) All Those Barbarians, Devon: Cista Mystica Press.

Turner, V.W. (1969) The Ritual Process, London: Penguin.

van Gennep, A. (1909) Les rites de passage, Paris: Emile Nourry.

Wattchow, B. and Brown, M. (2011) Pedagogy of Place: Outdoor Education for a Changing World. Monash: Monash University Press.

Chapter 5

The act of teaching, 'grown-up-ness' and eldership in the educational encounter

To Whom Does the Student Arrive?

Departure

Today, I went to the abattoir. I delivered sheep and goats for slaughter. It's an infrequent trip which also involves taking pigs and cattle. The journey always starts before dawn and I load up the stock either in the coldest dark, or on the brink of sunrise. The clatter of hooves on the metal ramp of the trailer always judders me awake to the fact of what we embark on; these beasts and I. By the time, I arrive at the lairage I am alert to the task, the bright strip lights of the depot bring me to account and within half an hour I am off home again, empty trailer rattling behind in the breaking day. Today, I intentionally took the concept of departure to the slaughterhouse with a view to education. Despite any apparent incongruence, I have found the juxtaposition instructive; its discomfort has provoked an insight that I have resisted, and noticed, seems overlooked in educational discourse. It concerns the departure of the student and the end of the teacher-student dynamic. What happens at the end of education? Indeed, is there such a destination? What remains of the relationship?

The etymology of 'departure' combines notions of separation, figurative and literal death, and a reference to 'granting a share', all of which resonate with me as I wait my turn in the queue. Whilst much has been written on the symbolism of birth and its connection with education, I have not come across a similar enthusiasm or interest in considering how the educational endeavour ends, and I am curious as to what that might reveal. Teachers leave, students move on, course programmes complete, groups finish; but does education 'die', and if not, what might that mean for it existentially?

Back at the abattoir, and I am keenly aware of two competing themes; responsibility and performance. This is one of those times when farmers

DOI: 10.4324/9781003407751-6

all take stock of their beasts. I have lived with these sheep and goats for all of their lives. For some, I brought them out into the world with my own hands, slippery with them; I witnessed their arrival. The older stock will have grown up with me across the seasons and for these, there is a weightier parting. As they trot off into the lairage, the waiting farmers, staff and duty vet watch the animals find their way to the pens. Sharp-eyed and officious, the vet assesses for correct tagging, good condition and spirit, passing comment to staff. On rare occasions, a question is raised about the gait of an individual animal, or missing ear tag, or errors in the paperwork. But most importantly, I listen out for any remark about the nature of the beast, good or otherwise. The waiting stockmen who lean over the barrier all know to keep their counsel, but each of us eyes up this finished stock; there's pride and shame wrapped up in this last catwalk.

I am often asked about this process, this final journey by other, non-farming folk. They wonder if the animals can sense what is happening, whether I feel loss, or numbness. (In my experience, the animals are indeed vigilant, not through fear of death, but because they are all reluctant travellers. And yes, occasionally I do feel the loss of a particular animal, a devoted mother, a characterful creature. I have never felt numb.) What I feel most is a peak in my responsibility. For all their lives, I have met them, at least twice daily, observed their growth, checked their feed, tended to ailments and worried away about weather and pasture. I have spent hours working around them, talking with them, planning their movement from field to field. There's an intimacy built up in these exchanges and a knowing of each other. When I set the date for the abattoir, I prepare for their leaving; the clearing of the trailer, last reckoning up of condition and maybe a last-minute change of mind as to which one goes, this time.

I had never really felt responsible for animals until we moved to Suffolk. We may have had an occasional pet, but the notion that animals truly warranted any significant responsibility was a peculiar notion. I could not understand the grief experienced when owners talked of the passing of a dog, or cat. As a vegetarian for some 20 years, I had made decisions so that animals did not feature in my life and I neither felt responsible nor especially caring towards them. Here though, in the midst of raising stock that all changed. David's presence gradually opened for me a new way of being in the world and one in which my relationship to other, non-human, sentient life was re-envisaged. It was through watching him walk around stock, hearing his soft murmuring or warning growls, his sense of duty towards their existence, that I chose to find my own way back to where I too had come from. This was a visceral experience of renewal, and death, by implication, accompanies the cycle. I only begin to realise that 'birth-only' cannot be sustainable, because the land must be replenished through such entropy.

After the incident with the newborn calf, discussed in my earlier piece, David and I embarked on an informal apprenticeship. For over a year, he and I would meet most days and he would teach me. I was taught how to lamb, operate a tractor, gather in livestock, manage the land and work in alignment with seasons. He introduced me to a shepherd who taught me how to train a sheepdog and helped me take the first steps in establishing a small pedigree herd of his beloved Red Poll cattle. Due to David's own long service, much of what he taught me came out of a pre-agricultural business culture, reflecting a strongly traditional approach to farming. Not only was his interruption of my life most unexpected, but also the direction in which I travelled with him was contrary to both my own inclinations and that of time and place. It should have been, in looking back, an entirely disorientating experience, and yet it became a process of 'coming home'. Several times I would catch myself sensing that this was how I was meant to be. That education might not be drawn as a line, but as an arc that eventually curves back on itself.

There is a tension I see in the notion of linking education with freedom. It is a common theme in educational discourse and one over which it is easy to stumble, like hard clods of turf in an apparently level meadow. I am struck by how education is promoted as a way in which the student is emancipated – for example from poverty, trauma, social oppression – and by doing so, somehow ransacks the place out of which the student arises. I remember visiting schools in Bhutan, in the capital, Thimpu, where I had been interested in hearing the ambitions of students. Most reported that they hoped to be engineers, doctors and pilots. They demonstrated such bright intelligence and capability that I had no doubt that they could achieve such qualification. The dilemma, however, is that Bhutan is one of the tiniest nations on earth; it has four airplanes and a handful of hospitals. It simply does not require hundreds of pilots and doctors. Students spoke of how they would leave for Canada, Indonesia, Europe in order to fulfil their ambitions. Educational freedom here equated with abandoning the land out of which the children were born. A similar theme emerged at a school in north-west England where a head teacher was bemoaning the struggle with engaging parents. He spoke of his hope that education provided opportunities by which students might see the world, escape the cycle of unemployment and avoid a life on benefits. The town had once been a productive industrial community, at the heart of the co-operative movement, but is now regarded as 'on its knees'. I spoke of the Pied Piper, the folktale character who stole away children from the townspeople, entranced by his music, led to distant mountains never to be seen again. Education is a plundering expedition, robbing a land sufficient enough to bear the future but not be renewed by it.

David's tutelage was generous. He bought me a secondhand tractor, shared the costs of the first breeding cows and frequently left small gifts for the children. When asked in the village how I was finding my elderly neighbour, I would tell people of his kindnesses. So I was surprised to learn that he had had a reputation as a mean-spirited and terrifically hard boss to work for in the past. I knew that his own family had left the county as soon they were able, despairing at the difficulties of making a living as untenanted agricultural workers. I gradually realised that in some way, through our educational encounter, David was engaging with a second chance at making the world his home. Despite these contrary impressions, I continued to enjoy the gifting of this educational endeavour. Not until almost two years passed did I begin to appreciate that there was another layer to this teacher-student dynamic.

For health reasons, David had been unable to drive a car which places particular limits on the elderly in rural communities. It caught my attention one day when I saw a car parked outside David's house. When asked, he explained that recent medical checks had shown an improvement in his health and that the doctor had said that he could now resume driving. He was clearly pleased, but not as surprised as the doctors had been at his improvement. David declared to me that his stable health was due to a single factor; the revival of his farm. He had not imagined that he would see cattle grazing in the fields, or 'draw' down lambs again. Watching the pasture cut in the summer heat had been beyond his dreams. Most importantly, he had given up on the possibility that he would ever be able to teach someone. My arrival as student had, in his opinion, given him, literally, the gift of a life he would not otherwise have had. This educational life had caught him also. Occasionally he would refer to me explicitly as a best possible student, someone with whom he could be at his very best as teacher, and I know what he meant in terms of being compelled to be alive through teaching. Teaching is not an act of altruism, or rather, if it becomes so, there's need for caution. Over investment by teachers in their students' ambitions is a dangerous folly, leading to an unhealthy symbiosis, disappointment, resentments and untimely ruptures. Recognising that there is something of my own teacherly desire to thrive in the act of teaching is, for me, both necessary and natural in this kind of education. David's acknowledgement that he was a teacher, in part because of my arrival into his life, did not minimise or reduce his agency but affirmed it. In doing so, there was not only the recognition of his physical frailty, but also an admission of the fleeting nature of the state of 'grown-up-ness' held by the teacher; it cannot be assumed or relied upon, it is earned and cultivated.

For a further year or so, David and I continued the teaching-and-taught-by relationship. At one point, as his health deteriorated again, he asked if I might brief him at the end of each day to tell me what had been done, as opposed to him coming over to take part. I was set out into farming, not adrift, but in view of the shore. It was at this time that the possibility of my family owning our own farm arose. An elderly couple who had allowed us to graze the sheep approached us. They had (again) been watching us for some months as we raised the stock, and they had wanted, as far as possible, to choose their successor. Their smallholding had long since run to ruin and, as land can, had turned their home into a prison, with the soil gradually reclaiming itself. When I let David know that moving to a new farm was being planned, he was delighted at the news. My journal records,

> When I told David that we were definitely going his first response was typical 'Well done! You're ready – man enough for the job. There's nothing more I can tell you. When I said how sad I would be, he said, 'Well, of course we'll be sad – I'm not sure what I'll do without you here. But you can't run your life on that situation – I'm living day to day'.

As I write these words again, I can feel my chest heave because I know what follows, and at some level, I knew it at the time also. We planned to move to the new farm on a Friday and on the Thursday, David died.

> And as if by some divine, scripted intervention, David died on this day, just before we opened a new page. As I suspect, we had given him a handful of years to have a second chance, and so he affirmed us in our new direction and then waved goodbye.

He died at home, overlooking his farm, his deepest desire accomplished and his greatest fear, that of dying in a distant hospital ward, avoided. When the doctor, who knew him well, arrived, he remarked that this man had 'stolen' four years of life. And I knew truly where he had stowed them for safe-keeping.

That following day, as I stood atop the new farm, taking in the dereliction, the ruined outbuildings, the unfenced meadows and knowing the sheer hard work that lay ahead, I was overwhelmed. Raw with the sadness at the death of my teacher, I worried myself sick at the enormity of it all. And yet, there was audacity in this moment too. I had only been able to imagine taking on this challenge by choosing to exist in such a way. That the origins of a desire to make this place a home lay in an educational encounter where the soil had mattered, and relationship meant giving up something that had once been everything. And this is what teachers do, and it's what education is for. To adapt Gibran's (2014) expression,

> Your students are not your students.
> They are the sons and daughters of Life's longing for itself;
> They come through you but not from you,
> And though they are with you yet they belong not to you...
> For life goes not backwards, nor tarries with yesterday.

That phrase, again, – Life's longing for itself – is at the heart of educational purpose. This is what the teacher creates the conditions for, not so much the student themselves, but the expression of life which they bring, no matter how camouflaged it may have become. The irony of recognising the significance of physis, the compelling desire to be alive, in this piece about death and departure, is not lost on me. In fact this is the point; that the role of the teacher is inextricably linked to physis. In a second reference to Gibran, if the students are the arrows, then the teacher is the bow from which they are sent forth,

> For even as He loves the arrow that flies, so He loves also the bow that is stable. (ibid)

I had been in flight as I arrived at the dilapidated smallholding and my 'bow', David had been stable enough in holding the tentative place out of which I might choose to fly, not knowing, or eventually him not seeing, where I might 'land'. By definition all teachers must depart, it is in the very nature of the task. There are matters of responsibility and performance in the leaving, but there's witness too, and presence. Teacher rooted in the place out of which the educational moment arises, and with a willingness for the student to create, out of freedom, the way in which their own life's longing for itself renews again the world, after which point departure.

This final phrase, describing the disappearance of the teacher, is somewhat misleading. In the literal sense of the working relationship, teachers do depart, take leave of the life of the student. However, I am interested in the phenomenon by which teachers continue to show up, sometimes unexpectedly, in our lives. I am intrigued by a very personal observation. David died in 2009 and since then, on our new farm, we have had countless visitors, young and old, who ask all sorts of questions. A recurring series of questions is how did we learn how to do things? Did we Google it? Was there a book? Did I do a course? I can only reply by telling the story of David, and as I do so, the educational purpose comes alive again, not just at the level of character and event, but also as a story about education, of the love for teaching and the desire to be taught by. The tale invariably moves people and I know that this is partly about the beautiful serendipity of David's passing, but it is also because it affirms a different narrative about teachers, of being taught by, and the nature of education.

A final observation is that each time I share the account I am reminded of a conversation I had with David a few months before his death. I had been attending a professional conference in South Africa where people had been curious about my new life as a farmer. As always, I told them of my apprenticeship and the importance of David as a teacher. I shared back to him their respect and interest they had for our partnership. David was struck at how people he would never know, in such distant parts of the world were impacted by his work. It was almost too difficult for him to accept, and he would turn the conversation back to whatever farm tasks were in hand. He saw himself as uneducated with no time for 'that college bunkum' and that besides, he didn't know anything of these faraway places and could not place himself in such a foreign context. Nevertheless, the educational impact of our joint process has extended beyond his death and beyond the boundaries of its East Anglian landscape, and I am often moved when I reconnect to the story; I suppose it is a way of re-framing the notion of life after death. Like mortar in a mosaic, the teacher occupies the spaces in-between where life's longing in the student, the fragments of coloured glass, might come shining through. The teacher is there, whether they ask to be, or not, and it is how they carry themselves that might matter most in the reconciliation of the student with soil, soul and society.

Introduction

In this chapter, I will be exploring how I conceptualise the role of the teacher in an alternative vision of education. If the first chapter is understood as being about arrival, and the previous chapter as being concerned with the liminal, then this chapter might be described as focused on the relational. I should point out at this early point that I am not referring to the 'relational' in psychological or systemic terms. My intention is to maintain the existential frame of reference that I have been pursuing throughout, and so I am interested in the relational dynamic in quite a distinctive way. I want to pay attention to the matter of to whom does the student arrive, or more specifically, with whom does the student's experience of subjectification occur? I regard this approach to the relational aspect as an existential question, rather than one of educational psychology or organisational effectiveness. So, in response to the considerations about the 'who' of the teacher, I am going to be drawing on a range of ideas, by which I mean that my understanding of the role of the teacher is understood in the context of place, as described in the previous chapter, and is centred on the event of the student's experience of subjectification which I presented in the first chapter. I am less interested with matters of teacher identity or personal vocation, both of which are worthwhile themes in themselves, but as I hope will become clearer are not central to my argument.

To open this chapter, I will be returning to the work of Biesta and in particular his more recent writings on the role of the teacher, the appeal to reclaim, or re-discover teaching and the notion of 'grown-up-ness' (Biesta, 2017). These discussions lead into a reflection on the theme of authority and its relation to freedom in the educational task, themes which I suggest are especially important to an integrating, connective vision of education. In keeping with the spirit of the previous chapter, I will turn to existing material that further illustrate the ideas that relate to the role of teacher and the act of teaching. To this end, I will introduce the concept of elderhood as a complementary aspect that offers an elaboration of grown-up-ness. Eldership literature is rich with insights into the relational domain (McNally, 2009), as well as the function and role of the elder, much of which is pertinent to my perspective on the teacher.

Having explored an understanding of the role of the teacher, I next move into a discussion of what I regard as key aspects of teaching that come from how I conceptualise the teacher. These refer to ideas that I think are helpful to have in mind when framing what happens, or are 'alive' in the relational domain between the student and teacher. Biesta offers the notion of dissensus (2017), which I find to be a useful way of making sense of the quality of unexpectedness that accompanies the experience of encounter. Connected to this is the tendency for 'passibility' – the capacity to feel, or be impacted by that of others – and I see this an interesting dimension, which counters the contemporary vogue for constructivism but chimes with my interest in how place, for instance, 'has its way' with human relationship, whether it is accounted for or not. If dissensus illuminates what occurs in the relational space between student and teacher, and passibility refers to the capacity of the student to be impacted, my discussion then turns more directly to the teacher. I offer a paradoxical position that captures the essence of how I see the intention of the teacher. On the one hand, I suggest that the teacher is a witness to the student's subjectification and that this is fundamental to the experience. Although this might suggest a passivity on behalf of the teacher, I will argue that to witness requires a particular intention which has an affirmative quality. On the other hand, in addition to witnessing, I will introduce the idea that a teacher offers direction to the attention of the student, that this is at the heart of the teacherly gesture (van Manen, 2015), and implies action on behalf of the teacher. This idea of paying attention to, and directing the student's attention towards the possibility of subjectification, in the context of place, is arguably both the hope of the teacher and the aim of an education orientated towards soil, soul and society. As I close the chapter with this notion of directing attention, the phenomenon of parallel process re-surfaces as my writing itself begins a shift in direction. I begin to point towards the purpose of this book as an 'educational object' and pre-empt my final chapter where the focus is on the extent to which it might direct the attention of the education community.

Introducing the Teacher

My intention throughout this chapter is to consider the question of how the teacher might best 'hold' themselves in the course of the kind of educational encounter I am developing. I emphasise that I am referring to the position of the teacher, as opposed to the generic 'educator', or 'facilitator of learning'. I will not only say some more about what I mean by the teacher shortly, but I also want to emphasise that, more specifically, I am interested in exploring the presence of the teacher, which in many respects is another way of framing the question about 'holding' the role of teacher. Teacher presence is perhaps an overlooked feature in teacher education even though it is arguably what many students recall most when reflecting on their experience of being taught. To pay attention to presence is to acknowledge the importance of someone in particular within the relational dynamic, and that this also refers to an energetic quality; this is not about the behavioural techniques employed by teachers. I am meaning that there is an attitudinal position that lends itself to how the teacher 'occurs' to the student which in turn gives rise to the experience, or event, of subjectification.

In their explorative paper, Rodgers and Raider-Roth (2006) describe the idea of teacher presence, suggesting that this is at the heart of how students are most impacted in education. Their discussion takes the matter closer to the work of educationalists such as Palmer (1990) and the observation that teachers teach out of 'who' they are. This attention to the 'personhood' or identity of the teacher is indeed an interesting theme, but not one that I wish to pursue here as it tends to look towards the territory of process, practice and technique, as well as identity. Instead I want to draw on Rodgers and Raider-Roth's observations about the notion of presence, and again, whilst their purpose is to investigate the impact of teacher presence on learning, as opposed to the relational in existential terms, nevertheless they describe the general field of experience that serves to introduce my own conceptualisation of the teacher. Of further relevance is that the authors regard the importance of teacher presence as being necessary, especially where education diminishes the uniqueness of the teacher. My previous critique of process-orientated education, and in particular the kind of education policy characterised by the global education reform movement (GERM), is intended to standardise education and by implication make it a homogenous process. By definition, the idea that individual teachers – or students – might appear as in any way remarkable is counterproductive. To even consider teacher presence as a legitimate factor, let alone seek to accentuate its impact might be considered subversive. Rodgers and Raider-Roth recognise the pernicious affect; 'When a teacher acts solely from an artificially constructed notion of who she should be, she becomes remote from herself and presence becomes difficult. There is a disconnection, a disintegration of self, that precludes bringing focused attention to bear', and they continue by focusing on the importance of integrity in establishing presence, 'Integration, wholeness, reliability and roundedness in a persona all speak to what it required for a teacher to able to trust herself and the actions which are an extension of that self' (Rodgers and Raider-Roth, 2006, p. 272). I have some further reservations about the use of the word 'self', because it can lead into a different discussion about identity and the question of 'who' am I?', which for my purposes is distinct from the question of 'how do I exist?' What I do find useful here is a recognition that in this approach to education there is limited capacity for the teacher to even ask, let alone address, the question of how to exist in relation to the student and place.

In touching on the theme of presence, I am aware that there is a delicate balance between describing what a teacher might do, from what I am more interested in, which is how the teacher might exist in relation to the student. I am attempting to describe the energetic quality of experience when in the presence of a teacher, which is different from describing the energetic impact of the teacher, which can imply and give rise to an intentional outcome. I acknowledge that this is a subtle dimension in the kind of education I am presenting and is perhaps the most nuanced concept of the vision I am developing. Whilst the construct of student subjectification might be understood as arrival, and that 'placeness' can have solidity to it, the notion of teacher presence is even more elusive and can be misunderstood in terms of how the teacher motivates the student to complete a process, or achieve an outcome. In addition to Palmer, other educationalists have recognised the importance of presence, or something closely associated with it, for example, Noddings (2005) and van Manen (2015); however, the tendency is that these accounts are in the context of the teacher having some kind of pedagogic objective. Instead, I am talking of a quality in the teacher's presence which is such that the student's capacity to be open to the possibility of subjectification might arise.

In some respects though I am getting ahead of myself and it might be useful to return to the understanding of my use of the term 'teacher'. In doing so, I am particularly interested in the work of Biesta (2017) in which he offers an exploration that distinguishes the teacher, and teaching, from 'learner' and 'learning'. Referring to Komisar (1968), Biesta outlines three levels in which teaching might be understood; as an occupation, an enterprise and as an act, and for the purposes of my work, I am most interested in this third possibility, that of the act of teaching,

> When a question has to do with what act is being done, then an answer in terms of 'teaching' is evasive. But when the question asks how the act fits in, asks after the manner of the doing, then 'teaching' is a proper answer.
>
> (Komisar, 1968, p. 175, author's emphasis)

I will be turning to aspects of the 'how', and the 'manner', of teaching later in this chapter, but for now, I want to draw out the feature of specificity in Komisar's description of the act. In other words, the act of the teacher is different from what could be regarded as general actions associated with teaching as enterprise or occupation, for example in terms of planning, assessment or student management. I am interested in regarding teaching as an act relating to a discriminatory intention on behalf of the teacher, which is revealed in its manner. This somewhat abstract explanation leads to a more elaborated understanding of what it is to teach, a theme that Biesta explores in his argument for the re-discovery of teaching. The act of teaching opens up the possibility of an educational encounter in which the event of student subjectification might arise. In such an encounter,

> ...is captured the idea that our existence as subject is precisely not in our hands, is not generated from the inside out, so to speak, but emerges in response to an address, in response to an experience of being addressed or being spoken to by what or who is other.
>
> (Biesta, 2017, p. 34)

From this, we might conclude that the addressive is one of the qualities associated within the manner of the teaching act and indicates the kind of presence to whom the student experiences themselves as a subject of their own existence. Questions then occur which include how does the teacher hold this quality? What is asked of the presence of the teacher in order that such an address might be offered? In response to these questions, I want to introduce the notion of 'grown-up-ness' which Biesta (2017) regards as a condition of the teacher. Suggesting that this term describes not a developmental stage, but a particular '"quality" or way of existing':

> What distinguishes a grown-up way of existing from a non-grown-up way is that the grown-up way acknowledges the alterity and integrity of what and who is other, whereas in the non-grown-up way this is not 'on the radar'. The grown-up way acknowledges, in other words, that the world 'out there' is indeed 'out there', and is neither a world of our own making

nor a world that is just at our disposal, that is a world with which we can do whatever we want or fancy.

And, in describing how the teacher might hold themselves, Biesta makes explicit that this relational stance extends beyond the social dynamic with the student:

'The world' here refers both to the natural and to the social world, both to the world of things and to the world of beings. It refers, more concretely, both to our planet and everything on it, and to the other human beings we encounter on this planet.

Finally, and in line with the contemporary eco-philosophical material of the previous chapter, Biesta also recognises that this 'concrete' world – or, as I have referred to earlier, the 'Lifeworld' – exists independent of whether, or not, the individual acknowledges it phenomenologically,

To acknowledge the alterity and integrity of this world is not to be understood as an act of generosity on my side to let what and who is other exist. It is in other words not a decision to let the world exist or not. It is rather my decision to give the alterity and integrity of the world a place in my life – or not, of course.

(Biesta, 2017, p. 8)

There is something evoked in this description of grown-up-ness that I experienced in the relationship with David, the teacher-farmer in the preceding vocative text, and which I have written about elsewhere from my own practice (Barrow, 2018). As Biesta makes clear, the term does not refer to an accomplished outcome of teacher training, or professional development; it describes a state of existence in relationship, a way of holding oneself. Consequently I am not concerned here with the task of explaining the steps by which a teacher 'achieves' the objective of grown-up-ness, but instead my interest is in elaborating the features and qualities associated with this way of being in relationship with the student, and with place. I want to draw out an aspect of Biesta's suggestion that I think is especially relevant which is the 'otherness' of the world. I mean by this that the event of subjectification can bring about an abrupt, or rude awakening, for the student, in that the 'world out there' is often not simply different from that which is anticipated, but also frequently antagonistic, or confronting, of how it has been hitherto understood. In my own account in the vocative passages, I have wanted to capture something of what might be even termed a hostile quality of the confrontation. The resistance to ensuring that the calf is properly fed, the fear and repulsion at the prospect of getting close to the cow in order to collect milk, indicate both the nature of the student's dilemma and the intensity of the experience when the world 'shows up' and is quite unlike that which is desired. This mention of desire also echoes a theme of Biesta's work around grown-up-ness in that a dimension of the event of student subjectification involves the individual reconciling (or not) their desire in relation to the world and especially when it is in contra-position to how the world appears before them. The choice for the student is whether they can accept this of the world, as being contingent on the student being part of it – to exist in their own grown-up-ness so to speak. Meanwhile, the tasks of the teacher, as I see it, are twofold; to exist in relation to the student from a state of grown-up-ness, and to cultivate the conditions by which the student experiences the freedom to choose for themselves, in the context of a sense of place. This, at the simplest level, is at the centre of the alternative vision of education presented here.

However, I do not want to over-simplify or minimise the challenges in advocating this educational perspective. What can be seen as a confrontation for the student in experiencing a sense of their existential subjectness can be similarly mirrored in that of the teacher's experience in the context of a product-orientated education system. To be more direct, in an educational culture which is 'encounter-averse' there is arguably a decreased opportunity for the teacher to be understood, or indeed, understand themselves, as capable of the kind of existential interruption that I am presenting here. A consequence is that the idea of 'grown-up-ness' becomes reduced to the more familiar and constricted discussion about how the teacher needs to be 'in authority', a disturbing feature which I see as an increasing threat to promoting the conditions by which encounter might be possible. This tendency, which I regard as a populist appeal to having teachers 'run the classroom', has seen a resurgence in measures by which to re-assert teachers as being in charge, in such a way as to diminish the prospect of grown-up-ness, as I am using the term. These practices include introducing systems where students are instructed as to when and how to raise their hand, precision in asking questions, walk in corridors and standing when teachers enter the room all accentuating a 'command and control' approach which quite literally keeps children in their place. However, these techniques are also designed to ensure that the 'desire' of the teacher goes unchecked. It becomes impossible for the teacher to act in their grown-up-ness and by doing so exercise the distinction between desire and what is desirable. The teacher is in a position whereby they can 'have their own way', whilst the student becomes the object of the teacher's desire. In this instance both student and teacher are caught, existentially, within an infantilised (and infantilising) dynamic. The over-riding premise is that the authority of the teacher becomes unquestionable and is embedded in a culture of systematic control over the movement and speech of the student. I have written elsewhere of the implications of this in terms of limiting the capacity for schools to practice effective pastoral care and, even more worryingly for those interested in freedom and education, advocating a reductionist policy of behaviour management to that of a 'zero tolerance' approach to pupil discipline (Barrow, 2017). Authority on these terms has a perverse appeal in this culture,

> For educators trained outside of this system, this is truly astonishing; for those trained within it, it is just common sense. Who would not want to be able to get kids to do what adults want them to do?
>
> (Barrow, 2017, p. 325)

The problem with entangling authority with control, which has taken hold in some educational debates and practice, and which is commonly associated with more technical models of product-orientated education, is that it has significant implications in promoting an education concerned with freedom. It also distracts from how the teacher might be authoritative, which I suggest, is implied in the idea of grown-up-ness and can too easily be misconstrued as authoritarian. The difference in the two words is significant; to provide authoritativeness is to bring a quality of reliability, trustworthiness and truthfulness to the teacher-student relationship, whereas authoritarian is defined in terms of enforcing strict obedience at the expense of personal freedom. This distinction is, I suggest, valuable in developing further how I am envisaging the role of teacher, and the act of teaching, in an education that pays attention to the soil, soul and society in the educational encounter.

Grown-up-ness and Eldership

In my previous chapter, I offered some illustrations of how place has been honoured in educational work by drawing on examples of what I began to describe as indigenous practices. In this chapter, I will now offer an elaboration of the role of teacher, the quality of teacher presence and the act of teaching, with reference to a similarly indigenous concept of eldership. It is a term that might be less familiar to a secular Western readership, but it is one that I suggest brings valuable insights to how the teacher might hold themselves in respect of the student. Typically the word elder is synonymous with that of an older adult, and indeed, in the States, it is a term of reference for those in 'elder care', whilst for many of us, we will be familiar with the phrase 'respect your elders' to denote behaviour towards older people. In some faith traditions, in particular non-conformist Protestant groups, the role of elder is given to individuals who are regarded as especially venerable or 'weighty' members of the community who maintain spiritual integrity. One of the few secular accounts of eldership can be found in the work of the Adlerian analyst, George Linden (2007) in his account of the ageing process. Whilst

Linden does not define eldership per se, he illuminates the concept through describing how ageing adults might navigate a path that distinguishes between becoming old and existing from a place of eldership.

> Elders can act as if their lives have had purpose and meaning. By so acting, elders can become exemplars and mentors, establish and maintain generational continuity, and create meaning in their lives and the lives of others.
>
> (Linden, 2007, p. 390)

The broader objective of the elder, in Linden's view, is to demonstrate how to exist as a citizen of the universe and contrasts this with how other ways of relating tend towards connection with career, personal accomplishments or status. The emphasis for Linden is that the state of eldership involves taking a position of ambivalence regarding aspects of life to which we might otherwise be firmly attached. As I will shortly suggest in my discussion of teaching as an act, this is a quality that is important to how the teacher presents themselves to the student. Another useful phrase that catches the sense of this lightly held attachment is that of 'creative indifference', a term originating in Gestalt psychoanalysis, and I offer a definition in which I have substituted reference to therapist for that of teacher,

> It is based on the idea that the [teacher] does not have a vested interest in any particular outcome. It is another way of facing the existential uncertainty of the unknown –not a simple task....The [teacher] is willing to accept whatever 'is and becomes'.
>
> (Joyce and Sills, 2009, p. 40)

One of the general themes in Linden's work is that existing as elder requires a particular 'creative indifference' towards the world, in terms described by Biesta earlier in this chapter. In other words, a state of eldership incorporates awareness of both the social and ecological spheres whilst remaining in relation with the arrival of the student.

The term elder is one that has been introduced into discussion of traditional communities as a way in which commentators have sought to understand the function of particular individuals, and a role that is commonly recognised by members of those societies. This concept of what I am referring to as an indigenous perspective on eldership I have found to be a useful resource for expanding the connection with how the teacher holds themselves in relation to the student. McNally (2009), in his account of elders in Native American communities, observes how the state of eldership is associated with an enhanced experience of connection. To be an elder is to be associated by others as inhabiting the good life; 'To live on the land, one must live well on the land, showing...a mastery of right relations with all other persons' (p. 25), which, for the community, includes the natural world. In exploring this tradition of eldership, a series of features can be identified which I think serve the purpose of my discussion on the question to whom does the student appear?

On the basis of my reading of McNally, I identify connections between eldership and the role of the teacher, the act of teaching and the state of grown-up-ness. I suggest that eldership means being less concerned with what needs to be done in practical terms and more interested in acknowledging possibilities for encounter. Whilst matters of curriculum, assessment and managing behaviour, for example, fall within the general remit of any teacher, this is not the territory of eldership. Similarly, whilst teachers often speak of what must be heeded, eldership does not obligate the student, put bluntly, the elder does not have to be listened to. Eldership seeks out and engages in encounters with uncertainty – the liminal space. In such a space competency and performance are less relevant to the teacher than professional wisdom and judgement. Eldership requires an awareness of personal fallibility. To exist as elder is not so much a goal for the teacher, but a possibility to hope for. If it occurs, I suggest that the act of teaching opens up the prospect for the student to encounter themselves as a subject in the world. It is also to caution that if such a way of being in relationship – as elder – becomes an intended outcome of the teacher then, in all likelihood, that possibility vanishes. It is arguably part of the mystery that comes with teaching, the elusive quality of why sometimes teachers touch into the lives of others and how occasionally education becomes remarkable and intimate.

The Act(s) of Teaching

I have introduced the general idea of teacher presence as a way of framing the existential relationship into which the student arrives. I have gone on to suggest that the notions of grown-up-ness, and a traditional concept of eldership, are helpful for elaborating how the teacher exists in relation to the student. In this section, I will consider two ideas – dissensus and passibility – to explain more specifically what I suggest is happening in that relational space, and which accentuate the existential experience of education. I want to emphasise my earlier remarks that I see the relational dimension in this vision of education to be elusive and nuanced. I have found that in this respect, the discussion can have an esoteric, or abstract tendencies, which is perhaps not surprising when exploring existential questions and is arguably where this perspective might contrast most sharply with a technical description of what to do, typical of product-orientated education. I am setting out to make sense of what is essentially mysterious about the educational encounter and to do so whilst being ambivalent in terms of avoiding to 'concretise' how what occurs between teacher and student comes about. Dissensus, I suggest, is an interesting way into understanding the surprise, or the unexpectedness of the encounter, whilst passibility suggests how the encounter is possible on behalf of the student, and it is to each of these ideas that I now turn.

Dissensus and Passibility

I have referred to the idea of arrival at several points, most importantly in relation to the 'arrival' of the student, by which I mean more precisely, the event in which the student experiences themselves as a subject in the world. I want to offer another take on the notion of arrival and in doing so introduce the phenomenon of dissensus. Introduced by Ranciere, in his work on politics and aesthetics (2010), dissensus is described as the appearance of something that could not previously be comprehensible, or conceived, and its occurrence brings new possibilities. Biesta brings this idea into the educational domain, explaining:

> Dissensus is not to be understood as the absence of consensus or as a moment of disagreement or conflict, but as the introduction of what we might call an 'incommensurable element' into an existing state of affairs... Dissensus occurs in education when we approach a child or student as subject precisely when this flies in the face of all available evidence, that is, of everything that can be seen and known. Yet... it is precisely this gesture – a teacherly gesture – that opens up a possibility for the child or student to appear as subject.
>
> (Biesta, 2017, p. 83)

We are arriving at the heart of what I see as the interplay in the existential dynamic among student, teacher, place and, importantly, the educational object, as discussed earlier in my methodological presentation. Aside from the story of my own experience of being taught as a farmer, offered in the vocative text prefacing this chapter, I have also written in an earlier vocative text, Beyond Arrival, giving an account involving a young man who is confronted by his fear of dogs. This unexpected experience leads to an encounter in which something occurs which is both unforeseen and also inconceivable, yet becomes entirely congruent with what is summoned, or called for, so that the student might experience themselves as subject in the world (Barrow, 2014). I want to return again to this encounter as a way of illuminating some of what I am offering conceptually.

In the account, I refer to how the young man, Alex, is terrified by my dog when visiting the farm on school trip. He lies on the floor crying whilst I, his teacher and others go to his aid. There is a moment when I felt disappointed in myself, believing that I made an error of judgement, and intended to send my dog back to the kennel, because it seemed the most obvious option within the parameters of what would be expected or anticipated,

> I was just about to put my sheep dog into its pen when in an unchecked moment I turned and walked toward Alex, my dog at my side, unleashed. In retrospect, I understand this now as a moment of misattunement in which I began to 'mind the gap', a wonderful phrase in Eusden's (2011)

work that I have found perfect for clarifying what sometimes happens if I am not being too careful.

(Barrow, 2014, p. 171)

This decision to stay in this moment is an illustration of how as a teacher I give rise to dissensus; resisting prescribing a certainty that explains or defines the experience of the student. It is the moment whereby acting in such a way, precisely by not taking action, the teacher creates a spaciousness for that which cannot be imagined to occur. There is a paradox here in that ostensibly I, as teacher, appear not to be doing anything, yet in that apparent passivity much becomes possible. In the instance of Alex, he grew increasingly curious about the dogs during his stay.

On the last day of the students' visit to the farm, early in the morning before the day had started, Alex and I walked into the field, and I asked if he would use the dog to move the sheep. With some caution he began to call the dog, moved it around the sheep, and successful had them gathered in the shelter. He declared it the best bit of the trip. I think I was pleased too. We had earlier both stepped into uncertain territory and both revealed something more of ourselves than we had initially known or were prepared to do.

(Barrow, 2014, p. 172)

There was no prior notion that such a task might be possible, or desirable and there could have been a number of ways in which such an opportunity might have been closed down. I suggest that it is a teacherly act to establish the relational conditions by which dissensus might occur.

To regard teaching as dissensus is to leave open the possibility for the unforeseen – not the impossible – but the arrival of what might be pregnant in the relational space and the ecological place. This is what it means to exist as teacher in the liminal, natal realm; expectant, and yet with no particular anticipation for what must follow. (In fact, to envisage the educative act as having any sense by which the student is 'to follow' is inimical to the understanding of kairos, the quality of time associated with the experience of encounter). Biesta gets closer to the mystery of it,

Teaching as dissensus, aimed at grown-up subject-ness is precisely characterised by such an orientation towards the unforeseen, that is, to what is not present, to what can be the object of hope and this requires a faith but can never be a matter of knowledge or certainty.

(Biesta, 2017, p. 84)

That education involves an act of faith is an important tenet in approaching the direction of my work here. When we gather in the education endeavour, teachers and students step into an unknown territory but one which is nevertheless rich with possibility; it is a way in which education contributes to the renewal of the individual, the other and the world itself. I am talking of dissensus here from the teacher's perspective, relating to the spaciousness that is created in the educational encounter and in which the student might choose to exercise freedom. This is not the same as saying that the teacher has a sense of what the student could 'do', but instead, that the teacher has no expectation that the student performs in a specific way and instead pays attention to dissensual possibility. It is as if the entire world awaits, hidden within the educational task when orientated towards soil, soul and society. However, to have faith in the existential possibility of the educational task is just one aspect for hope in this dynamic; it is also necessary to have faith in the student's capacity to 'hear' the call.

At its most straightforward, the term 'passibility' (Roth, 2011) refers to an aptness to feel or to suffer and includes being susceptible to the 'impressions from external agents, capable of being changed'. If I, as teacher, am paying attention to the spaciousness of the educational encounter, then simultaneously, the student experiences a capacity for passibility. In the example of Alex, despite his upset and the recurrence of an earlier incident, he has a capacity to be 'affected' by the world, to experience the impact, or be impressionable to the influence of the external world, and, in this instance, in a most unexpected and uncomfortable way. This capacity, I suggest, has a quality of passivity that might be seen as a counter-point to the possibility of dissensus created by the teacher's ability to not take action. Passibility is then also a key feature in the experience of arrival. To be born into the world involves a heightened sense of being susceptible to the potential of how it occurs to the individual. It – the world – cannot be renewed by the individual if it has not affected the sensibilities of the newcomer, for then any attempt at renewal would be baseless. The nascent event is primed for passibility and again, in relation to Alex, there is an abundance of possibility in how he might experience the impact of the world.

Teacherly Gesture and Gaze

Having introduced the ideas of dissensus and passability to conceptualise the reciprocal predicament of the teacher and student, I want to offer a little more detail about how the teacher shows up in this dynamic, whilst resisting the possibility of them becoming too direct or prescriptive of what the teacher must 'do'. This is more a reflection on how it is for the student to be experienced by the teacher; it is important to remember that in my discussion of the act(s) of teaching, I am referring to teacher presence, the phenomenological state by which the teacher 'interrupts' the world of the student. By means of illustration, the type of teacher act, or teacherly gesture, I am referring to is when, in the story of Alex, I make the decision to

walk towards him with the dog unleashed. It is also there in the earlier vocative text when David, the old farmer, breaks his silence and announces to me
that he can teach me all he knows. In neither instance can these be defined
as an 'intervention' in the sense that they determine what must happen next
or are orientated towards an anticipated outcome. In both encounters, the
student remains free to be taught, or not, in spite of the teacher's capacity to
teach. I want to identify two more aspects in supporting my consideration
of the teacher perspective, the first of which refers to what I am referring to
as the teacherly gesture and the second which is explaining what I mean by
the teacherly gaze.

The idea of teacher gesture can be found in the work of van Manen (2015)
who takes a pragmatic view which is that through particular actions, the
teacher impacts the student in such a way that acknowledges the 'concern
of the inner life', 'senses the meaning of this concern' and 'intuits the ethical limits and possibilities' and then 'acts accordingly'. Whilst this is a little
too prescriptive, or sequential, for my general purpose, what I value in van
Manen's writing is his attention to the phenomenological experience of the
teacher on the student. This forensic account leads into discussing gesture to
create a sense of what van Manen calls 'tact',

> Indeed there is no manual, blueprint or technology to tact. But we can
> say that pedagogical tact (1) manifests itself in everyday life as instant ac-
> tion; (2) forms a way of acting that is first of all dependent on an intuitive
> sensibility and sensitivity - in other words, a feeling-understanding; (3) is
> sensitive to the uniqueness of the child or young person; (4) is sensitive to
> the particularities and context of the situation; and (5) is unique also to the
> personal character of the teacher....
>
> (van Manen, 2015, pp. 78–79)

Again, I have a reservation about the implications of the word pedagogy,
but putting this concern aside, van Manen is capturing some of the qualities
associated with teacher presence, as outlined earlier and the characteristics of
eldership. However, an important difference between van Manen's perspective and the one that I am developing here is the purpose to which such tact
is orientated. For my discussion, the focus is not the developmental progress
of the child (which is, of course, a legitimate concern for many school teachers). To clarify my understanding of the teacherly gesture, I will turn again to
the work of Biesta.

In Biesta's reflection on teaching and artistry (unpublished paper), he offers
an analysis of 'teaching', referring to an Old English word, 'Taecan' carries
such meanings as 'to show', 'to point out', 'to instruct', 'to warn' and 'to persuade'
and goes onto suggest that perhaps then teaching has something to do with
'providing signs', (p. 3). Consequently, an act of the teacher comprises a
gesture that re-directs the student or, more precisely, (re)directs the attention

of the student. Drawing on Benner's (2020) consideration of this kind of gesture, Biesta explains further,

> Whereas Benner approaches teaching in terms of the (re)direction of the student's gaze and thus approaches teaching first and foremost in terms of looking, a slightly broader term that is useful here is that of attention, as one could argue that the basic gesture of teaching is that of trying to (re) direct the attention of the student to something.
>
> (Biesta, unpublished, p. 4)

I will focus on a different view to Biesta's a little later when considering the teacher as witness, but for now, it is this movement of re-direction that is of interest, which as Biesta indicates, might be towards the possible experience of subjectification,

> This 'something' can, of course, be content, or knowledge or some specified task. But teaching can also be about (re)directing the attention of the students to themselves, for example in order to encourage them to pay attention to their own actions or to consider their own complicity in a particular situation.
>
> (Biesta, p. 4)

As a passing observation, in my earlier chapter on methodology, I refer to the three-part dynamic of teacher-student-educational object and referred to how seduction can be an effect of the teacher on the student. It may be useful to bear in mind that this is another way of creating the kind of re-direction of attention by the teacher, in service of dissensus. If I return to the case of Alex, there is a moment, when I walk towards him with the dog unleashed, where there is the possibility of a redirection of the boy's attention. I don't mean simply in the literal sense, but existentially. In other words, by maintaining the presence of myself and the dog, a possibility opens up by which he might choose to exist in relation to the world in a way which need not be fearful, but different. There is an invitational signal from the teacher; 'that this might matter and you can make you own sense of it'. To summarise, I suggest that to re-direct the attention of the student is one example of a teacherly gesture, which, in turn, opens up a field of possibility, or dissensus which is an act of teaching. I will turn now to a related aspect by which the teacher is experienced by the student, which is to consider the gaze of the teacher.

When I refer to the gaze of the teacher, I think it is important to distinguish how I am using the term because it is possible to misunderstand what can be implied when we think about teachers watching students. There is an established body of work that considers the use of the teacher's use of eye contact in relation to student surveillance and behaviour management (see, for example, Yamamoto and Imai-Matsumura, 2013). This research is interested in tracking the duration and movement of how the stare of the teacher influences student outcomes and serves a highly technical perspective on improving teacher performance, none of which is of interest for our purpose here. Instead, my interest in the gaze of the teacher is about how the student is 'held' in the eye of the teacher. The notion of gaze implies an intensity and wonder which, I suggest, is associated with the nascent event of subjectification. I want to introduce another way in which 'arrival' is experienced which is that it is subject to the gaze of the teacher and that this is done on behalf, so to speak, of the world into which the student is arriving.

I appreciate that this is perhaps a very particular way of referring to gaze, particularly as an act, but in considering the phenomenological dimension of my perspective on education, it is useful to have in mind. For instance, prior to breaking his silence, David had neither been absent nor 'doing nothing'; he had been watching me and in doing so held in the present moment what future possibilities might arise. Similarly, I held in my gaze what was occurring not just at the time between myself and Alex, but also the possibilities of what could happen next. More importantly, the student has an awareness that one quality of who they encounter is that they are held by the gaze. (I am reminded here of how a sheep dog 'holds' the sheep through the power of their 'eye'). I will write some more later about what is incorporated in this gaze when I turn to the theme of love in education. For now though, I want to extend the discussion about the gaze of the teacher by introducing the act of witness. We are perhaps familiar with what it is to witness, which can be defined as to 'attest to fact or event', but there is a further etymological connection with the Greek word, martyr, which refers to 'one who bears testimony to faith'. I am interested in this association because of the link with my previous reference to teaching being in part an act of faith. To act as a witness to what occurs for the student is what this act of faith entails for the teacher. For an individual to be witnessed confirms their existence and, in the context of education, is a way in which the teacher 'shows up' in the life of the student, in readiness as witness. I want to introduce a variation for understanding the act of witness which accounts for the existential quality I am speaking of here. 'To witness', in English, suggests an objective stance on behalf of the teacher-as-witness, but I want to offer a potentially more appropriate term – sakshi bhaav – which is a Hindi phrase. Whilst 'sakshi' means 'witness', the full phrase refers to a sacred witnessing of all phenomenon experienced, mindfully, through the senses, including those of the teacher and not solely that of the student. It involves the teacher being on the one hand aware of thoughts, feelings and sensations, but not identifying oneself with them (for more discussion of this idea, see Barrow and Pandya, 2021). This is what I was referring to earlier, in the discussion of eldership, where the teacher might be described as being detached from ego. It is, essentially, the practice of selflessness.

The Lives of Children (Dennison, 1969)

In the following section, I will explore a further example of teaching which illustrates aspects of what I have been so far describing as the acts of the teacher. I am featuring the work of George Dennison in his account published in The Lives of Children (1969). Dennison chronicles his experience of establishing a 'street school' in the Lower East Side area of New York City during the 1960s. The story comes out of an inner city, urban landscape, one quite different than that of my own account in rural East Anglia. Nevertheless, Dennison frequently describes his experience of being in the role of teacher in ways that strongly resonate with how I have been explaining my understanding of the student-teacher dynamic. The small school that Dennison and his colleagues set up might be categorised as typical of the alternative education projects of the that time, some of which, like Dennison's, were influenced by A. S. Neill's experimentation at the Summerhill School. The staff team were motivated in creating a less formal approach to education as a reaction to what they regarded as the brutality and anti-educational public school system. Dennison's criticisms of standardisation, student alienation and objectification reflect much of my own argument presented in the opening rationale, albeit nearly 50 years on. However, my reason for featuring The Lives of Children in this chapter is neither to repeat these criticisms, nor to advocate for the pedagogy developed at the school. My purpose is to focus on the way in which Dennison describes his experience of being a teacher, in relation to the students and the environment in which he was working.

There are several points in Dennison's commentary where he describes in detail the specific circumstances of individual students and the challenges he faced by their intense antagonism to being in school and the prospect of being educated. The students were from a culturally diverse community, in terms of ethnicity, but all of them were from economically and social deprived backgrounds. In many respects, they were quite different from Dennison, who frequently records his own sense of being culturally apart from the students, which heightens the challenge of relationship. Much of what he sets out to teach, in the conventional sense of the term, initially fails to engage students and frequently he shares a sense of futility in making a tangible impact on their learning. However, gradually Dennison begins to recognise the false logic of cause and effect in relation to the educational relationship,

> And here we come to one of the really damaging myths of education, namely, that learning is the result of teaching: that the progress of the child bears a direct relation to methods of instruction and internal relationships of the curriculum. Nothing could be further from the truth. Naturally we want good teachers. Naturally we want a coherent curriculum (we need not impose it in standardised forms). But to cite these as the effective causes of learning is wrong.
>
> (Dennison, 1969, p. 73)

Furthermore, that this 'damaging myth of education' is counter-productive and, in a brief reference to Dewey, Dennison explains,

> The continuum of experience and reality of encounter are destroyed in the public schools (and most private ones) by the very methods which are for the institution itself – the top-down organisation, the regimentation, the faceless encounters, the empty professionalism, and so on.
>
> (ibid, p. 74)

Instead, Dennison attempts to explain what he notices and what might be seen as the beginnings of an existential frame of reference, stating that

> The child is always finding himself (sic), moving toward himself, as it were, in the near distance. The adult is his ally, his model – and his obstacle (for there are natural conflicts, too, and they must be given their due).
>
> (ibid, p. 24)

It is a sentiment found earlier in the account in which he is outlining a series of important understandings about the school, one of which is that education is situated in the real – or material – world. He suggests that a body of knowledge – the educational object, in my terms – does not exist in a vacuum, 'But rather all knowledge is possessed and must be expressed by individuals; that the human voices preserved in books belong to the real features of the world' (ibid, p. 9). After which Dennison points towards what might be associated with the concept of physis and a natural tendency for renewal,

> and that children are so powerfully attracted to this world that the very motion of their curiosity comes through to us as a form of love; that an active moral life cannot be evolved except where people are free to express their feelings and act upon the insights of conscience.
>
> (ibid, p. 9)

There is some difference here in the choice of terminology, but again, I suggest that Dennison is writing out of a similar field as to that of my own work. I will pick up on the reference to love and education later, but for now stay with the focus on the student experience, encounter and subjectification.

Dennison provides examples of his own anecdotal writing in which he offers narratives regarding individual student situations. For example, Kenzo is a nine-year-old boy who puts great effort in presenting as 'self-sufficient hipster' and the appearance of a 'sophisticated fourteen-year-old'. He spends lots of time at the school in squabbles about rules, defying others' efforts to control situations, acting with arrogance in opposition to teachers and frequently ending up in fights with peers. After several months of this, Dennison writes,

> Kenzo is making some kind of breakthrough....today he haggled and haggled about one of the rules and said, at last that he was only nine years old and needed the protection of the rules. It was a really significant kind of self-exposure and was the first genuine exchange he's had with me, speaking directly in his own behalf.
>
> (Dennison, 1969, pp. 48/49)

Kenzo is frequently featured in the reflective passages, along with references to other students and their respective position to the authority of the teacher. I want to emphasise some of what Dennison offers on this theme because it demonstrates what I was previously discussing in relation to the teacher being prepared to open up the spaces in between themselves and the student. In a section addressing the theme of freedom, again in relation to Kenzo, Dennison observes that 'What may not be so obvious is that freedom also allows moral considerations to enter into the life at school' (p. 86), adding that 'right action' cannot be addressed if the student is unable to voice their feelings and be respected for doing so. But this requires a quality of presence in the teacher,

> It is worth mentioning here too, that when children are allowed to work out their ethical problems, adults no longer appear to them as mere figures of authority. They are removed from the central position of actors and become interested observers, in which position they appear as the elders of the community rather than the heads of organisations. Where the pronouncements of authorities are often repugnant and damaging to children, the opinions of elders are just as often respected, and are sometimes eagerly sought. Here again the natural authority of adults is thrown into optimal relations with the needs of children.
>
> (ibid, p. 87)

Despite the opportunity to exercise a different way of being in relationship with students, Dennison finds there is no room for complacency, and that educational encounters are often uncomfortable and unpredictable. Describing his work with Jose, Dennison describes the intense resistance of the student to be taught how to read. However, as the boy's teacher, he confronts this reluctance, 'When I thought the time was ripe, I insisted that we begin our lessons', and in doing so recognises that 'My own demands, then, were an important part of Jose's experience'. Dennison then makes the following observation, which echo both David's exhortation of me to draw milk from the cow, or my walking towards Alex with the dog unleashed,

> They were not simply the demands of a teacher, nor of an adult, but belonged to my own way of caring about Jose. And he sensed this. There was something he prized in the fact that I made demands on him. This became all the more evident once he realised that I wasn't simply processing him... And when he learned that he could refuse – could refuse altogether, could terminate the lesson, could change its direction.... We became collaborators in the business of life.
>
> (Dennison, 1969, pp. 112–113)

I find a significant overlap between how Dennison is describing his reflection on the role of teacher and what I have earlier explained in terms of dissensus and passibility. I also see this in conjunction with the teacher act of re-directing attention, with the possibility that the student might know that they have a choice in how to exist when called by the world through the teacher. Dennison is sensitive to the tension he experiences in the urge to compel the student to attend class. In what I find to be an especially powerful insight into the role of the teacher, and by implication, the state of grown-up-ness, he shares that

> if I had made no demand – had simply waited for him to come to class – I would in some sense have been false to my own motives, my own engagement in the life of the school and the community.
>
> (ibid, p. 113)

Then, brilliantly capturing the essence of what this chapter has been concerned about, Dennison finishes by declaring that if he had not made such a demand,

> In his eyes I would have lost immediacy, would have lost reality, as it were, for I would have seemed more and more just like a teacher. What he prized, after all, was this: that an adult with a life of his own, was willing to teach him.
>
> (ibid, p. 113)

The teacher holding back from directly intervening is a recurring theme in Dennison's approach and one that is increasingly associated with care. At one point, he asks rhetorically of himself, 'But what of my own refusal to intervene?', and 'Did it mean that he didn't care?', answering,

> They knew that I did care, and they knew very accurately (probably better than I) just where my caring ended. My refusal meant the most obvious thing...[that] I was not withholding myself, but was in fact putting myself in relation with something much larger... their independent life in the world...

The effect of this was to locate all questions of ethics and conduct in the experience itself, that is, in the boys themselves, and not in some figure of authority.

(Dennison, 1969, p. 202)

Finally, Dennison comments on the existential challenge that comes when the student must choose how, or whether to discern their desire with what might be desirable,

The further effect of this important shift in responsibility was that each boy was able to experience the necessary relationship between his own excitement and the code of conduct which joined him with others in a social group.

(ibid, p. 202)

Alongside what I see as the rich interplay between Dennison's account and my own description of the role of the teacher, there are also many references to the themes of love and care in his reflections and it is to this that I now turn in bringing the chapter to a close.

Love in Education

Before I begin to conclude this chapter, I will offer a summary of the discussion so far which has been to answer the question; to whom does the student arrive? My emphasis throughout has been to consider the role of the teacher when the education encounter is orientated towards matters of soil, soul and society. I have suggested that most importantly, the teacher exists through a particular presence, or state of existence, which I have connected to the concepts of grown-up-ness and eldership, and that can be described as features of the act of teaching. I have been clear not to suggest that this is in terms of action, by which I mean that the teacher implements an intervention with an intended outcome in mind. Instead, I have explained that the teacherly act is to cultivate the conditions by which dissensus becomes possible, and where the capacity for passibility in view of subjectification is heightened. In support of this, I have introduced the idea of the teacherly gesture, which involves a re-direction of the attention of the student to what might matter, and the gaze of the teacher, which I regard as a particular kind of witnessing, the practice of sakshi bhaav.

The combinations of ideas presented in this chapter have been intended to describe the general experience of what it is to be a teacher, and what teaching means, when incorporated into a vision of education that connects soil, soul and society. It is an attempt to describe what is essentially a state of 'being with' the other, and with what might be possible in the here and now interplay among teacher, student and place. I have suggested that there is a mystery in this which might tolerate only so much analysis before such abstraction begins to limit the understanding of the phenomenological, existential and relational experience of the teacher. In a final attempt to make sense of what it is to be the one to whom the student arrives, I want to turn to the theme of love in education and in doing so intimate the next and final chapter.

Discussions of love in education have tended to focus on either matters of care for children and/or the human potential of the individual student. This is especially reflected in the literature concerned with pastoral care in education and holistic education. When addressed theoretically, the tendency has been to refer to pedagogical love (Maatta and Uusiautti, 2013) or 'educational caritas' (Noddings and Shore, 1984). In these instances, the reference to love is embedded in an idea of education which remains product-orientated, with the teacher positioned as having a loving intention on behalf of the student. Whilst I recognise that this attention to love is well placed and much needed in education, these do not address the role of love in the terms of an existential view. For my purposes, love exists in the gaze and gesture of the teacher for the possibility of what might become. It is a notion of love that is not so much bound up with individual self/selves but understood as a particular kind of social action. In other words, and in the educational context of which I have been writing, the teacher has love for the possibility of renewal that educational encounters bring to the world, ecologically, socially and existentially. The love in education I am referring to is for what might occur in the space among teacher, student and place. Love as social action involves the teacher letting in (or letting go) of something that is beyond their control, and outside of the student's awareness. Love, in education, involves letting loose the impact of place, the movement of physis and the interplay of presence and passibility. There's faith, not certainty, in such a love, and there's hope there too, not for the 'who', but the 'how' the world might be renewed, in its beauty, duality and unpredictability. Fromm (1957) in my view gets close to this understanding of love in writing about the act of giving,

> Giving implies to make the other person a giver also and they both share in the joy of what they have brought to life. In the act of giving, something is born, and both persons involved are grateful for the life that is born for both of them. Specifically with regard to love this means: love is a power which produces love.
>
> (Fromm, 1957, p. 20)

The reciprocal experience that Fromm speaks of lies at the heart of what my work has been moving towards – the circularity of renewal and gifting that becomes possible through the educational encounter. A view of education that looks to possibility, not by framing outcomes, or processes, but by paying attention to what is created out of the present situation, by responding to the call; what matters most, here, now and in relationship? This is perhaps the closest I come to declaring the hope in this view of education and in doing so raise a subsequent and final question: for whom is such a harvest?

References

Barrow, G. (2014) Whatever! The Wonderful Possibilities of Adolescence, Transactional Analysis Journal, Vol. 44, No. 2, pp. 167–174. DOI: 10.1177/0362153714543077

Barrow, G. (2017) The Case for Natality in Pastoral Education and Why It Matters, Pastoral Care in Education, Vol. 35, No. 4, pp. 284–292. DOI: 10.1080/02643944.2017.1350201

Barrow, G. (2018) For Whom Is the Teacher and for What Is the Teaching? An Educational Re-Frame of the Parent Ego State, Transactional Analysis Journal, Vol. 48, No. 4, pp. 322–334. DOI: 10.1080/03621537.2018.1505113

Barrow, G. and Pandya, A. (2021) Beej Raksha: Re-framing Cure in the Sacred Domain, Transactional Analysis Journal, Vol. 51, No. 3, pp. 292–302.

Benner, D. (2020) Umriss der allgemeinen Wissenschaftsdidaktik, Weinheim: Beltz/Juventa.

Biesta, G.J.J. (2017) The Rediscovery of Teaching, London: Routledge.

Dennison, G. (1969) The Lives of Children: The Story of the First Street School, New York: Random House.

Fromm, E. (1957) The Art of Loving, London: Thorsons.

Gibran, K. (2014) The Prophet, London: Oneworld Publications.

Joyce, P. and Sills, C. (2009) Skills in Gestalt Counselling & Psychotherapy (4th Edition),London: SAGE.

Komisar, P. (1968) Teaching: Act and Enterprise, Studies in Philosophy and Education, Vol. 6, No. 2, pp. 168–193.

Linden, G. (2007) An Adlerian View of Aging, The Journal of Individual Psychology, Vol. 63, No. 4, pp. 387–399.

Maatta, K. and Uusiautti, S. (2013) Many Faces of Love, Netherlands: BRILL.

McNally, M.D. (2009) Honoring Elders: Aging, Authority and Ojibwe Religion, New York: Columbia University Press.

Noddings, N. (2005) The Challenge to Care in Schools: An Alternative Approach to Education, New York: Teachers College Press.

Noddings, N. and Shore, P. (1984) Awakening the Inner Eye: Intuition and Education, New York: Teachers College Press.

Palmer, P.J. (1990) The Courage to Teach: Exploring the Inner Landscape of the Teacher's Life, San Francisco: Jossey-Bass Publishers.

Ranciere, J. (2010) On Ignorant Schoolmasters, in Bingham C., Biesta, G.J.J., eds., Jacques Ranciere: Education, Truth, Emancipation, London/New York: Continuum, pp. 1–24.

Rodgers, C.R. and Raider-Roth, M.B. (2006) Presence in Teaching, Teachers and Teaching: Theory and Practice, Vol. 12, No. 3, pp. 265–287.

Roth, W.-M. (2011) Passibility: At the Limits of the Constructivist Metaphor, Dordrecht: Springer.

van Manen, M. (2015) Pedagogical Tact: Knowing What to Do When You Don't Know What to Do, London: Routledge.

Yamamoto, T. and Imai-Matsumura, K. (2013) Teachers' Gaze and Awareness of Students' Behaviour: Using an Eye Tracker, Comprehensive Psychology, Vol. 2. DOI: 10.2466/01.IT.2.6

Implications for an education orientated towards connection with the existential, social and ecological domains

For Whom Is the Harvest?

For Whom is the Harvest?

Last Tuesday was my birthday. In between phone calls wishing me well and relatives coming by, I caught snatches of weather warnings on the radio; the 'Beast from the East' was due to arrive, bringing with it some new kind of meteorological chaos. By Wednesday, our farm was under a few inches of snow, by Thursday, it was a foot deep and the water supplies both outside and inside the house had frozen solid. Blizzards whirled around the house, gusts of wind rushed up our fields dispersing flurries of new snow into high drifts. As the temperature fell to minus six, and that's without calculating the wind chill, my work appointments began to be cancelled and I found myself with a week at home, snowbound. (This piece of writing is not really about the weather.)

Life on a farm is generally good; virtuous, healthy, it involves regular physical exercise and gives plenty of opportunity to be aligned to the turning of the seasons. Then, at times, as at the end of winter, it enters a 'thin time', a liminal period between deep winter and the first edge of spring, where it becomes doubtful if there is sufficient fodder for the animals to seek out until sun, warmth and new grazing return. Occasionally it can slip suddenly into a different type of existence all together, and a swift sharp turn in the weather can bring real danger with what feels like vengeance. Ruminants – cows and sheep – by definition must have grass, or some such roughage on which to ruminate, or they will die. Perhaps, surprisingly, in cold weather, dehydration is as likely a cause of death as in hotter times – regular access to water in winter is crucial for livestock, so frozen water supplies create another threat.

Within a few hours of snowfall, the temperature fell sharply and the winds picked up. This is the time where stock are totally dependent on

DOI: 10.4324/9781003407751-7

what fodder can be taken to them – no vegetation is accessible. Sheep would scratch at the ground to expose ragged grass, but this will not suffice. Cows drink water by the gallon and once taps have frozen, the only alternative is to bring water by the bucket, each carrying approximately two gallons. A cow requires at least a couple of gallons a day, which, with six cows in the herd that equals 24 gallons, is 12 buckets per feed. The water has to be drawn up from a pond nearby to their field, which is also frozen over and has snow on its banks. A gallon of water weighs just over half a stone. Pigs are also dependent on water to help digest their dry feed and require another gallon or so a day. We have a sow with piglets and, as with any lactating animal, require more water than usual to maintain her milk. Sheep can last much longer without water, but there is a particular concern in that the frozen pond is at the far end of their field and now it is possible for a thirsty ewe to venture out onto the ice and risk drowning. Ensuring that fresh water is safely available hopefully coaxes them away from the steep bank. Our ewes are pregnant and with lambing due in a couple of weeks' time, the growing lamb draws huge resources from the ewe in these final days of pregnancy. This is a time of 'twin lamb' disease, where, in the latter stage of pregnancy, the mother loses all condition, falls to the ground and dies, in vain, and the unborn lambs are lost too.

Each morning and evening, the feeding tasks take an hour and half – the best part of 4 hours a day. For a range of reasons, this week the tasks fall much to myself, and for several days, a significant amount of my time is spent outside in that weather, trudging through snow, humping bales of hay, drawing water into buckets and circulating around the stock, counting and checking, and checking again. To remain outside for hours in these conditions is possible, and even comfortable, providing several layers are worn, adding several pounds in weight to whatever else requires carrying. Care has to be taken not to expose fingers for too long when tying twine, or fiddling with hurdles. Staying dry at all costs is critical, and not losing equipment in the snow is another trick to learn. (But this piece is not really about looking after the stock in bad weather.)

This week, the world showed up and it was inhospitable. It failed to remain in its constant and familiar shape and form; it was neither comfortable nor in line within the normal range of what I could control or understand. Instead it cut right across how it ought to have been and then remained there, just outside my door menacingly. Nevertheless, I was obliged to be there with it, despite, or in spite of, its contrary nature. A farmer is called to farm, even when it – the world – is at its most hostile to the notion of farming. There is no escape from this without the likelihood of decline and death, either literally with regard to the stock, or the farmer's experience of themselves in relation to that role. The world calls me from outside to show up, whether or not it is how I would prefer it to be. I want to be clear – this has a quite different quality of obligation from that of simply not being interested in 'going to work today'. This situation challenges who I am capable of being – or whether I even can be – in relation to the world, and in this process, something will have to either live, or die.

So, this piece of writing is about my experience of remaining obliged, in relation to the world, in circumstances that defy personal inclination and my belief in my capacity to succeed. I remain thoughtful of this whilst in the process of doing so. I notice my reluctance, the reserves of energy and strength that this work costs me, the points at which my skills and capacities are insufficient and I have to moderate the pace at which tasks are undertaken. I am simultaneously aware of the question; what is being asked of me in this inhospitable circumstance? and the answer to this is simply to be who I am called to be. This may sound grandiose, or too enigmatic, but put more succinctly, it means that there are times when to be a farmer is only really understood is only properly clear to the world, when it is most difficult, or improbable to be a farmer. I find in this insight, something that relates directly to the role of the teacher in the wider educational vision at the centre of my writing. At many other times, choosing to be a farmer is easeful; on a balmy sunny day, or at the point of gathering the fruit. Even in the mundane tasks of mucking out, feeding up, weeding and planting out vegetables, there is a familiar expectation of toil and duty. However, the question of what it is to farm, and whether to be even called a 'farmer', is not in demand; the stakes are not high enough to experience it, and anyone can be a farmer on those kinds of days.

Back to this week, and the heavy snow is coming at me on the horizontal, and I shuffle down to the pond, break a bucket-sized hole and begin the half hour task of gathering the cows' water. I bring it to them and wait alongside as they take turns to drink it up, bucket after bucket after bucket. The howling wind dies and we find ourselves together, they and I, in an unexpected calmness. The evening light is still sharp enough and catches the glint of the snow on their chestnut red thick coats. As I stand close in amongst them, I catch the warmth of their breath on my hands as I remove strands of straw from about their eyes and muzzle. There's an intimacy in these small gestures and I realise that I never get as close to these beautiful creatures as when it is as hard as this. They munch down on the fresh fodder I have brought, and we are held by this place. On this particular evening, I look up, and from the hedgerow, a pale barn owl takes flight and glides towards us, around and just above us. I fancy to myself that it is an intimation of the spring to come, a blessing perhaps. The ancient bird gazes down, then circles and departs and we are left – the cows and I – still gathered, silent, in the falling snow.

There's a peculiar sense of harvest that comes from being in the world when it is like it has been this week. I have re-discovered a resilience in myself and kindled a trust again between me and the animals, and the land too. I have, more importantly, re-experienced what it is to call myself a farmer, to inhabit a way of being in the world when so much is at stake. This is not the first time this has happened, but I am struck by how forgetful I have been of previous, similar episodes. It seems that such an experience has to be born again. Like many other people this week, I have entreated the gods to stop the storm, to bring the thaw and make way for the spring. Sure enough, as the weekends, the temperature gains and now it rains and we return to the familiar. I feel the exhaustion of the past week, the animals return to their wary independence and there is a collective sense of relief. But I do not feel quite as alive as I did when the world was not mine to take for granted.

Introduction

As I settle to write this concluding chapter, I look outside and see a landscape gripped in thick ice and blanketed in hard snow. There's an easterly wind that has formed drifts at the edges of the open fields and the whiteness is broken only by the black fingers of trees reaching out of snow-covered hedgerows. It is bitterly cold outside and the land remains virtually invisible; what ground can be seen is a tangled mess of flat, matted grass on frozen soil. The notion of harvest seems ridiculous on days such as these. To set about writing on the question of such a thing might appear optimistic at best, futile at worst. Yet I know, that in a matter of months this view will be full of sharp green, corn standing tall, apples blushing and fat lambs grazing on rich pasture. In the short, dark days of winter though, such things seem improbable and it is as if the prospect of a harvest requires an act of faith.

Sitting with this reflection, I recognise in myself a paradox of sorts; I know full well that the seasons will turn and yet in the here-and-now, I experience a sense of disbelief that it will occur. In this paradoxical moment, it becomes possible to explain the educational vision which I have been creating over the course of these pages. To be educated is to know about what might be anticipated, whilst being subject to what remains immediately before us. Such a view of education is intrinsic to the renewal of the world, and one by which we – student and teacher – might make our home in the world in the meantime. This is the possibility that lies within the educational task as I see it, and the act of the teacher is to re-direct, accompany and be a witness to the student as they choose how to live well and be connected to others and place.

In this final chapter, I will be considering the question 'For Whom is the Harvest?' and in doing so present a two-fold response. First, I want to conclude the discussions of the previous chapters about my educational vision. I have set out an alternative perspective from that of a product-orientated model of education and have been indicating what such a position might mean for teachers and students. So, in the opening section of the chapter, I will speak more directly to the question of what harvest might there be for an education orientated towards soil, soul and society. I will summarise specific elements of what has already been presented, including extracts from the vocative texts. I will also be returning to the material from the discussion about what I see as 'most at stake' in offering such an alternative educational vision. My hope is that the reader may have a more complete view of what has been gathering over the course of this work and an understanding of how I have been defining the purpose of education and its implications for the teacher and student. I frame this as a hope, impart due to my ability to adequately explain my vision, but also because it cannot be guaranteed that my view will be shared. That despite my hope to turn attention towards this direction it fails to do so. Sometimes the crop withers, the lambs do not arrive and fruit falls, unripened. Herein lies the risk I have been referring to throughout the book and this closing chapter, with its gathered conclusions, is a telling time.

So, what I hope for is that the reader understand that I have been defining education as an encountered experience, one in which the student is called to act out of their own subjectification, that is, not as an object of the teacher's authority. Education, for the student, means to decide from their subjectness 'how we are, how we will exist, how we will lead our life, how we will respond to the challenges that come our way' (Biesta, 2021, p. 50). Whilst this educational moment might connect the student as existing with themselves, so to speak, I am also suggesting that this experience is always located and that this also matters. The student exists as subject because of, and in connection with, the specificity of the place in which it occurs. Education, as I am describing it, cannot be uncoupled from the biosphere, nor understood as being apart from it. To do so is to estrange education from the world and have it exiled as increasingly irrelevant. Finally, subjectification is not only particularly located, but it also occurs because of, and into, relationship with the teacher. That this happens at all might require an act of faith, but it can also be invited through how the teacher exists in relation to the student. The teacher is experienced however transiently, as someone equally irreplaceable as the student and location. This is the essence of what I have been moving towards, offering vignettes and vocative writing to elaborate, illuminate and enliven a sense of an education which is encountered and orientated towards connection with soul, soil and society. What follows in the first section of this chapter is a more detailed exploration of what this means for the student, the teacher and the world.

My second response to the question For Whom is the Harvest? is the extent to which the work might be useful in terms of its research contribution. In doing so, I will be focusing predominately on the methodology and the concept of parallel process. I want to return to some of the previous concerns I raised about the limitations and inappropriateness of adopting a pseudo evidenced-based method to what I have been offering as an existential-phenomenological approach to understanding education. In bringing this aspect of the conclusion to a close, I will highlight possibilities for future research and in particularly raise a question about the function of this work as an educational object.

Again, I have a hope in that this chapter might be understood as inviting a shift of attention in the reader towards the work, enacting the kind of encounter described in the content. Similarly to my previous comments about defining education, I cannot make certain whether this book re-directs the reader's sense of how they might exist in relation to the material; lambs fail to thrive, storms wipe out crops, fruit goes bad on the branch, and this is the educational risk. So, in the second section of this chapter, I will share some more about how I see this project informing the wider field of research and also report on my experience as a researcher in the process. In doing so, I will return to my beginning, both in terms of the opening rationale and the metaphor of the margins, and my own encountered experience as a teacher whilst undertaking this work.

Soil, Soul and Society in the Education Encounter – For Whom Is This Harvest?

In the following discussion, I set out an understanding for how an educational perspective, based on encounter, and orientated towards soil, soul and society, might yield a harvest. In doing so, I think it might be necessary to describe how I am using the term 'harvest', so as to make a distinction from 'outcome', and I will also return to some of my earlier critique of product-orientated education in order to emphasise not only what has been at stake, as such, but also the impact of understanding how else education might be imagined. In other words, for a teacher to hold in their mind's eye that an alternative is imaginable can in itself constitute a kind of harvest, not dissimilar to my being able to imagine that summer is possible when I am trapped indoors on a dark wintry day when the land is clad in ice, as described in the opening of this chapter. This latter observation will become increasingly important in scoping out what I mean by education and its implications for teachers, student and the world. I am interested in offering a view of an education that, at a 'sub-symbolic' level (Bucci, 1997), is cyclic and, symboli-cally, is one of renewal. These comments are discussed more fully later, but at this point, I want to return to the problem of 'harvest' in the context of product-orientated education.

Harvest, 'Product' and Education

To talk of harvest might suggest a culmination of what has come before, a reaping of the reward of hard labour and effort. To be more specific, harvest might equate with outcome and in this respect lends itself to conceptualising education as being product-orientated. In the opening chapter, I emphasised my concern that such an approach has significant negative implications that creates disconnection and that one way this occurs is through advocating concrete outcome measures as key indicators of a successful education. Fur-thermore, that by doing so the teacher is obliged to design and lead, facilitate or, at worst, coerce the student to arrive at a pre-determined destination. The harvest, in this frame of reference, refers to the yield of exam results, for example, that mark the end of the educational activity and the departure of student and teacher. At a more symbolic level, there is a kind of satisfaction to be had from meeting the end of a journey that might have spanned a few weeks or several years, as if teacher and student have reached point B, having left the earlier point A and thereby a linear trajectory is completed. I suggest that this feature of 'linear-ality' is deeply embedded, systemically, in how education is commonly understood to exist. The implication of this is that educational 'harvest' is associated with finality. I want to resist extending this reprise of my earlier critique of product-orientated education but have offered these remarks as a preface to engaging in the problematic issue when talking of harvest in educational terms.

Throughout the book, I have been arguing for an alternative way of un-derstanding education and one which draws attention to a range of ideas, including arrival, natality, liminality and witnessing amongst others. How-ever, I am mindful that the reader may remain unclear as to who, or what, is being served by this alternative perspective. If not the outcome, what might be the aim of such a vision of education? I recognise that it might be ir-responsible to avoid this question, and that in itself would undermine an important intention of my work which is to argue for an education by which teacher and student engage more responsibly in service of the world. So, in response to this question, I want to return to the idea of harvest and in doing so address a more fully framed question; for whom is the harvest when edu-cation is encountered with soil, soul and society in mind? As I do so, I hope to provide a summary position, not so much of what has been 'achieved' in educational terms, but what appears as most clearly important and available for consideration, for now.

Harvest as Renewal

To regard harvest as an end point, at which some kind of gain is accomplished might well be an understandable use of the word in conventional terms. However, to do so misses a broader understanding of how harvest applies to a phenomenon that is somewhat more complex. The Old English root of the word means 'autumn', the period of time between August and November, the time of the year which, in temperate zones, sits between the heat of summer and the winter cold weather. In other words, harvest is originally associated with a seasonal shift, rather than a given end point. I want to stay with this meaning of the term and look more closely at what occurs during autumn, which is something other than completion. Whilst there certainly is an association of harvest with the tasks of 'gathering-in', or 'plucking-from', it is perhaps as important to acknowledge that what is being collected is the promise of future renewal. Much of what is taken for consumption are basically seeds; whether it be the fruit, crops, fattened stock or vegetables – what is being harvested is the kernel of a life to come. To dwell on this detail is important because it reframes what is actually happening at the point of harvest. It is the intentional act of observing the capacity of the world to renew itself. An additional term worth considering, alongside harvest, is the idea of 'yield'. This, again, is a word that has a common meaning related to payment and production and might seem more appropriately set within a product-orientated educational perspective. But the word also refers to 'surrender' and for my purpose, this is of greater interest in the context of how I am using the notion of harvest. The gardener, or farmer, is paying attention to the surrendering that will often naturally occur, but by paying attention to it, the horticulturalist exists both as witness and partner, knowingly in relationship with the world's enduring cycle of renewal. To recognise this tendency towards renewal, to exist in alignment with the experience of arrival, to relate and connect, and then return is, I suggest, also of educational concern. I would add that in the current circumstances, it is a profoundly important educational matter when it is understood as the basis for living a connected life.

The reference to renewal may seem self-evident to the reader and we might in general terms recognise the need to address issues around climate collapse and other problems that signal a broader deterioration in the capacity of the planet to sustain a species determined to maximise its consumption. However, this rather misses my educational point, which is that the widespread adoption of product-orientated education philosophies and pedagogies remains steadfastly aligned to a linear trajectory. The problem with this is that the teaching function, and the student experience, is caught within an educational imaginary that valorises growth in pursuit of personal autonomy, which is formed in a space and shape that runs contrary to the perspective of renewal that I am suggesting is more relevant and necessary. Furthermore, that this limits the possibilities for student subjectification and the teacher's capacity to establish a relationship rooted in 'grown-up-ness'. I might go further by suggesting that the function of product-orientated education – especially in its more technical form – is antagonistic towards such freedom and is structured so as to eliminate the principle of an educational encounter that accounts for soil, soul and society. A consequence of such a limited educational vision is to 'bend out of shape' how educational work might more appropriately serve community life, address climate collapse and promote individual agency. In other words, it restricts the ability to address how education might connect teachers and students in exploring the task of existing in a cyclical and rhythmic world, as opposed to the linear.

I want to offer a short exploration of an idea that is relevant here, introduced in the work of Wilma Bucci (1997) and in particularly, her observations about the connection with somatic, unconscious and verbal levels of experience. Put briefly, Bucci suggests that how an individual creates verbal – conscious – meaning is underpinned by a symbolic, non-verbal, understanding, which may take the form of image or figurative form. Bucci argues that there is a further layer of experience, at the bodily level, that she refers to as the sub-symbolic, which is revealed through movement and shape. Whilst the objective of her work was to support psychological and psychotherapeutic interventions, I have been interested in how these observations might be helpful in relation to education and have written elsewhere on the somatic and environmental impact in educational work (Barrow, 2018). However, my intention in referring to Bucci's material here is to make more explicit my exploration of educational harvest.

I am suggesting that one feature of harvest when advocating for a view of education orientated towards soil, soul and society is a shift from a linear sub-symbolic movement, towards a cyclic form. This is, I am aware, potentially challenging for those accustomed to the rigour and regulatory world of formal education where policies and practices are steadfastly outcome-based and directed towards a linear trajectory. However, for educators familiar with some of the illustrative material featured earlier in my study, for example in the work of Cajete, or that described in Bhutan, it is offered as a view into practices which occur from movement that forms a cyclical arc. To exist within this educational work is to become experienced in the 'reach out' and 'return' that is intrinsic to the human condition. In other words, it is to engage in education existentially because it asks of the student how, or if, they might choose to engage with it. By re-directing education towards soil, soul and society, my intention is to heighten the possibilities for teachers and students in deciding how to exist in relation to this cyclic arc.

However, it is not sufficient in my view to simply encourage a shift from the linear to the cyclic. I want to emphasise again that the function of the rhythmic movement is renewal. Product-orientation, almost by definition, operates in denial of the necessity of sustaining processes and, by its own volition, drives an appetite for greater, consumption. I discussed in my opening rationale the importance of sufficiency as a corollary to 'growth' and I mention it again in relation to the need for renewal and understood as a feature of harvest when education is directed to matters of soil, soul and society.

I am arguing that whilst much of my concern has been to explore existential matters in education, such dialogue tends to remain at the verbal, conscious level and by paying attention to the symbolic and sub-symbolic levels, I am seeking to 'get under the skin' of cognitive discourse. As will become clear when I discuss the research implications of this work, part of its educational harvest is to consider how else education might need to be understood and described, at the 'felt' level; to know it existentially, so to speak. This means that part of the harvest will be experienced only when we fall away from using the familiar words.

So far I have been discussing in general terms how I understand the term harvest, the way in which it can be problematic and appropriated into product-orientated thinking about education, and then applied differently in the context of the themes covered throughout this work. I have suggested that shifting from the linear to the cyclic and aligning with renewal are particular features that are significant when stepping into this alternative educational frame. I want now to turn to the more specific questions as to what the nature of this harvest might mean for the teacher, how it can be understood from the perspective of the student, and what does it bring for the world?

Harvest for the Student

In considering the question of harvest with regard to the student, I suggest that it is not defined as some 'thing' but understood in the context of the previous discussion regarding renewal. To recognise that arrival, departure and return are integral to living in alignment with the biosphere is not simply a task of knowledge and understanding. It is an existential matter and there is a decision to be made as to how to exist in the world in which renewal is core. To be educated is to both experience this recognition, phenomenologically, and to decide how to act in response to this, which is to say, to be a subject in the world. In a culture where the educational imaginary is linear, to become aware of the cyclic movement is in itself a re-direction of attention and one which orientates the student towards renewal. An aspect of a harvest for the student might therefore be understood as a particular kind of noticing. It is a word that used both as verb and noun and I believe proves helpful in developing an idea of how education impacts the student in relation to the role of the teacher. A 'notice' refers to 'information, knowledge, intelligence', coming from a combination of Old French, notece and the Latin notitia, which refers to 'being known', whereas when used as a verb, notice means 'to point out, refer to, remark upon'. The harvest can be the point of realisation which involves knowing that to exist is possible, or perhaps more tentatively, that there is the possibility of such a realisation. My emphasis on the value and function of this realisation might be clearer if I refer back to specific moments in the earlier vocative texts. For example, a harvest is intimated in the first transaction between myself and David when he approaches me whilst I am digging and declares; 'I'll teach you...'. It is an early instance in which he both puts me 'on notice' and also ushers in the possibility of my 'being known'. Later, in the episode of concerning the birth of a calf, David expresses his initial anger at my reluctance to be involved in supporting its first suckling. It is a rude awakening for myself, as I had been full of fear and self-doubt, but the 'harvested' realisation is in how David explains that his anger is with himself for not having been properly in relationship with me at such a moment. It is precisely in this moment of separation that I experienced having the choice to step into the world differently, or not. He demonstrated, by walking away from the calf and I that afternoon, that I could act on my own volition. The noticing of such an opening is what might be termed harvests 'along the way', that is moments when the attention of the student is set towards choosing how to be in the world in a response to a call to act.

I have offered several accounts of what might be described in terms of student subjectification in the course of these chapters, including the woman in the east European training programme, Alex encountering the sheep dog and my own experience with David. In each of these stories, the student is 'caught' or might even feel ambushed by the sudden arrival of their subjectification, or to be more precise, the point at which the possibility to act as a subject occurs. I have already written in the previous chapter about the unanticipated feature of dissensus and the capacity for passibility in the student as ways in which we might explain a little of how this surprise might be understood. However, I suggest that this combination of noticing and existing in relation to what is noticed can also be explained in terms of a gift, and in particularly a gift not asked for. This, I argue, is another way of framing the harvest for the student when education is defined in relation to subjectification.

Biesta (2021) writes of three gifts of teaching, two of which, 'Being given what you didn't ask for' and 'Double truth giving' can be associated with the two dimensions of education featured in earlier writing (Biesta, 2014), and one of which is connected with subjectification, described as 'Being given yourself'. Re-introducing the use of the term subjectification, Biesta explains,

> Again, put simply, subjectification refers to the existence of students – or human beings more generally – as subjects and not as objects. Subjectifciation thus refers to the educational dynamics that have to do with the existence of students-as-subjects, and the word 'existence' is helpful here, because subjectness is precisely to be understood as a way of existing. It is located, in other words, on the existential plane which means that it is a first-person matter – my existing as subject is something no one else can 'do' for me.
>
> (Biesta, 2021, p. 50)

On this premise, to encounter one's subject-ness carries both a responsibility and a particular kind of freedom. It comes out of a view of education where an unexpected gift of oneself is possible but that it comes from being called forth by the world which is external to the individual. Bearing in mind my own experience of David's opening declaration to teach me, or calling for the calf to be fed, Biesta's observations resonate,

> ...our subject-ness is not something that we contract from the inside-out so to speak, but that it is in response to this [call]...that the self is given to itself. This then is the third gift of teaching where we are not just being given what we ask for, and not just being given the conditions under which we can recognise something as true or meaningful, but where we are given ourselves, our subject-ness, which...is basically an act of emancipation.
>
> (ibid, p. 50)

Here then is a harvest for the student, whereby the student meets themselves again and differently. The character, or substance of this harvest, is twofold, first the recognition, or re-connection to the arc of renewal, and second the freedom that comes with choosing how to exist in response to the call of a renewing world, and one in which the student might matter in relation to such renewal.

Harvest for the Teacher

I want now to turn to the notion of harvest in relation to the role of the teacher and offer possibilities for how the alternative vision of education that I have been presenting might be of value. Most practically, for the teacher whose experience of teaching is defined within the context of product-orientated education, the possibility of discovering an alternative frame of reference may serve as an important benefit in itself. I discussed earlier in my rationale that the teacher in such a context is in peril of disappearing as a person who exists capable of freedom, both in terms of their professional 'act' and in relation to their role with the student. In this dynamic, the teacher might be understood as a technical operative, who is replaceable and at as great a risk of objectification as the student. Whilst the teacher is destined to perform necessary interventions in order to cause a pre-determined impact in terms of student performance, they too are the focus of a similar performative drive (Ball, 2003).

What is at stake in this alternative situation is the teacher being experienced as someone with the capacity to 'occur' in the life of another, and for that to be potentially important. I hasten to clarify at this point that I do not mean that the teacher is important in the sense that they make something happen to the student, which is perhaps outside of the permitted remit of the curriculum, or indeed come along unexpectedly and 'save' the student from an undesirable situation. I am aware of the dangers regarding the teacher as an altruistic, well-intentioned saviour, and this is quite contrary to the point I am seeking to make. This is, I would argue, a mistaken strategy for some teachers who, disillusioned with the restrictions of an overly technical approach to education, set out to 'do well by the poor student', by offering a version of an escape route, perhaps through re-directing the student to some alternative curriculum option or withdrawal into a pastoral care intervention that distracts or avoids the 'imprisonment' of a mainstream education. In these circumstances, despite the shift in tone and style, the symbolic quality of the educational experience is barely changed. The teacher continues to position themselves as knowing what's best for the student and designs a route which remains both product-orientated and lacks opportunity for the student to freely determine, or not, their way of existing in the world. In terms of harvest, it is akin to stealing a handful of potatoes from the edge of the field.

Instead I am interested in what a harvest for the teacher might mean which puts aside satisfying a sense of altruism or acting as saviour. If it is not to deliver something for the student, or experience a vicarious sense of achievement via that of the student, how else might the teacher experience harvest? In exploring a response to this I will return to the story of David, and in particular some of the observations in the vocative text, Departure. It is one of the more surprising aspects of the story that, for a period of time during our time together, his condition improved and he claimed he had a new lease of life:

David declared to me that his stable health was due to a single factor; the revival of his farm. He had not imagined that he would see cattle grazing in the fields, or 'draw' down lambs again. Watching the pasture cut in the summer heat had been beyond his dreams. Most importantly, he had given up on the possibility that he would ever be able to teach someone. My arrival as student had, in his opinion, given him, literally, the gift of a life he would not otherwise have had. This educational life had caught him also. Occasionally he would refer to me explicitly as a best possible student, someone with whom he could be at his very best as teacher, and I know what he meant in terms of being compelled to have life through teaching.

Teaching is not an act of altruism, or rather, if it becomes so, there's need for caution. Over investment by teachers in their students' ambitions is a dangerous folly, leading to symbiosis, disappointment, resentments and untimely ruptures. Recognising that there is something of my own teacherly desire to thrive in the act of teaching is, for me, both necessary and natural in this kind of education. David's acknowledgement that he was a teacher, in part because of my arrival into his life, did not minimise or reduce his agency, but affirmed it.

To be compelled to teach is as much a desire to be understood, and calibrated, by the teacher, as those desires of the student. Understanding education as an existential lesson offers a unique harvest, not to be found in a product-orientated culture. David would tell me often how for him to have taught was life's late gift. I, however, spent much of my time being quite unaware of this yield for David, especially early in the relationship. I think that this indicates an important distinction between the student's and teacher's experience of harvest. Whilst the teacher remains thoughtful of the existential possibility of the student, in addition to being mindful of moderating their own desires, motivations and presence, the student remains for the most part, concerned with the impact of their subjectification.

Before widening the discussion of harvest, I want to consider a way of framing what I have been suggesting in terms of the subjectification of the teacher. Little attention has been given to this idea in the literature regarding subjectification which appears to be entirely associated with that of the student. Biesta's account of the role of the teacher focuses on the act of teaching and grown-up-ness, both of which I recognise as useful ways of describing the relational quality in the teacher-student dynamic. But these cannot be described as a harvest for the teacher in any sense of the term. As I reflect on the narratives featured in this work, the challenge of deciding how to act is as valid for the teacher as the student. On frequent occasions, David might have become authoritarian instead of demonstrating authoritativeness, and I have certainly experienced enough self-doubt and grandiosity win my own practice, that the capacity for the student to act as subject has been jeopardised. The fallibilities of the teacher remind us that the task of finding a home in the world is on-going, that when we refer to subjectification it is not a state of completion, and that grown-up-ness has little to do with age or seniority.

When I think of the moment when Alex chose to work the dog, or the East-European woman stood and left the room, or on numerous other occasions when the phenomenon of subjectification has been let loose in the relationship, I too have experienced an encounter – it is not a one-way occurrence and this is, for the purpose of the study, an especially important factor. To encounter implies to be met by the other, or risk doing so, and this involves not only a sense of 'Where are you in this?', from the teacher to the student, but also 'I am here in answer to your call', in the response of the student to the teacher. For education to be connective, it requires the existence of one to not only be witnessed, but also to possibly confer the other's existence too. In other words, the harvest for the teacher is their subjectness, which cannot be taken for granted.

As I commented earlier in my response to Dennison's reflective chronicle (1969), he understood that he, too, was at risk of becoming the object of the student. I have already suggested that the role of teacher is arguably in more danger of objectification than 50 years ago, with the increase in technocratic education, in which to exist as subject is counter-cultural. So, David experiences an unexpected choice as to how to exist in relation with myself as his student, and he is also risking being recognised anew. I might push this a little more and propose that what is at stake in this view of education is the renewal of the teacher as emancipated. Far from a saviour offering salvation to the student, this kind of encounter reaffirms not so much 'who' the teacher is, but that they might act in the life of another and there is an intimacy that comes with this. By intimacy, I mean that the inmost, or intrinsic, quality of the individual is made known through their action, by how they choose to exist, or not, in relationship. This is as applicable to the teacher, as to the student, and is intrinsic to connective education encounters where someone appears, a phenomenon Berne refers to in explaining the importance of recognition,

> The implications are: (a) Someone is there; (b) Someone with feelings is there; (c) Someone with feelings and sensations is there; (d) Someone with feelings, sensations, and a personality is there; (e) Someone with feelings, sensations, a personality, and in whom I have more than a passing interest is there.
>
> (Berne, 1961, p. 85)

To conclude my reflection on the harvest for the teacher, I see how framing education as an existential task can support the teacher resolving the impasse of what Ball refers to as 'values schizophrenia'. This is where the intensity of performativity, endemic in technocratic education, is keenly felt, where 'commitment, judgement and authenticity are sacrificed...' and a 'splitting' (Ball, 2003, p. 221) occurs in which the teacher is emptied of their capacity for their own subjectness. By considering education as I am suggesting, there is the possibility for re-installing the hope that teaching might be connected to ecological and social renewal, and it is to this wider agenda that I now turn.

Harvest for Education

The harvest I am most interested with is that of education itself. I appreciate that this might suggest grandiosity so I should state clearly that I am not coming to this discussion with a view that education has 'lost its way' or is in some kind of crisis and that the vision I am setting out is intended to somehow 'save' education. Far from it, in fact I have argued that generally education is understood to be set on a well-marked, linear path in which destination is clear, supported by discourse, much of which reinforce the premise that education remains focused on production. When I talk of how my work might offer a harvest in relation to education, I mean that it can indicate how education can provide a harvest in the wider context of ecological and social renewal. I think I have been clear enough that renewal is a distinctive feature of my education vision and this is because this cyclic arc is the most suitable form, if education is to connect with the world in mind.

In the opening chapters, I featured the work of Arendt, and in particularly her writing on natality, the event of arrival and the challenge through which individuals exist in the world, explaining that 'It is an unending activity by which, in constant change and variation, we come to terms with and reconcile ourselves to reality, that is, try to be at home in the world.' (1994, pp. 307–308). There is a close alignment in this sentiment with some of the features covered in this book, namely the acknowledgement that this is 'work in progress', and not one that is ever concluded and that there is an external world with which the individual has to determine relationship, even if it is to choose to be in a non-relationship. Much of how Arendt describes the world also aligns with how I have been understanding the concept, although I believe I have accentuated the ecological and material qualities which, in my view, are underplayed in Arendt's writing, that nevertheless have been a significant influence on my thinking. However, as I have been pulling this work to a close the phrase, to 'try to be at home in the world', has become troublesome in my mind. This is in part because there is the slightest hint that by succeeding at being at home in the world it might then be owned by me, and secondly, and more importantly, it doesn't quite acknowledge the transience of my being at home here. Whilst Arendt (1958) also writes on the theme of renewal, as I have discussed earlier, and the inevitable entropic schema by which all organisms deteriorate and die, there is a dimension to this existential account that is overlooked, which is the fact that the individual is, so to speak, simply passing through, or staying awhile. I think it is useful, in gathering the book to its close, to focus a little more on transience in educational terms. As I have mentioned, 'to find a home in the world' suggests that I might be here to stay and in doing so might imagine a proprietary claim on it, even whilst I experience its challenge to my state of immanence. I understand that Arendt refers to the world as a pluralistic one, that this is such a necessary confrontation, and that the individual might have wished it otherwise. Nevertheless, to meet the world, to try and find a way of being with it, I am arguing, means also understanding and figuring out how to exist because life in such a world is also transient.

On our smallholding, we have an ancient oak tree set out in the field. It is majestic and at just under 400 years is one of the oldest in the village. It was most likely planted in the reign of Elizabeth I, around 1573. Its central bowl is big enough to accommodate a dozen small children and over the years a number of individuals have slept up in its boughs. Occasionally visitors ask me what it is like to own the tree and I have to be clear that it is impossible to own such a tree as this. I explain that at best I would hope to curate it well enough, but that basically we are just living with it awhile. To exist, as fully as one might dare to, is to not only know that at times the world can be antagonistic to what we anticipate or expect, but also that arguably the greatest confrontation is that we, not the world, are passing through. To exist in this state of awareness is to know our place in the myriad of inter-connection, not through stewardship nor mastery, but simply as another expression of physis. Hence the challenge, in existential terms, is to choose how, or whether, to show up on this transient basis, and do so anyway.

This has significant implications for an educational imaginary that is preoccupied only with exponential growth and the valorising of individual ambition (and, by way of reference to Jantzen [2010] in denial of death). The purpose in gathering themes together is, to remind the reader, drawing the wildlife from the margins and perhaps I am getting closer to describing the harvest for, and of, education. To refer back to Biesta's (2021) idea of the gifts of teaching, I will borrow and adapt the notion of the third gift, that of being given oneself. I have wondered whether, as the book begins to close, what opens up is the possibility that education might be 'given back to itself' if it is orientated towards re-connecting soil, soul and society. My concern throughout the study is that education has been heading in a direction that not only disconnects but also anaesthetises and in doing so establishes a kind of 'cultural immanence' that resists the very kind of interruption needed by which it might be free from generating and amplifying disconnection. Put more bluntly, that the gift of itself shifts education from being the problem of disconnection and contributes to solution through re-connection.

I recognise that I have been discussing in broad terms how these ideas might provide a harvest to education and perhaps it would be useful to propose a more specific way in which this can be understood. I suggest that the existential position I have been presenting would be best framed as endeavouring to be a good guest in the world. It is a phrase common to shamanic practices, used as an expression of hopefulness for what might be possible in the meantime. In other words, in educational terms, the direction of attention that the teacher might point towards calls the student to recognise that not only are they not at the centre of the world, but also that they are connected transiently. It is in part why I have wanted to emphasis the concept of liminality alongside those of arrival and the relational in the study. To be a good guest is to know that we do not own the home in which we stay. It requires us to be sensitive to how it might differ from what we might otherwise expect. It also means we are open to the hospitality, the sense of welcome that might be offered. I have used the term 'good' guest, in a similar vein to Biesta's decision to refer to a 'beautiful' risk in relation to education (2014) because I see that this is also a matter of aesthetics. In other words, that there is a judgement to be made, a discernment required, which reveals how the student appears as subject. In referring to the role of a guest, I hope to draw attention to its existential and relational implications. As a guest I might be encouraged 'to make myself at home' during my stay, in the understanding that of course, it is not my home. In doing so, I am connected with the place and others and that calls me to make choices in how to exist in these circumstances. For the student to exist as subject in the context of being a good enough guest is, by implication to be re-connected with and in relationship with soil, soul and society.

Life's Longing for Itself

I am aware that so far I have been pushing back on the idea that harvest implies a completion of a process, preferring to emphasise that the term can describe a period of transition, and one during which there is a surrendering of what is required for the renewal of the world. I have done so in order to avoid slipping too swiftly into the language of product, which would be counter to my vision of education. However, it might be somewhat dogmatic to entirely dismiss the fact that something happens in autumn that does not occur at other times, and that this involves a closure of sorts. So, I therefore want to offer some final observations about the yield of this work.

To talk of harvest is not, in my view, synonymous with departure, although there is an understandable association which in the world of education is easily recognisable. The end of the academic year is typically marked with the announcement of examination results and the leaving of older students and retiring members of staff, so it is unsurprising that such a connection is part of a common cultural experience. The academic year is divided into seasonal terms, each of which builds upon the other in order to culminate in the final semester where ending is inevitably marked in valediction. I have explored the impact of departure in an earlier section that dealt with the death of David and I want to return to some of that material to further illustrate the educational harvest.

> Life's longing for itself – is at the heart of educational purpose. This is what the teacher creates the conditions for, not so much the student themselves, but the expression of life which they bring, no matter how camouflaged it may have become. The irony of recognising the significance of physis, the compelling desire to be alive... the role of the teacher is inextricably linked to physis.

In that description, I offer the closest to what I dare in defining the kernel of what this book has been about; a vision in which education is understood where the student's attention might be caught in a moment where 'Life's longing for itself' occurs, in plain sight. This is not at all in the form of ambition, or personal glory, or some other version of individual autonomy. It is a point in which the soul of the student is experienced in concert with a myriad of others, nested in a place that is simultaneously and uniquely understood, and collectively shared. And, for the teacher, to know that such a thing might be possible, without them bearing responsibility for either making it so, or defining its shape. This is what I am meaning by education when soul, soil and society matter most; to exist as one's Life longs for itself in relationship with another rooted in place, here on Earth. To do so is an act of renewal, existentially of the student and teacher, collectively in community, and literally, in relation to the land.

There is then a point, I suggest, where harvest and sowing, arrival and departure, roles of teacher and student suddenly and imperceptibly switch. That which appeared student becomes teacher, what was understood as a departure ushers an arrival, and the reaped harvest yields fresh seed to sow.

> That following day, as I stood atop the new farm, taking in the dereliction, the ruined outbuildings, the unfenced meadows and knowing the sheer hard work that lay ahead, I was overwhelmed. Raw with the sadness at the death of my teacher, I worried myself sick at the enormity of it all. And yet there was audacity in this moment too. I had only been able to imagine taking on this challenge by choosing to exist in such a way. That the origins of a desire to make this place a home lay in an educational encounter where the soil had mattered, and relationship meant giving up something that had once been everything. And this is what teachers do, and it's what education is for.

> By definition all teachers must depart, it is in the very nature of the task. There are matters of responsibility and performance in the leaving, but there's witness too, and presence. Teacher, rooted in the place out of which the educational moment arises, and with a willingness for the student to create, out of freedom, the way in which their own life's longing for itself renews again the world, after which point departure.

> This final phrase, describing the disappearance of the teacher is somewhat misleading. In the literal sense of the working relationship, teachers do depart, take leave of the life of the student. However, I am interested in the phenomenon by which teachers continue to show up, sometimes unexpectedly, in our lives. I am intrigued by a very personal observation. David died in 2009 and since then, on our new farm we have had countless visitors, young and old, who ask all sorts of questions. A recurring series of questions is how did we learn how to do things? Did we Google it? Was there a book? Did I do a course? I can only reply by telling the story of David, and as I do so the educational purpose comes alive again, not just at the level of character and event, but as a story about education, of the love for teaching and the desire to be taught by. The tale invariably moves people and I know that this is partly about the beautiful serendipity of David's passing, but it is also because it affirms a different narrative about teachers, of being taught by, and the nature of education.

I have written with interest and enthusiasm about natality in my study and have made little mention of mortality. I am aware as I return to these observations about the departure of the teacher that there may be a suggestion that part of the harvest for the teacher in my vision of education is the prospect of immortality, and this would be mistaken. The notion that by intervening in the life of the student the teacher might achieve a 'life after death' is again, another version of outcome attainment, and a particularly grandiose one at that! To teach might mean that the teacher is remembered fondly or otherwise, but that it is not quite the point here. Bearing in mind my discussion of grown-up-ness in the previous chapter, for the teacher to seek immortality through their role is arguably not to have come to terms with one's mortality and is an indicator of the infantilism that can limit both student and teacher. For the teacher, the harvest comes from knowing that the educational task might return nothing, and yet much may get carried forward.

Finally, I turn my mind to the vocative text preceding this chapter in which I embark on showing up as a farmer when conditions are most inhospitable, and the experience of discovering at close hand, what 'Lifes' longing for itself' asks of the individual. This is not so much what another person might ask of the other, but what the world calls of us, individually and collectively. The kind of education I have been writing about is a response to such a call. The call is there when I struggle to feed my cows in bitter winter, or in the sense of futility, the teacher experiences when working with the cynical student, or in the frustration of the student in the face of a new problem. In each of these moments so the world turns up another unexpected opportunity by which it might educate us once more in what it is to exist within it. To teach is to direct another's attention to such a possibility in such moments. To become educated is to choose to do so.

For Whom Is This Book a Harvest?

In this final section, I will be turning to the second dimension to the question of harvest. This time I will be focusing on why I think that this has been a valuable project in terms of education research, how it contributes to discourses on education and what further research might be worthwhile. In bringing the book to its conclusion, I also want to summarise some of the themes that I suggest have become most significant in developing a view of education orientated towards soil, soul and society.

From the outset of this writing, I have argued against the preoccupation in education with attempts to formalise the impact of the teacher on the student, whether this be in terms of academic attainment, levels of competency or developmental maturation, for example. I have discussed earlier that this kind of education is prone to fall into a trap in which teachers and students are caught in a collusive dynamic whereby the student adapts to the teacher's view of what constitutes a successful education should look like. Such a view of education, in my view, is based on a false premise of 'cause and effect', which leads to freezing the teacher and student dynamic in the service of productivity and the deification of teaching and learning objectives. I do not want to rehearse again here the concerns I have with this way of framing education suffice it to say that in ecological, sociological and existential terms, it is highly problematic. Instead I have wanted to research not only an alternative approach to envisioning education, but also explore a methodology which is congruent with its themes.

One of the important features that I have been paying attention to is the layers of parallel processing between the content and the research components. I want briefly to revisit the concept of parallel process and then emphasise how congruence, between the subject of the research and how it is researched, has been an important aspect of establishing integrity and coherence in developing the vision of education. In other words, because the research has been focused on the problem of disconnection in education among individuals, people and place, I have wanted to avoid creating a parallel disconnection between my research themes from my method. I have set out an approach that connects content with process. Consequently this has involved remaining close to the phenomenological experience of what I am exploring as a best effort to resist drifting into a disconnected, overly intellectual explanation of what has been directly experienced. The use of vocative texts has been one way in which I have attempted to maintain a connecting thread throughout the format of the book. Another part of my method is to draw on material from educational practices that, in my view, are rooted in connection with soil, soul and society. A recurring intention has been to explore what might otherwise be regarded as abstract ideas from 'the inside out'.

To be more precise, because I have been addressing a range of existential aspects of education – arrival, liminal, relational – my intention has been to explore how each of these 'exists' in the teacher – student – place dynamic. It has been more important in the context of the writing to open up the field of possibility, rather than define for the reader how to understand each component in order 'to do' this kind of educational work. Perhaps this is the more counter-intuitive feature of this book in that it resists the conventional tendency of educational research to provide a practical 'how to' approach to teaching and learning. In fact, it might be important to state that this is the contra-position; I would not want to be advocating, for instance, a scheme for establishing educational encounters that address soil, soul and society. To do so would undermine the substance and intention of what has been explored throughout these chapters.

One of my intentions in developing this visioning exercise has been to pay attention to some of the existential matters of education, which I have argued, tend to be overlooked in an educational culture dominated by a product-orientated view of education. Much of the writing has been set out in such a way that it might re-direct the attention of the reader towards the importance of place in the teacher-student dynamic, a particular view of freedom in education and a re-framing of the role of the teacher. Furthermore, that by signalling these ideas I have been attempting to pay attention to what appear to be useful questions, whilst not seeking to provide specific answers to them. This is perhaps in contrast to research where the aim has been to 'capture' data in order to demonstrate, or prove a particular hypothesis.

Here, though, my intention is that the 'harvest' of the work is to open up discourse so that, for example, teachers might discern for themselves questions about educational practice that matters to them and their students. To generate a spaciousness in which this exploration might be undertaken is a hope of this book because in doing so there is a possibility that educational work could be re-imagined and re-connected.

Spaciousness and the Liminal Opportunity

In these final sections, I pursue a tentative approach to exploring the spaciousness that I have set out to create for the reader, that is different from a familiar educational discussion, and which gives a particular account of liminality and the wildness that comes from stories. I will be referring back to earlier aspects of the study and will focus on what I see as an opportunity, a moment where the attention of educators is re-directed towards how education can re-connect with soil, soul and society. Here is an encounter...

> They say that once there was a soldier who entered a forest on his horse, and as he made his way along the path a wolf appeared and accosted the solider. The wolf pulled him off his horse, overpowered the man and was about to kill him when he pleaded mercy. The wolf offered a deal and told him that if he turned back to his village and promised not to venture out again he would let him free, or he could decide to continue his journey but that the wolf would return and take the life of his horse. The solider, immediately relieved at the prospect of escape, but also seeing an opportunity to follow his ambitions, took the latter option. The wolf released him and the soldier set off. At first he was grateful that he had his life back and then as he trotted deeper into the forest, felt quite smug at how he had escaped to live another day. Just as he began to forget the meeting with the wolf, and when he was a long way from home, the wolf reappeared. Within a moment the wolf had shaken the soldier off of his horse, slaughtered it and began to take his fill. The solider was aghast and suddenly aware of how isolated he was, alone in the forest. 'What shall I do?', he asked. The wolf replied, 'The time of the horse is over. Now if you are to live, you must ride with me'.

It is an old tale and one that tells a 'truth crooked'. In the world of story, the horse is associated with the familiar world, harnessed to the ambitions of their rider, held in high regard as a symbol of accomplishment, hard work and dutiful. They are a beast of domestic affairs, times when priests and politicians serve to explain how we got to where we are. But the wolf is quite a different creature altogether. When the wolf arrives in a story, we know that we are in the presence of wildness. To ride with wolves is to not know the destination but to cover the ground with intent as we do so. This is a time when prophets point to where we might arrive, if we hold tight.

I introduce this brief interlude about story to the discussion as a way of returning to the potential of the liminal space and how I see the relevance of this work at this particular time. I began to develop the ideas of this vision of education back in 2016 in what can, I think, be reliably described as a very different time. The completion of the work though has been undertaken during the period of global pandemic and a series of lockdown arrangements. Whilst disruptions to normality are a continual feature of life, and certainly the pandemic is not the only, or arguably the most important one of our times, it is difficult to downplay the extent and duration of the impact generated by the pandemic and education has certainly experienced a significant interruption. Similarly, in a book that declares itself interested in existential matters it would be peculiar not to consider an event that has provoked doubts and challenged how to exist in political, organisational, cultural and personal domains. I want to focus on the educational opportunities that might open up as a result of this interruption and consider how the ideas I have been discussing might contribute to such an opportunity. I am coming from the position that the pandemic instigated a substantial liminal experience and that this has potentially important implications for teachers, students and how we might envisage education.

If I refer back to the features of liminality, it might become clearer as to how this work could serve education, because to my mind much of what was familiar and understood has become less reliable, relevant and can no longer be understood to serve. In other words, the information about education – the body of knowledge about schooling, for example– has been somewhat undermined. What was assumed about curriculum delivery, assessment and standardisation has tumbled in the light of mass home-schooling experience, the failure of algorithmic levelling and a return to teacher-based assessment. What were familiar strategies for managing the challenges arising in education – acknowledging and responses to stress – have also needed revision. In other words, the shift away from the civic authority of local government towards the private sector, for example, proved insufficiently robust to counter what communities needed from their schools. The relevance of pre-covid educational thinking and options, especially in terms of curriculum and assessment, has become increasingly irrelevant when staggering the attendance of groups of students, blended curriculum delivery formats and on-line classroom management. Finally, and perhaps most important to the purpose of the alternative vision of education explored in this work, the issue of power and authority in education relations has also been disrupted. The data-orientated rubric by which schools and colleges have been regulated has also been significantly sabotaged by what will be several years of inadequate student data returns. My point here is that much of what was recognised and understood as the educational imaginary has been thoroughly disturbed and the question of how education might exist is arguably more pertinent now than it was when I first set out on this project.

I am aware that just because I frame this situation in such terms evidently does not mean that the opportunity to encourage change will come about. The reaction, 'to return to normal', is one that is understandable but overlooks the point of a liminal experience which is that, like the horse-less soldier, a return to the old times is no longer possible, despite best efforts to contrive to do so. However, a strategy to combat or resist this is denial and I suggest that education, if it is to be worthwhile, might be especially concerned in confronting such denial. Biesta (2020) in commenting on options for responding educationally to the pandemic crisis focuses on how the situation might be helpful for us to return again to the existential questions that are at the heart of a teacherly gesture and 'to say no' more than 'look, there is something there that I believe might be good, important, worthwhile for you to pay attention to' (Biesta, 2020). This is, in effect, what I am seeking out to do in this study; to invite a consideration of how to act in connection with the social and ecological place in mind and in the context of opportunity. Not to do so is arguably anti-educational, in the sense that it involves embedding further in an education that deepens disconnection and limits the possibility for the student to experience subjectness. Biesta explains what is at stake here, and I would suggest that his position is applicable to that of teacher as it is to student,

> If the aesthetics of education seeks to awaken students for the work and, through this awaken them for themselves – which is the question of emancipation – it follows that the anaesthetics of education does the exact opposite. Rather than awakening students and trying to keep them awake, it induces a state of slumber.
>
> (Biesta, 2020)

In an echo of the challenge presented to the horseman, a choice presents itself; 'For education all this raises the question whether the school will act on the side of aesthetics or the side of aesthetics' (Biesta, 2020). I wrote at the outset that I have positioned the book at the margins with a view to bringing it to the centre and in many respects, the pandemic crisis and its subsequent disturbance of education provide the event by which that might occur. It is on this basis that I suggest that this work might be seen to offer a gift of education back to itself.

Finding My Way Back Again

I mentioned that I began writing several years ago at a time when I felt well established as an educator. I knew education in the sense that I found my home in the professional community and some success that had come from doing so. However, the experience of developing these ideas of an alternative vision of education has become an encounter in its own way and one in which I have found myself returning to myself as teacher. In the opening rationale,

I referred to how, in the field of transactional analysis, I had begun to create a space in which its educational application might extend beyond that of a useful educational psychological model. Nowadays it is also acknowledged that educational TA can raise existential possibilities through educational experiences (see for example, Dijkman, 2019). In carrying out the work what was not thought of before has materialised, including, as a further example, the development of ecological transactional analysis (Barrow and Marshall, 2020). These are instances which have come about through paying attention to the theme of connection with regard to soil, soul and society.

In most respects as a research project, this work has been an exercise in paying attention and provides a series of encouragements to the reader to have regard for what is paid attention to. I have resisted an approach that relied on 'capturing' data and rendering it into a concrete form for analysis. An important point throughout my writing has been to make a shift from the 'destinational' account of education and explore a more 'horizonal' approach, which in my view, means paying attention to the ever-changing landscape whilst making choices as to how to be in meaningful connection with it. The use of anecdotal writing has been my strategy for integrating process with content and I have found at times that this has, to my mind, resonated and felt 'true', whilst at other points this has not been the case. For instance, I have a keen sense that the pieces, From the Margins, Natality and For Whom Is the Harvest?, each have an energetic resonance which quickly takes me to the phenomenological level, or truth in what I am exploring. However, when I reflect on other sections, I notice that there is a something less sure of itself in Arrival, or wandering in Beyond Arrival, and perhaps somewhat sentimental in Departure. This is not so much to say that these 'fail' as anecdotal contributions, but that encounter belongs outside of a manufactured experience, is elusive and resists entrapment.

In terms of what might remain beyond the reach of this current work, I am mindful of two possible areas for future consideration. Whether it is anecdotal writing, or a similar ethnographic approach, I believe not enough is available of direct accounts of teachers – and students – of the experience of subjectness. Whilst there is a range of writings on the theoretical importance of subjectification, and existential education, it would appear that most of this falls short of giving an insight into it phenomenologically. At times, therefore I have wondered how I might be still hunkering at the margins; it would be helpful if this book title might have some company! A second and related observation is that in looking to the opportunities ahead, I wonder if the time has come to disrupt further the academic 'register'. I have spent numerous hours reading texts, many of which refer to vital, exciting, energetic and radical ideas. Yet, the language by which this is communicated is full of dead words and this ought to be of a concern to those interested in matters connecting soil, soul and society. There is a fundamental disconnect embedded into a bloodless text that continues to alienate research – and educational research in particularly – from the phenomenon it seeks to illuminate. This is especially dangerous when it relates to practices that involve people and places. Some indigenous writers refer to the cancer of intellectualism that has infected the sensibilities to such an extent that ecological despoliation, social injustice and mental ill health are endemic. Strong words indeed, but after several years seeking out words that speak out of, and to, the human condition, it is rare to find a pulse. This, I suggest, ought to worry the research community more than I believe it does currently. My concern is that in addition to schooling, academia might also be entranced by the attraction of homogeneity, indicated in part with a too easily franchised language register. Consequently, I have taken what opportunities arise and chosen to bring the lyric and poetic to the foreground, turns of phrase that judder occasionally and perhaps irritate at times, but are alive nevertheless. What this has meant is that as a researcher I have felt some risk, not only in featuring some aspects of the material, but also in choosing the style of writing. However, the risk, the content and style are precisely aligned to the purpose of this book and to not do so would be to open it up to a significant critique.

When I first set out to write the rationale for the book, I opened with a brief account of a student – a nine-year-old boy – who visited the farm. I eventually decided against using it in my introduction for some reason and now, as I bring this work to a close I understand why – because it was what I must end with. Liam was described as a 'reluctant writer' and would come to visit the farm occasionally, with other recalcitrant students. Their school was in the county city and they were bussed out for a series of afternoons in the summer term. They could choose how to spend their time whilst they were on the farm, rounding up sheep, making fires, cooking a meal, fishing or climbing trees. The invitation each time was that towards the end of the visit they could find a place for themselves and niche there whilst they either drew or recorded in some other way, about their experience. I was not to know that Liam had never climbed a tree, but he could not resist clambering up that majestic oak which has stood in the field for hundreds of years. I found myself his witness, and he a good guest in that place. When he returned back to the ground, he had become a writer, opening his book and these fresh forged words: 'I climbed a tree... I was trembling with fear, but my courage fought back. Mother Nature has given me her power! May Mother Nature give others her power!'

References

Arendt, H. (1958) The Human Condition, Chicago: Chicago Press.

Arendt, H. (1994) Understanding and Politics (the Difficulties of Understanding), in Kohn, J., ed., Essays in Understanding 1930–1954, New York: Harcourt, Brace and Company, pp. 307–327.

Ball, S.J. (2003) The Teacher's Soul and the Terror of Performativity, Journal of Education Policy, Vol. 18, No. 2, pp. 215–228. DOI: 10.1080/0268093022000043065

Barrow, G. (2018) A Body of Knowledge: Somatic Encounter and Environmental Impacts in the Educational Encounter, Transactional Analysis Journal, Vol. 48, No. 1, pp. 7–17, DOI: 10.1080/03621537.2018.1391681

Barrow, G. and Marshall, H. (2020) Ecological Transactional Analysis – Principles for a New Movement, The Transactional Analyst, Vol. 10, No. 2, Spring, pp. 5–9.

Berne, E. (1961) Transactional Analysis in Psychotherapy: The Classic Handbook to Its Principles, New York: Grove Press.

Biesta, G.J.J. (2014) The Beautiful Risk of Education, Boulder: Paradigm.

Biesta, G.J.J. (2020). Have We Been Paying Attention? Educational Anaesthetics in a Time of Crisis, Educational Philosophy and Theory, Vol. 54, No. 3, pp. 221–223. DOI: 10.1080/00131857.2020.1792612

Biesta, G.J.J. (2021) The Three Gifts of Teaching: Towards a non-Ecological Future for Moral Education, Journal of Moral Education, Vol. 50, No. 1, pp. 39–54.

Bucci, W. (1997) Psychoanalysis and Cognitive Science: A Multiple Code Theory, New York: Guilford.

Dennison, G. (1969) The Lives of Children: The Story of the First Street School, New York: Random House.

Dijkman, B. (2019) What Is This Asking From Me? Transactional Analysis Journal, Vol. 50, No. 1, pp. 93–100. DOI: 10.1080/03621537.2019.1690249

Jantzen, G. (2010) Place of Springs: Death and the Displacement of Beauty, Vol. 3, London: Routledge.

Coda

Aftermath (n.)

Old English

New Growth Following the Harvest

One evening when I was locking up the hens for the night, David told me I need not worry about doing so. I replied that despite being a city boy even I knew that foxes would take off hens if they were not shut away properly. He assured me that no fox would come close to the yard and that the hens would be safe whether or not I locked them up for an evening. He was right – in the time we lived at the farm, we never saw a fox, nor lost poultry. Whilst it was a peculiarity we grew used to the fact and though we knew foxes lived in the surrounding woods and might patrol the far reaches of the field, they gave no trouble closer to home.

David died in November and soon after a heavy snow fell and remained on the ground for months proving a hard challenge for us as we established ourselves at our new farm which was in much need of restoration. It was during this winter that I had a most strange meeting. Whilst visiting our local town, I saw the family that had taken on the tenancy at the old farm following our departure. I asked how they were finding their new home and they spoke of how they were enjoying the place and looking forward to the spring and warmer months. However, the father asked, 'Tell me, what did you do about the fox when you lived there?' I was confused and asked what he meant.

'Well,' he continued, 'since we have moved in we keep seeing a fox in the yard. Now the snow has come we can see its tracks and it sometimes comes right up to the back door. Sometimes we see it strolling around – a big bright coated fox. In fact, only this week I saw it and it looked back at me *as if it owned the place.*' I said something about not having ever seen a fox and made my way home.

What to make of such a thing? In the years since I have often wondered on the meaning of this encounter. How could it be that a fox arrives, strutting about the yard, as if it owned the place? Perhaps the cold weather drove it seeking food closer than it might prefer? Maybe it was a new fox to the area, bolder than the others and determined to mark out its territory? Or could David have been mistaken and that foxes came by the house and we just never saw them? And why now, after the old man had gone, does such a thing occur? When I let my mind wander to the margins of the imagination and

DOI: 10.4324/9781003407751-9

settle awhile in the rough banks of the tidied field, other possibilities arise. Was this as much a fox as a shape-shifting farmer, returning in spirit to take stock of how its land lies? Might this be how ancestors reclaim their place in the world, care-taking what had been so precious and should remain so for future generations? When I first told people the story of how I came to be a farmer I would leave out this coda to the tale. I felt self-conscious, wary that it would undermine the beauty and credibility of my apprenticeship. However, as the years go by, and when I have the opportunity, I have offered the account of the fox. Invariably people 'ooh' and 'aahh' as they also wonder what it means.

I have no idea what led me to pause when Alex fell to the ground and I decided to bring the dog towards him, unleashed. I can only speculate why the woman in the east European training group stood up, took courage and left the room. I do not know why it was 'that' moment when David decided to approach me to tell me he would teach me to farm, and I cannot explain my immediate acceptance of the challenge. I know that each of these occurrences was both uninvited and unexpected.

As I moved to closing the study I became acutely aware of the thousands of words, hundreds of concepts and dozens of cases, all of which served the desire to explain and understand the educational task, the experience of the student and the role of the teacher. I have come as close as I dare in my closing chapter to offer tentative insights and conclusions. However, as this project has unfolded, I have developed a growing reverence for the mystery that lies at the kernel of education, and indeed the call to existence. Sometimes, like the appearance of a fox, red-set against the snow, claiming connection, I have had to accept that not everything can be brought down to clarity and explanation. There's acceptance in this, and beauty too, if we can bear it.

Index